CHARLIE SHAFFER · BILLY CUNNINGHAM · CHARLIE SCOTT · DA

BBY JONES · WALTER DAVIS · JOHN KU

NCAA

2009
DIVISION I

BRAD DAUGHERTY · STEVE HALE · JOE

D WILLIAMS · DANTE CALABRIA · JEFF MCINNIS · VINCE CART

AY · MARVIN WILLIAMS · BOBBY FRASOR · DANNY GREEN · TY

MEN'S
BASKETBALL

LENNIE ROSENBLUTH · TOMMY KEARNS · YORK LARESE · LA

DAVID CHADWICK · BILL CHAMBERLAIN · GEORGE KARL ·

AL CHAMPION

JAMES WORTHY · JIMMY BRADDOCK · MATT DOHERTY · B

COTT WILLIAMS · GEORGE LYNCH · ERIC MONTROSS · BRIAN R

ANTAWN JAMISON · JAWAD WILLIAMS · RAYMOND FELTON · S

NSBROUGH · MARCUS GINYARD · WAYNE ELLINGTON · TY LAWS

WN · CHARLIE SHAFFER · BILLY CUNNINGHAM · CHARLIE SCO

OO · BOBBY JONES · WALTER DAVIS · JOHN KUESTER · PHIL FO

N · BRAD DAUGHERTY · STEVE HALE · JOE WOLF · JEFF LEBO · SC

D WILLIAMS · DANTE CALABRIA · JEFF MCINNIS · VINCE CART

AY · MARVIN WILLIAMS · BOBBY FRASOR · DANNY GREEN · TY

N · LENNIE ROSENBLUTH · TOMMY KEARNS · YORK LARESE · LA

CBS

DAVID CHADWICK · BILL CHAMBERLAIN · GEORGE KARL ·

SPORTS

JAMES WORTHY · JIMMY BRADDOCK · MATT DOHERTY · BUZZ

WHAT IT MEANS TO BE A TAR HEEL

WHAT IT MEANS
TO BE A TAR HEEL

ROY WILLIAMS
AND NORTH CAROLINA'S GREATEST PLAYERS

SCOTT FOWLER

TRIUMPH
BOOKS

Library of Congress Cataloging-in-Publication Data
Fowler, Scott.
  What it means to be a Tar Heel : Roy Williams and North Carolina's greatest players / Scott Fowler.
     p. cm.
   ISBN 978-1-60078-378-4
   1. University of North Carolina at Chapel Hill—Basketball—History. 2. North Carolina Tar Heels (Basketball team)—History. 3. Williams, Roy, 1950– 4. Basketball coaches—North Carolina—Chapel Hill. 5. Basketball players—North Carolina—Chapel Hill. I. Title.
   GV885.43.U54W48 2010
   796.323'6309756565—dc22

                                                    2010027854

This book is available in quantity at special discounts for your group or organization. For further information, contact:

   TRIUMPH BOOKS
   542 South Dearborn Street, Suite 750
   Chicago, Illinois 60605
   (312) 939-3330 • Fax (312) 663-3557
   www.triumphbooks.com

Printed in U.S.A.
ISBN: 978-1-60078-378-4
Design by Nick Panos
Editorial production and layout by Prologue Publishing Services, LLC
Photos courtesy of University of North Carolina

CONTENTS

Foreword: *What It Means to Be a Tar Heel* by Roy Williams vii

Acknowledgments xv

Introduction xix

The FIFTIES 1
Lennie Rosenbluth, Tommy Kearns, York Larese

The SIXTIES 23
Larry Brown, Charlie Shaffer, Billy Cunningham, Charlie Scott

The SEVENTIES 51
David Chadwick, Bill Chamberlain, George Karl, Bob McAdoo,
Bobby Jones, Walter Davis, John Kuester, Phil Ford

The EIGHTIES 97
James Worthy, Jimmy Braddock, Matt Doherty, Buzz Peterson,
Brad Daugherty, Steve Hale, Joe Wolf, Jeff Lebo, Scott Williams

The NINETIES 149
George Lynch, Eric Montross, Brian Reese, Donald Williams,
Dante Calabria, Jeff McInnis, Vince Carter, Antawn Jamison

The NEW MILLENNIUM 197
Jawad Williams, Raymond Felton, Sean May, Marvin Williams,
Bobby Frasor, Danny Green, Tyler Hansbrough, Marcus Ginyard,
Wayne Ellington, Ty Lawson

FOREWORD

What It Means to Be a Tar Heel

by Roy Williams

WHAT DOES IT MEAN TO BE A TAR HEEL? There are many ways for me to answer that because I have loved all my experiences at the University of North Carolina, and I have had a lot of them. I have two diplomas from Carolina, and my two children and wife graduated from here. I am now the head basketball coach and have been part of the basketball program for a long time, so I understand what that means, too. When you say "Chapel Hill," those words always bring a smile to my face. I'm part of this town. I'm passionate about this university, and it is a passion that grew naturally. I'm a Tar Heel and proud to be a Tar Heel.

When I was growing up in western North Carolina near Asheville, I never even thought about going to college until I was in high school. It just wasn't part of what we talked about in my family. I thought I would go to work in a sawmill like everybody else. But Buddy Baldwin was my high school basketball coach and my history teacher, and he was also a UNC graduate. He loved the Tar Heels.

I started my first basketball game for him as a sophomore. By the time I was a junior at Roberson High, I was listening to his tales about North Carolina and watching Larry Miller and Bobby Lewis on television. One day, Buddy came to school after seeing a UNC–Wake Forest game. At the end of that game, Miller made this great acrobatic shot, spinning it in off the backboard from some unbelievable angle, and that shot won the game. That day at practice, Buddy was trying to show everybody that shot and make us understand how unbelievable it was. That started it for me.

The first time I set foot on UNC's campus was in 1967 during the fall of my senior year. I was on our high school square-dance team. I know it sounds comical, but it's true. We came to Durham for a performance at Cameron Indoor Stadium. Yes, I square-danced at Duke. It was the Duke Folk Festival. Joan Baez and Janis Joplin were there, too, as headline acts. You can bet the Roberson High square-dance team wasn't a headliner, but we did perform on stage in Cameron.

I had never been to either Duke or UNC. The next day after our performance, Miss Weir, the teacher who was the sponsor of the square dance team, brought us to Chapel Hill. She pulled me aside after we saw the campus and said, "This is where I want you to go to school. This is where you belong." By then, I had decided I wanted to go to college. So I came to Carolina, mostly because Buddy Baldwin and people like Miss Weir felt it would be a great place for me. The next time I came to campus was for freshman orientation.

At first, college was difficult. I had no preconceived notions about what was going to happen and didn't know where I would find my niche. No Williams had gone to college before me. I had come from a small pond where I was a very big fish, but as a freshman, I felt like a number. I was nobody and struggled for the first five weeks. Honestly, I did not know if I was going to survive. My future wife, Wanda, was also a freshman. We were not dating, but we were friends, and she helped me through those first weeks of college life. And then, on October 15, 1968, I tried out for the freshman basketball team. That opened up a whole new avenue. Basketball just exploded in importance for me after I made the freshman team.

My involvement with basketball helped me fall in love with the school and grow in other ways. Chapel Hill was the kind of place where you could find someone to do something with you, no matter what that something was— good or bad. The late '60s was a very turbulent time. If I wanted to protest and carry a sign, I could do that. If I wanted to go to the library and study six hours, I could do that. If I wanted to go to the bars every night, I could do that. If I wanted to go to the gym every night and play, I could do that. I chose the gym. The gym was my escape, a place where I had fun.

With each day, week, month, and year, I became more aware of what was going on in the world. I became more educated and more worldly, even though I was living inside this little village. Carolina pushes you to grow as a person, yet it allows you to do so at your own pace. It taught me to keep an open mind. When I graduated, I was much better prepared for life. I had a great experience in the classroom, but I also had great educational experiences outside that helped me mature. There are special places on campus like the Bell Tower, the Old Well, the Arboretum, and downtown Franklin Street. Those places meant a lot to me when I was a student and still do today. I know that's corny. But a lot of times, I am corny.

I'm proud our school is nationally ranked as one of the top public institutions and one of the top universities in the country. I'm proud of our chancellor, Holden Thorp, who is young but has accomplished so much. I'm very proud of what our former student body president Eve Carson stood for. There is a wonderful program called the Carolina Covenant, which allows low-income students to attend debt-free. That would have been such a helpful program to have at Carolina when I was in school. So I support the Carolina Covenant with a deep passion.

When you're a Tar Heel, you support all Tar Heels. When I watch the highlights of other sports events, I pay particular attention to the Tar Heels. Maybe I'm watching the NFL highlights on a Sunday night, and Vonnie Holliday makes a big play. He played here. He's a Tar Heel. Like all of us, he gave his sweat, his focus, everything he had. He sacrificed to be a great player.

I cannot stand the Boston Red Sox. I have been a fan of the New York Yankees my whole life. But when Daniel Bard comes in to pitch for the Red Sox, I watch him because he's a Tar Heel. I say, "Gosh, he just threw that 98 miles an hour!" I watch Davis Love with great interest when he's in contention at a golf tournament, because he's a Tar Heel. In my office, I have a picture of Larry Brown and me with three of the UNC women who won the gold medal in soccer in Athens, Greece, at the 2004 Olympics. I'm so excited for all the Tar Heels' successes. It's that camaraderie, that fellowship, that care you have for every other single athlete who played in any sport here. To me, that emotional tie is unique.

I'm passionate about Carolina, but nobody ever told me to feel this way. My mom and dad didn't say, "We're going to be Tar Heel fans." They didn't put a Tar Heel jersey on me and have me wave a blue-and-white pom-pom. The feeling I have for the university just came naturally, through what this place did for me and what it has done for so many other people. Many times you hear, "Why'd you go to that college?" And people say, "I grew up going to the games with my parents. It was just part of my life." My life was not like that. My love for Carolina grew because of my experiences here.

And to me, that made it even stronger. It happened just because it happened. That's neat.

And yet, in my case, all of those things are a bit overshadowed by Tar Heel basketball. They are overshadowed because the University of North Carolina has allowed this basketball family to grow, prosper, and excel—to be a model that makes so many other people around the world jealous. I know that's a blunt way to put it, but it's the truth. Our players go to the NBA, and other people say to them, "Oh, it's really not that good at Carolina. You guys just agree to say this stuff." And our guys just laugh at them because they know it *really is that good*.

I was an assistant basketball coach at Carolina from 1978 to 1988, and I heard Coach Smith talk so much about his alma mater, the University of Kansas. He talked a lot about Dr. Phog Allen, the father of basketball coaches. Then I went back to Kansas to coach and found it really was a wonderful place. I've always said this—the people at Kansas have no idea what we have in Chapel Hill. And Tar Heels have no idea what they have in Lawrence. Coach Smith took what Doc Allen did in Kansas as a blueprint and built it in Chapel Hill, not only as this enormously successful basketball program, but as a family and community.

When I went to Kansas, I told Bob Frederick, the KU athletics director, "If you're just looking for me to be a basketball coach, I'm not the guy. But if you want someone who will coach and try to build the program and make the program really big, that's what I'm going to try to do." During my 15 years at Kansas, the Tar Heels were my second-favorite team, and I loved every single accomplishment of a Carolina team—except one. When the Tar Heels beat my Kansas team in 1993 in the Final Four, I didn't love that. But I still had so much pride in the Carolina program.

When I came back to North Carolina in 2003, my first job here was to win games. There is no question about that. If I don't win games, I'll be fired. But my second job was to get the Carolina family back together. There had been a bit of a split, a fragmentation, and some unhappiness. I needed to get the former players back together. I needed the old-timers back in the program. I needed to honor Coach Smith in my own way by trying to continue his vision. I wanted to continue what he built. I wanted to make people remember that it wasn't just about wins, losses, points, and rebounds with Coach Smith. It was about people. We held a reunion for all the players during my first season in 2004. I said, "Guys, this is your program." And it is. It

Coach Roy Williams, whose UNC teams won two national championships in his first five years as head coach, celebrates the Tar Heels' 2009 national championship with some of his players.

is the program of the former players and the general fan. It is not just the program of the alumnus who gives a lot of money. This is *the* state university, *the* University of North Carolina. I have a tremendous amount of pride in trying to promote that.

I have felt enormous pressure at UNC. It has been a challenge to continue what Coach Smith put in place. You know what the bottom line is? I'm not as good as he was. I'm not being humble; that's just the truth. Coach Smith was the best there's ever been on the court. Yet he was far better off the court. He was so good with personal relationships. He did so much with every former player. I try. But I can't even come close to what he did. I'm just blown away by what he was able to do with every former player. I admire everything he did.

Wanda and Buddy Baldwin say there are so many other responsibilities for a coach nowadays. I believe that's true. I believe that's why Coach Smith left as early as he did, retiring at age 66. If he could have just coached his team and taken care of his lettermen, he would have stayed much longer. But there are so many other responsibilities now that it's harder to concentrate only on that.

It would also be more difficult for Coach Smith now because he was such a private person. Now you can't be anywhere without someone knowing. I can leave a prospect's home, and Wanda can look on the Internet and know what I said there before I get back. That lack of privacy on a home visit would have driven Coach Smith crazy. Coach Smith and I have had some wonderful conversations when I was at Kansas and when I first came back here. I'd say, "Coach, I chose not to do that because I don't want to do it like you did it. That wasn't right for me."

Pressure aside, I'm happy about the joy we've been able to give our fans with the two NCAA championships we've won at Carolina. I think there was more passion involved with the first title in 2005. Maybe that was a result of the hardships the program endured in the previous years. Our fans adopted that group once again as their team. The joy and the fun they had with the win in St. Louis were truly off the charts.

Then we did it again four years later, winning the national championship in a way that felt vastly different. It was a more challenging year because of the adversity, injuries, and expectations we faced. A lot of people felt we might go undefeated and that we were destined to win, but it was not destiny to us; it was hard work. Overcoming all the adversity we faced made winning the 2009 championship very satisfying.

Tradition is very important to me. That's why we celebrated the 100th year of Carolina Basketball throughout the 2009–2010 season. I said to Dick Baddour, our athletics director, "We've got to make it a year-long celebration because it has been such a wonderful 100 years." Carolina has accomplished so much. I wanted to celebrate how successful and fortunate we've been, because it's not like that everywhere. People need to be reminded to appreciate that.

We held an alumni game with our current professional players and coaches in September 2009 that drew more than 20,000 fans. I was covered with cold chills when players like Antawn Jamison, Raymond Felton, and Tyler Hansbrough were introduced and I heard the ovations they received. I was at center court when Coach Smith was introduced. It dawned on me that I was standing between Michael Jordan and Dean Smith. That was one of the neatest feelings I've ever had in my life.

As amazing as that evening was, the reunion weekend we held in February 2010 was even more remarkable. More than 200 former players and 100 managers came to renew friendships and celebrate the program's wonderful history. The "Celebration of a Century," as it was called, felt like part old-timers game, part Academy Awards. Nearly 70 former Tar Heels played, including four guys who were in their seventies and eighties and were on Carolina teams in the 1930s and '40s. That's how much being a Tar Heel meant to them—and to Bobby Jones, Walter Davis, and Phil Ford, out there running the Four Corners again. And in the process we made new memories that will last forever.

When the game ended, and not surprisingly it was a one-point game that went down to the last shot, the 20 or so players in attendance whose jerseys are either retired or honored passed a ball from one end of the court to the other. It was the first time so many celebrated Tar Heels from that many generations had ever been on the court at the same time. Tyler Hansbrough, who said he's never felt such pressure, made a layup at the end of the "fast break," and all the players gathered at the center circle for one more huddle. It was an incredible moment.

But the one moment I will cherish forever came during halftime. Every player who came back for the reunion gathered at the edges of the court while they played a video in tribute to Coach Smith. There could not possibly have been a dry eye in the house when they were showing the video. The lights came up, and I had the honor of joining Bill Guthridge and Eddie Fogler, all of us assistants under Coach Smith, to escort him out to center court.

The love that poured from the crowd and the players was unbelievable. The players circled around Coach Smith and started to hug him and thank him for all he had done for them and for Carolina Basketball. I remember having to step to the side for a tearful hug with Al Wood, our great All-American from my first three teams as an assistant coach. The video, the reaction from the crowd and players, the moments we shared together at center court brought emotions that I will never, ever forget.

Fortunately, our 2010 Tar Heels went out the next day and beat N.C. State, which allowed me to fully enjoy the reunion banquet and receptions we had after the game that capped a truly unforgettable celebration.

So what does being a Tar Heel mean to me? It's family, education, passion, integrity, competitive spirit, togetherness, hard work, class, opportunity, tradition, success…all of the above and more. I'm a Tar Heel and always will be. I'm not just the coach here. I'm a Tar Heel. It is in my blood. It is part of me. And it always will be.

Roy Williams, a member of the Naismith Memorial Basketball Hall of Fame, has won two national championships as the head coach at North Carolina (2005 and 2009). He has also led his teams at North Carolina and Kansas to a total of seven Final Fours.

Born August 1, 1950, in Asheville, North Carolina, Williams has spent most of his life in his homestate. He attended college at UNC and earned two degrees. He served as a high school coach in North Carolina and then was a trusted assistant coach on Dean Smith's staff for 10 seasons before leaving to become Kansas's head basketball coach for 15 years, from 1988 to 2003.

Williams is the only coach in college basketball history to lead two schools to at least two appearances in the national final (Kansas in 1991 and 2003; UNC in 2005 and 2009). Nine of his college teams have won 30 or more games, and his overall winning percentage has long been the best among active coaches. Active in many charitable endeavors, Williams and his family have contributed more than $250,000 to the Carolina Covenant, which allows low-income students to attend UNC debt-free.

Williams' family includes his wife, Wanda, daughter Kimberly, son Scott, daughter-in-law Katie, and grandson Aiden Allen.

ACKNOWLEDGMENTS

Dean Smith once told me in an interview that Bobby Jones added a fine twist to the longtime North Carolina tradition of pointing to the player who provided you with the key pass when you scored a basket. This "thanking the assist man" was a UNC tradition for years before Jones came along in the 1970s. It was a gesture designed to promote the "team-first" philosophy Smith always taught.

But Jones—who is personally close to my heart because he's a Charlottean, a committed Christian, and one of the finest men you will ever meet—added something to it. As Smith recalled with a laugh: "In Bobby's sophomore year, we started the 'Bobby Jones Rule.' George Karl threw him a pass, he missed a pretty tough layup, and he came back pointing at George anyway. We liked that so much we decided we wanted all of our guys to do that."

I am instituting the "Bobby Jones Rule" for this set of acknowledgments. A lot of people have thrown me gorgeous passes along the way for this book. If I miss the resulting layup, that is my fault, not theirs. So now I'm going to start pointing.

I have long enjoyed a friendship and a fine working relationship with Steve Kirschner and Matt Bowers, who serve as the sports information gurus for men's basketball at UNC along with their many other duties. They are two of the best in America at what they do—helpful, professional, and exceedingly efficient. Thanks to both of them for helping me arrange interviews, for making the process of getting good photos into this book so much easier, for untold other assists and for making me still look forward to every trip to Chapel Hill after all these years.

Thanks to the Hugh Morton family. Mr. Morton, who died at age 85 in 2006, was one of North Carolina's true Renaissance men—the owner of Grandfather Mountain, an environmentalist, a superb promoter of the state, and a splendid photographer. Mr. Morton was kind enough to allow me to use some of his pictures in a previous book. His grandson, Jack Morton—who is also an excellent photographer—gave me permission to use more of them here. Several other photographers are also represented in this book (via basketball pictures provided by UNC that span the past 50 or so years). And although I don't know all of their names, they all have my thanks.

Thanks to my bosses at the *Charlotte Observer*, particularly Gary Schwab, Mike Persinger, and Harry Pickett. I hope to continue my great job at the *Observer* (www.charlotteobserver.com) as a sports columnist for many more years—I've worked at the newspaper since 1994—but it is nice to write in a longer format like this occasionally. Gary, Mike, and Harry have allowed me to pursue book projects for years as long as I do them on my own time. I appreciate that so much. They are the rare bosses who always try to think why something can be done rather than make an excuse for why it can't be. Think of the boss in the *Dilbert* comic strip—they are his polar opposite.

Thanks to Coach Dean Smith, such a towering figure that he seems to leap from these pages in one story after another told by his former players. Although Smith rarely grants in-depth interviews anymore and was not able to for this project, several one-on-one talks we have had about his career and his players in the past helped me understand my subject matter much more clearly. For that, I am grateful.

Thanks to everyone at Triumph Books, including Tom Bast and Don Gulbrandsen, for seeing the potential in this book from the beginning. This is the fifth book I've written but the first one published by Triumph. I have found the people at Triumph to be friendly, talented, and very committed to producing quality sports books.

Thanks to all those who have contributed in some way to my personal website—www.ScottFowlerSports.com. Check it out. A number of pictures that didn't make it into this book are posted there, as well as a lot of my favorite sports stories from over the years. Another place you should check out is the UNC Basketball Museum, which opened in 2008 adjacent to the Smith Center. It is free, fun, and very informative. I learned several details there that found their way into this book. All Tar Heels fans owe it to themselves to visit at least once.

Thanks to the newspaper sportswriters—my wonderful "ink-stained wretch" colleagues—who came before me. They saw many of these players play firsthand before I got to Chapel Hill myself in 1983 for my own freshman year at North Carolina. Thanks to non-fiction authors like Art Chansky, Barry Jacobs, and Adam Lucas. All three have written excellent books that chronicle UNC basketball in whole or in part. I am indebted to all of them, consider each of them friends, and recommend their work highly.

Thanks to all those wonderful PR folks and intermediaries who helped me track down a player or two along the way. I am particularly grateful to B.J. Evans and Josh Rosen of the Charlotte Bobcats, since so many former Tar Heels either play or coach for the Bobcats or else play against them in NBA games and show up in my hometown because of that connection.

Thanks to my parents, Abby and Steve Fowler, and my wife's parents, Frances and Jim Mundy, who are great babysitters and sounding boards. They were very supportive during this project, as they have always been.

Thanks to all 43 of the former Tar Heels who provided their memories in my interviews for this book—42 former players and current Carolina coach Roy Williams. They all quickly grasped what I was trying to do with this project and were very generous with their time. They made the Carolina Way easier to understand for an old *Daily Tar Heel* sports editor like myself.

No one was paid to be interviewed for this book. All these men interviewed gave up their time, quite literally, for free.

A special thanks to every fan of Tar Heels basketball. If you didn't have the same relentless passion for your team that these Carolina players demonstrated on the basketball court, no one would have ever wanted me to write this book.

Last and most, I would like to thank my own family—my wife, Elise, handsome sons, Chapel, Salem, and London, and gorgeous daughter, Georgia. They are extraordinary, and I love them very much.

INTRODUCTION

I F YOU'RE LOOKING AT THIS BOOK RIGHT NOW, you probably have some deep connection to the University of North Carolina. So let me ask you a simple question: what does it mean to be a Tar Heel?

That was also the central question I posed to more than 40 men who know exactly what it means, having each worn a Tar Heels basketball jersey for some of the program's most significant moments. Their first-person memories form the heart of this book—an uncensored and affectionate oral history of the Carolina program. I have structured each chapter in a way so that you can almost imagine the Carolina player in question sitting across from you at a coffeeshop or restaurant, telling you stories you never knew about the basketball program that you love.

Consider these men your tour guides on a journey through the last 50-plus years of Carolina basketball—from the championship of 1957 through the championship of 2009 and beyond. James Worthy is here. So are Tyler Hansbrough, Lennie Rosenbluth, Antawn Jamison, Vince Carter, Billy Cunningham, Eric Montross, and Phil Ford.

Walter Davis tells you all about the famous eight-points-in-17-seconds comeback win against Duke in 1974. Worthy guides you through the 1982 title season. Sean May and Raymond Felton talk about what it was really like during the 2005 championship run. Charlie Scott lets you know how it felt to integrate the basketball program. And current Tar Heels coach Roy Williams, who has already won two national championships at his alma mater, graciously agreed to write this book's foreword to help fans understand what it means to be a Tar Heel for him.

Neither Williams nor any of the 42 players that I interviewed for this book were paid for this reminiscing. They did so freely. In fact, when I had the opportunity to explain the concept of this book to former UNC players in a one-on-one conversation, not a single former player ever turned me down for an interview. They were eager to talk about a subject very dear to them all—their Carolina family.

In a number of cases, I also asked the players to describe their single favorite game in a Carolina uniform. You will find many stories about those battles here, as well. Some of the players' choices will surprise you. Some won't—close to half of them mentioned some win or another over Duke.

You also get an inside play-by-play of the 1957 championship game—about how Tom Kearns really felt when he was asked to jump center against Wilt Chamberlain. Montross describes how the Tar Heels came back from a 21-point second-half deficit to beat Florida State. Donald Williams tells you about the 1993 NCAA title win over Michigan. Five key players from the 2009 team—including Hansbrough, Ty Lawson, and Wayne Ellington—give you the inside story on that championship.

The former UNC players I tracked down for this book weren't terribly difficult to find in most cases, although they sure were busy. Many have gone on to great successes both in and out of basketball following their careers. Besides the numerous NBA All-Stars and famous head coaches like Larry Brown and George Karl, there are also men like Steve Hale, a pediatrician and father of four who lives in Vermont.

And whether they are in or out of the sport, all of the players remain committed to the legendary UNC basketball family. "It's the greatest fraternity of sportsmen in the world," said Karl, an NBA head coach. "I'm convinced of that. And most of that is due to one man—Dean Smith. When you meet someone else, just for 15 minutes, there's something there if you both played for UNC. It's a brotherhood. An automatic respect."

Said Brad Daugherty, the Tar Heels' center of the 1980s who became the NBA's No. 1 draft pick in 1986, "I will never forget what Magic Johnson said once to me. He was laughing and he said, 'What is it about you North Carolina guys? I'm sick of you! Every time I see one of you, there's another one of you right behind him. It doesn't matter how old you are, you're always hanging out together.' The thing is, that's true. We're just a big family."

A big family always has its big moments—the stories that relatives tell time and again, punching each other on the shoulder when they get together. The

Tar Heels are no exception. You get to share those stories here. I'm only sorry I couldn't include more players. Certainly, in the 100-year history of North Carolina basketball, there were hundreds more very worthy candidates.

The book is laid out chronologically, beginning with several players who played in the 1950s and ending with those who have starred in the new millennium. But this is not a book that must be read from the first page straight through until the end.

Skip around as you like. Each chapter is self-contained and lets the player tell his own story in his own words. Each chapter also includes a picture of the player during his UNC playing days and a postscript that I wrote to tell you what happened to the player once he left Chapel Hill.

I did all of the research for this book on my own time, and it was a pleasure. The interviews were conducted in person when possible and on the phone when necessary.

I have a passion for UNC basketball history, which is why I have written or cowritten two previous books about this subject as well. Those were *North Carolina Tar Heels: Where Have You Gone?* in 2005 and *Jimmy Black's Tales from the Tar Heels* in 2006. So this book represents the end of my own personal trilogy of Tar Heels basketball books.

Listening to these players tell their stories was a privilege. I hope it will be for you, as well.

So take a journey with all of us. Join more than 40 of the best players in UNC basketball history. Discover what it means to be a Tar Heel.

The FIFTIES

LENNIE ROSENBLUTH

FORWARD

1954–1957

I'M SO VERY PROUD TO BE A TAR HEEL now and have been for a long time. But when I came down to Carolina with Coach Frank McGuire for the first time, I knew nothing about the University of North Carolina. Nothing at all.

People would ask me in New York all the time where I was going to school. I'd say, "North Carolina," and they'd say, "You mean N.C. State?" That's because N.C. State was the basketball program everyone knew back then in the South. I'd tell them, no, it was North Carolina. They'd say, "Where is that?" And I didn't really know—I didn't even know where Chapel Hill was.

When I saw the campus, though, I immediately fell in love with it. To be a member of that team and the extended Carolina basketball family today, it makes me both proud and humble. I go back now and say to myself, *Wow, I actually played for this team!* I try to go back now every year since I retired. I've been going to the ACC tournament every year for the past five years or so. It's hard to believe when I get back on the campus and walk on Franklin Street how it was when I was back in school.

Believe it or not, there weren't many places selling T-shirts on Franklin Street back in the 1950s. About the only thing you could really pick up was a UNC shirt. There was hardly any UNC basketball stuff. There were a lot of eating places and a lot of clothing places. Chapel Hill really was Franklin

Street back then. I had made many friends from the people in town, and I'd go to the Goody's shop—that was a restaurant. In the 1950s you couldn't get into that place at 8:00 PM. All the ballplayers were there. I didn't drink, but people who wanted a beer and a sandwich would go there. The Varsity Theater was there for movies, and there was a bookstore. Franklin Street was a unique place then, just as it is now.

That I still hold any basketball records at all at Carolina is mind-boggling to me. They have the three-point shot now, and they play more games. My late wife, Pat, was really big on that. She would look up the names and say I'm still on there in the scoring chart or something. I'm still remembered after all these years, and so is our 1957 team. That's unique in itself, that we were part of a one-of-a-kind ballclub that went undefeated. How many people can say that?

The players today are so much bigger and stronger than we were. When we were playing in the 1950s, you didn't lift weights. You didn't do anything other than run. Today the 6′10″ guys run the court the way our backcourt men did and can jump to the moon. I don't know if they are better shots than we were, though, or if they are as fundamentally strong as we were.

I didn't start playing basketball until junior high. I grew up in New York and loved baseball first. I was a typical New York kid—I played a lot of stickball. My dad and I went almost every weekend to either Yankee Stadium or to the Polo Grounds to watch a major league game. You could get in there for 50 cents. Sometimes, just the neighborhood kids would go. We'd get together, get some sandwiches and a dollar, and that could last you all day. It was 50 cents to get in. The subway was a nickel, and drinks were about a dime. You could get a scorecard for a dime, too. The games started at 1:00 PM, and we'd get there at 9:00 AM to watch batting practice. We'd sit in the bleachers all day long. I saw Joe DiMaggio, Ted Williams, Willie Mays in his later years—it was great. My dad was a big Yankees fan. He was there the day Lou Gehrig said good-bye to everyone in Yankee Stadium. I saw Babe Ruth at the same place, saying good-bye to everybody in 1947.

The way I got started in basketball was one day my father got tickets to Madison Square Garden for a college game. The Garden was packed, and it sounded like a good Duke-Carolina game. The next day in gym class at school I started trying to play basketball, dribbling with two hands. This was in junior high. I was 6′1″ but couldn't play at all.

I tried out for the junior high team and was cut every year—in seventh, eighth, and ninth grades. Then I tried out for the J-V team as a 10th grader

3

Lennie Rosenbluth (left) guards Kansas star Wilt Chamberlain in the 1957 national championship game, which the Tar Heels ultimately won in triple overtime.

and couldn't even make that! In 11th grade, I got cut again. But I loved the sport, so I was playing almost every day in the park. We had a neighborhood team that I played on, and I still remember the first time I scored in double figures—10 points.

Halfway through my junior year, the high school coach called me back. He was getting some calls from other coaches who played our neighborhood team, saying, "Lennie Rosenbluth is not on your varsity? Why is that?" So pretty quickly I went from not making the team to starting on the team. I got in six to eight games my junior year but didn't really do that well. But one time we got to play at the Garden, and I had a good game against a team that went on to win the public school city championship. I bumped into a guy called Harry Gotkin, and everything changed from there. He was sort of recruiting for N.C. State and said, "I'd like to keep in touch with you. How would you like to go up to the Catskills and play basketball for the summer?"

I did that, playing for a team at one of the resorts. I didn't start at first, but then three of the starters got hurt in an accident, and I was forced to start. Before long, I was playing for some other teams up there, too. That's when I played for Red Auerbach's team for a while. I actually got to train with the Boston Celtics for a while after that. I roomed for two weeks with Bob Cousy. And then, of course, Everett Case was recruiting me to go to State. I knew McGuire, but I never thought I'd play for him. He was the head coach at St. John's, and I didn't want to go to the city. I wanted to get out of New York.

Case brought me down to N.C. State at one point. It was supposed to be a recruiting visit, but it was really a tryout. I didn't even have sneakers with me. I had to borrow some when I realized he wanted to try me out against a lot of other guys before he committed to a scholarship. I can see why he said no to me after that tryout. I was in terrible shape at the time. But it all worked out. I think even if Case would have given me the scholarship, I would have sat on the bench a lot there.

5

In the meantime, McGuire was about to leave St. John's and become the head coach at either Alabama or North Carolina. Harry Gotkin told him I was a good player and, even though McGuire had never seen me play in person, he trusted Gotkin enough that he promised me a scholarship. I would have followed McGuire to either place. He ended up at Carolina, and so I did, too. I took a prep-school year and then enrolled at UNC in the fall of 1953.

McGuire was great for me. We never really had any plays at all at UNC, except for a couple of inbound plays. I was used to playing in the New York city parks in games without a lot of structure. I probably wouldn't have been nearly as good in a more structured system like the one Dean Smith had. But McGuire was a great coach for what I did.

There was a freshman team back then, and we played in Woollen Gym. For our first game, we put on our jerseys somewhere nearby, ran up the stairs to get into the gym, and the gym was locked! The opposing team was milling around, all trying to get someone to open the door. The place could sit about 4,500, and I think there were about 10 people there. At first, I had trouble even giving away my comp tickets for games we were playing. But that got better.

The 1957 season is the one everyone remembers now—that was my senior year. When you look back on it, we had so many close ballgames. I believed right from the beginning we'd have a unique team. We had had a really good team the year before, too, in 1955–1956, but we got blown out by Wake Forest in the ACC tournament by 21 points. Coach McGuire never let us forget that humiliating defeat.

At the beginning of the 1956–1957 season, when he made me captain, I thought the only thing that would hurt us would be dissension among ourselves. So we had weekly meetings, trying to stay on the same page. We thought there was no reason why we couldn't win the whole thing, because we really didn't have a weakness on our ballclub. We were great shooters. We'd light up a zone and were very hard to match up against in a man-to-man.

In the locker room after we got off to a good start in the season, I started counting down how many wins we would need to have a perfect season— the 32–0 mark we were shooting for. It used to drive Coach McGuire crazy. I'd say, "Twenty more, Coach. Nineteen more." Like that.

But after the Maryland game that season, I believe he started to believe it, too. In that game, he called timeout toward the end just to tell us to shake hands with them like gentlemen after the game, that our streak was over and to act the right way about it. And we came back and won that game. We had several games like that, when we escaped. How many times could a team have made one foul shot to beat us and then they miss the foul shot? Many times, teams seemed to just self-destruct against us.

McGuire didn't do a lot of Xs and Os. Like I said, we didn't run plays. We just played schoolyard basketball. We practiced at night that whole season— from 7:00 to 9:00 PM, because we had to share the gym. We did a lot of practicing of "time-remaining" situations—what to do when you only had 10 seconds or five seconds left to shoot. They didn't keep turnover statistics back then, but we really just didn't turn the ball over. That was a no-no. He didn't believe in crazy passes. McGuire always said the basketball was gold, and that you never throw away gold.

McGuire held firm on other things, too, like he never wanted the ball thrown into the middle from the top of the circle—we always threw the entry pass from the side. He believed in angles. You take a shot on one side, you better have teammates over on the other side, because that's where the ball would usually bounce out. We were good rebounders, smart ballplayers, and good shooters.

I averaged 28 points per game my senior year, and I did things pretty much the same way every time. If they played me man-to-man, I always went inside. I'd get the ball, dribble, and boom, my shot was up. It was a very fast shot. If they played a zone, I'd just go outside and shoot over them. I didn't waste much time creating a shot.

My teammates didn't have to do this, but they bought into giving me the ball. A lot. I owe them so much for that. As I've said before, when I came down to Carolina, I realized a whole lot of students had two first names, like Jim Bob. If I had had two first names, they could have called me Lennie "Shoot-a-Lot" Rosenbluth, because that's what I did.

I was a little bit different than some of the other guys on the team that year. For one thing, I was engaged my whole senior year. Pat and I were married in June of 1957, right after the season.

I lived in Joyner Dorm and just roomed with a regular student, not a teammate. I loved that. I loved being part of the campus and being with the students, that's the way to go, as far as I'm concerned. I was Jewish, and that was considered unusual at the time in Chapel Hill, but I never felt any prejudice because of it.

We had an incredible Final Four that season. Both our games went into triple overtime. In the one that everyone remembers, the national championship, we beat Wilt Chamberlain and Kansas by a single point in Kansas City. It was amazing.

7

I only have two regrets about my college career. One is that I didn't go back with the team on the plane after we won the title in 1957 to see and experience the celebration. Instead, Coach McGuire and I went to be on *The Ed Sullivan Show* for a few seconds. I would have much rather been in Chapel Hill. And also, I wish I could have played on the 1956 U.S. Olympic team. But those Olympics were held in Australia, and the Aussie summer is our winter. So it didn't work out in terms of our college schedule, and I was not given a chance to make that team. I would have had a chance to make it. So even in a perfect season, not quite everything works out perfectly.

That 1957 championship and undefeated season was really the highlight of my basketball career. I played for two years in the NBA, but unfortunately I got picked by the wrong team. Philadelphia drafted me, and that was exactly the wrong place for me to go. They already had a guy in Paul Arizin who was just my size and did the same things I did, only better. He was 6'5", and so was I, and he didn't come out much. He would wind up in the Naismith Memorial Basketball Hall of Fame. I played for two seasons.

I wasn't enjoying it much, and the NBA money wasn't very good back then, so I quit. I was invited back the third year, but it was on the West Coast, and I said, "I think I'm going to hang it up." And that was it. To me, basketball has always been a game. I love it. I still do. But in the scheme of things, it's just a ballgame. People live and die with it, but it's not life and death. Something like Iraq—that's life and death.

After retiring, I ran a bowling alley back in North Carolina for a while and then I became a high school teacher and coach. That turned out to be a great job. I mostly taught and coached in the Miami area. The best player I ever had was Chris Corchiani when he was young, before he became a star at N.C. State.

One trip to Chapel Hill I really enjoyed was in February 2007, when both our 1957 team and the 1982 title team were honored together and had reunions. That was a fantastic weekend. It's so heartwarming to be recognized 50 years later.

In 1957 if McGuire had come to us and said, "I want you to meet the 1907 Carolina team," we'd have looked at him like he was out of his mind. We would have thought, *A bunch of old men—what do we need to meet them for?* But the current players didn't seem to mind meeting us when we had that reunion. And James Worthy, Sam Perkins, Michael Jordan—all the 1982 guys came over to us and thanked us for starting everything at Carolina. That was just tremendous.

Lennie Rosenbluth was the National Collegiate Player of the Year in 1957 (over Wilt Chamberlain). Rosenbluth averaged 28 points per game on the 32–0 UNC team of 1957, which won back-to-back triple-overtime games against Michigan State and Kansas at the Final Four to win the national title for the Tar Heels.

Rosenbluth's career scoring average of 26.9 points remains the highest in Tar Heels history. Although he played only three seasons due to freshmen being ineligible during his career, Rosenbluth still ranks No. 4 in career scoring at the school, trailing only Tyler Hansbrough, Phil Ford, and Sam Perkins. He is one of only four players in conference history (along with Hansbrough,

Antawn Jamison, and Duke's Christian Laettner) to win ACC Player of the Year, ACC Tournament MVP, NCAA Regional MVP, and National Player of the Year honors in the same season. Most of his post-basketball life was spent in Miami, Florida, where he taught and coached at the high school level for decades. Rosenbluth's wife, Pat, died in July 2010 of cancer. The two were college sweethearts and had been married 53 years. Rosenbluth now lives in Chapel Hill and says his favorite current role is the one of grandfather.

TOMMY KEARNS

GUARD

1955–1958

O NE GAME. ONE POINT. IT CHANGED MY LIFE, and so many others. Because we were NCAA champions in 1957, that win keeps getting resurrected. They say winning isn't everything, but in this case, it sure as hell would have been different if we hadn't won. I'm talking about our win in the NCAA championship game, of course—the 54–53 victory in triple overtime we had over Kansas and Wilt Chamberlain.

Being a Tar Heel means lots of things, of course, but when I think about it, that's the first thing that comes to my mind because I've been asked about that game so much over the years.

I'll back up a bit. I came from New York, like so many other players in the 1950s on Frank McGuire's "reverse railroad." I grew up in the Bronx in a neighborhood that was mostly Irish and Italian. My father was a policeman. I played for Louie Carnesecca in high school—I've always had the great fortune of having great instructors and teachers. My school was Catholic, and we were encouraged to attend a Catholic college, too. But McGuire was a master salesman. His hair was slicked back, his suit was always immaculate, his cuff links were always flashing, and he was always pulling on them. He came to the house, visited with my parents, and convinced them that all of us Catholics were going to go down to the South and convert the heathens. Sort of like we were missionaries or something.

When I got to Chapel Hill, it was a culture shock. I'd be walking down Franklin Street, and people would say hello me out of the blue, for no reason. I would think, *What's the con here? What do they want from me?*

I played some as a sophomore, but I was kind of my own worst enemy. I thought I was a lot better than I was. I was probably more self-centered than I should have been, which means you sit on the bench. Frank McGuire, who became a great friend, handled me very well. He let me sit down and think about things. My junior year, right from the get-go, I played a lot and was more team-oriented.

That year we got to the Final Four, in 1957, I was a guard. People forget sometimes, but we actually had two triple-overtime games in that Final Four. We started against Michigan State on a Friday night, then played Kansas on Saturday night. And in that Michigan State game, I was just terrible. It was the worst game I played all season. I barely could score at all—I think I had six points and four fouls. I don't know where I was, but I wasn't there. Michigan State had this guy who could really jump—his name was "Jumping" Johnny Green. They almost beat us several times. At the end of regulation, with the score tied, one of their guys threw it up from about 60 feet, and the damn thing went in. I knew the buzzer had sounded, but you never know how the officials are going to rule in that situation. That would have been an unusual way to have lost.

But the officials said it didn't count, and so we went into overtime. Then, with 11 seconds remaining, we were behind 64–62. Green was at the line for two free throws. If he made either one, we were dead meat, because there was no three-point line at the time. We were 30–0 at the time, and this Michigan State guard sidled up to me before Green shot and whispered, "Thirty and one."

But Green missed them both, Pete Brennan went down and hit a shot for us, and we got to keep going. Eventually, we won in triple overtime.

So we had to play Kansas in the final. And they had Goliath. That was the first thing. They had Goliath, and we all knew it. Who was going to beat Wilt Chamberlain? They had absolutely annihilated San Francisco the night before the championship game. We played our game first on that Friday night—the triple-overtime game where I played so badly and we were very fortunate to win—against Michigan State. That was the first semifinal. When that was over, we went out to watch the first half of Kansas–San Francisco.

I thought we'd stay for the whole thing, but Coach McGuire didn't want us to. He told us to leave at halftime. I think he was worried we would get intimidated.

We weren't a bunch that got intimidated much, though. On Saturday Coach McGuire went around to each of us before the game and asked us if we were scared of Chamberlain. He was great at zeroing in on opponents and what we needed to do. He was our motivator. Buck Freeman, our assistant, was an Xs and Os genius. So everyone was saying, "No, Coach. We're not scared of Chamberlain." A lot of us had played against him before in the summer. When he asked me if I was scared of Chamberlain, I said "Hell, no!" Coach said, "Good. Good! Then you're jumping center against him."

And that was it. One of the most famous moments of my life— I'm sure it will be in my obituary—and that was it. We didn't diagnose it 10 different ways. The reality was no one was going to get the jump over Chamberlain, so why not try to play a mind game with him a little bit? It was just a ploy. I really think that was a Buck Freeman move—he said later he had seen a game in the 1930s in Brooklyn or something where a team did that. It just stuck in Buck's head for 20 years until he decided there was a good time for it. Buck was very cerebral like that.

We were staying only a couple of blocks away from the arena in Kansas City. On the morning of the game, I ran into Jerry Tax. He later became a great friend of mine. He was covering the game for *Sports Illustrated*. He and I sat down and had a cup of coffee. We were just talking, and he was convinced that we really didn't have a chance. I said, "We've just come too far for this thing. There's something out there—a force, looking out for us." I really believed that.

In a lot of places, we were eight- or nine-point underdogs, even though we were undefeated and No. 1. It was clear that we were playing practically on a home court for Kansas. And they had Wilt. It seemed like we had a lot of things working against us. When we came out and looked at the crowd, it was amazing. The night before, it had been more evenly divided, because there weren't many fans from Michigan State, either. But this time? We had maybe 50 to 100 people in the stands. That included my father and my then-brother-in-law. And the governor of North Carolina, too—Luther Hodges. He actually sat on our bench for a while, much to McGuire's chagrin. But just about everybody else in the place—and there were about 10,000 squeezed in there—was rooting for Kansas.

So we started with the jump ball. I pretended like I was really going to jump for it, but then I dropped back on defense. We were going to collapse on Chamberlain the whole game and dare them to shoot 15- to 18-foot jump shots. It seemed like they had the same strategy. They were going to try and take away Lennie Rosenbluth. They opened up in a box-and-one.

We started out great. We loved that sort of defense, because it meant we'd get a lot of open jumpers from the corners over the zone. Pete Brennan and Joe Quigg were hot early, and we were up fast, 9–2.

We were sagging on Wilt at every chance, but he was such a good player, even then. He got his points, but we made him work for them. At halftime, we were up 29–22 and playing perfectly. We had shot incredibly well for the first half [64.7 percent]. We knew we couldn't keep that up forever, but we were confident.

In the second half Kansas made it closer. We didn't shoot as well. Lennie got into foul trouble. I didn't do the jump ball for the second half or any of the overtimes, either—I guess our coaches decided that once was enough. Kansas went to a man-to-man, which was a little more effective. And with about 10 minutes to go, Kansas was actually up by a few points [40–37]. That's when Kansas' coach called for the stall. We were happy to see it. We had played a triple-overtime game the night before, remember, and we could use the rest. So we didn't guard them—we just let them stand out there—until there were about five minutes to go. It was a strategic error on their part. They let us rest.

We went out to guard them again, but we still didn't catch up right away. Then, with a little under two minutes to go, Lennie fouled out. Everyone thought we were done. But not us. We actually caught up [to 46–46] and had the ball on the final possession of regulation but missed a shot.

That put us into the first overtime. We each made an early basket and then had the ball and ran down the clock. We weren't doing that much out there. Given the way they were content to lay back and let us come to them for a lot of the game, I think we could have played six or eight overtimes—it really wasn't as tiring as you would think. No one scored after those early baskets, and so that put us into the second OT.

No one scored a point in that one. But there was one very significant thing that happened. Wilt almost got into a fight with Cunningham and Brennan after a hard foul. Both Coach McGuire and Coach Harp came off the benches and got into it a little with each other before everyone got calmed down. Wilt missed the free throw, though. No one could score. And so we went into the third overtime.

Finally, in that one, I sneaked in for a layup [to put Carolina up 50–48]. Then I got fouled and made a couple of free throws. But Wilt scored on a three-point play, and it got close again. Tensions were high. On one play with it tied 52–52, I was trying to intercept a pass, and instead I came down right on top of this guy [Kansas's Gene Elstun] in front of the Kansas bench. I may have pushed him a little when we collided, too. They probably could have kicked me out of the game. That created some more spontaneous combustion, but it got calmed down again. Elstun made one of two free throws, and that put us down a point with less than a minute left.

We spread the floor. I had the ball up top, and then I beat my man and was dribbling to the basket. While I was on the move, I remembered what Coach Freeman said to me. "What you want to do against Wilt," he had said, "is get an angle and use the backboard. If it's a straightaway shot, there's a significantly higher chance of a block."

Well, I thought I had an angle. I went to the right side. I just *knew* I was going to make it. And Wilt came out of nowhere and knocked it into the grandstands.

We still had the ball, though. Quigg got it and drove. Wilt recovered and blocked that, too, but Maurice King had come over to help and had gotten Joe with the body, and they called the foul. There were six seconds remaining. McGuire called a timeout and told us in the huddle, "Now, when Joe makes these...." He was giving Joe confidence there. And Joe did—he knocked them both down.

On the last play of the game, they tried to feed Wilt again. The ball was a little too low. Joe tapped it. I got the ball just before a couple of Kansas guys, and I threw it high in the air. I knew there were just a couple of seconds left. I knew intuitively that by the time the ball came down, it would be over.

And that's what happened. By the time the ball came down, we were national champions. We were just a bunch of guys from New York—I don't think any of us knew what the hell we had done.

After the game, we all had to walk two or three blocks to the hotel to change. There wasn't really a locker room for us to use in the arena—well, there was one, but it was tiny. It was rainy and cold outside on that walk home, but we were so happy we didn't care. Kansas' guys had to walk back to the hotel, too— I remember Wilt had this British driving cap he was wearing while we walked.

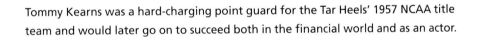

Tommy Kearns was a hard-charging point guard for the Tar Heels' 1957 NCAA title team and would later go on to succeed both in the financial world and as an actor.

After we changed, we went up to McGuire's hotel suite, ready for a late-night supper. McGuire had been sharing the suite with three other coaches—one of them was Dean Smith, who was an assistant at Air Force at the time. Dean had actually been cheering for Kansas during the game, because Kansas was his alma mater, but McGuire obviously didn't hold that against Dean. He would hire him later as an assistant.

Governor Hodges was in the suite, too. He was a real mover and shaker, and he was trying to promote the whole Research Triangle thing at the time. He kept saying how we would be a big boost for the plans for that.

We went out to eat as a team. Kansas' players made the drive back to Lawrence late that night. I have seen tapes and read stories later about how they had a "welcome-home" party at the Kansas Student Union. Louis Armstrong was there as a performer, and when they came in, he and his band played "When the Saints Go Marching In." This was obviously going to be their great return as the triumphant warriors. Well, they returned, but they left the trophy behind.

We went home the next day, and thousands of people gathered to welcome us at the Raleigh-Durham airport. That's when we started to realize the significance of what we had done. Sports on TV was still a very new thing back then—but C.D. Chesley had set up a small network and had broadcast the game in North Carolina on several stations. So a whole lot of people saw it live. And we had gone from being kids from the Bronx and Brooklyn—kids who just loved to play basketball—to being overnight heroes. That year really helped establish the tradition of Carolina basketball as we know it today. At the time it was a great experience, and the best part of it was coming back to Chapel Hill.

It was a big deal in North Carolina, but not so much nationally. Nothing like it is now. There was a little squib in some of the New York papers and that was it. Nothing much, really.

We thought we could repeat in 1958, but we lost Lennie Rosenbluth to graduation and Joe Quigg, our big man, to an injury, and that was too much to overcome. We didn't even win the ACC the next year, so we couldn't go to the NCAA tournament.

I'm really proud to be associated with the University of North Carolina. I joined a fraternity when I was down there, mostly guys from North Carolina, and they took me into their lives. They are great friends of mine to this day. I'll always have such a wonderful, warm feeling about the institution and the friends I made there.

I had a very brief NBA career before the Syracuse Nationals cut me. That was devastating for a while, because basketball was my life. But then I ended up working on Wall Street and doing some other things as an investment banker. I even developed a friendship with Wilt over the years. We stayed at each others' houses some, and I helped him invest some of his money. We saw each other at a basketball game years after that game in Kansas City, exchanged pleasantries, and it went from there. I've had a very blessed life, and I'm so glad I went to Carolina. That was the key to so much of it.

Tommy Kearns was a gritty, 5'11" point guard for the Tar Heels in the mid-1950s and has stayed closely connected to the university ever since. He won the school's Distinguished Alumnus Award in 1996. He was 14 inches shorter than the 7'1" Wilt Chamberlain when the two jumped center at the start of the 1957 title game.

A third-team All-American in 1958, Kearns was selected in the NBA's fourth round but ended up taking only one shot in his NBA career. He made it. Then he left basketball and rose rapidly in the financial world.

Kearns married a Duke alumna—the former Betsy Wright—and turned her into a Tar Heels fan. The two of them have three children. Kearns remains active on the boards of several companies and with a number of fund-raising and artistic endeavors at UNC. He still plays golf occasionally with Roy Williams. Now retired, Kearns has lived in the greater New York area since 1969 and for years was a successful investment banker on Wall Street.

Kearns also has dabbled in acting. He had a prominent speaking role as a high school basketball coach in the 2000 hit movie *Finding Forrester*, which starred Sean Connery as a reclusive novelist.

YORK LARESE

GUARD

1958–1961

H EAVEN. THAT'S WHAT I THOUGHT OF when I first saw the campus at
Chapel Hill. I'd never seen anything more beautiful in my life.

I grew up in New York, so the South was really new to me. I went to the
same high school as Tommy Kearns—St. Ann's, which was a Catholic school
in New York that eventually became Archbishop Molloy. Lou Carnesecca
was my high school coach there, and Tommy's, too. I was two years behind
Tommy in school, and we played one year together, when he was a senior and
I was a sophomore. I lived in Greenwich Village and had to take three subway trains to get to school, so I could get from the west side of Manhattan to
the east side.

There was not a lot of athleticism in my family until me, but there were a
lot of hard-working people. My father's name was Oswald, and he had a business in New York City, where he catered to the big restaurants, supplying
them with copper pots. He was a tinsmith. He and two of his partners did
that for a long time. But he could do just about anything with his hands—
plastering, bricklaying, you name it. My mother's name was Valentine. I had
one older brother. The family was originally from Italy.

By the time I was in eighth grade, I was about 5′11″—taller than the rest
of the kids in my class. People kept saying, "Why don't you try basketball?"
So I tried it, and from then on it was in my blood. It still is today.

Frank McGuire had quite a recruiting pipeline into the New York area then. He got interested in me, and I came down for a visit. Tommy Kearns showed me around since I knew him. It was something else. The beauty, the kindness people showed you, all the fans so interested in college basketball—I never seriously considered going anywhere else after that visit.

When I got to Chapel Hill, of course, the freshmen could still only play on the freshman basketball team. Tommy and that 1957 team won the national title in my freshman year. Then in my second year, when I thought I was going to get to play with Tommy again, I ended up having several operations on my knee and basically sat out that year. Then I had three years on the varsity after that, from 1959 to 1961.

Frank McGuire was a great man to play ball under. He was our surrogate father. He was always looking out for us if we needed anything. It was our first time out of the New York or New Jersey area for most of us who came down in those years. Maybe our first plane flight. So the South was something to get used to.

I was a pretty good shooter. Coach McGuire and Duke's coach, Vic Bubas, both called me the best shooter they had ever seen while I was in college. I don't think I really was the best, but I was pretty good. I wasn't that good at handling the ball, though—fortunately we had guys like Larry Brown and Donnie Walsh who could do that.

19

What I also became known for, after one game in 1959, was free-throw shooting. Starting in that 1959–1960 season at UNC, I would get the ball for free throws and shoot almost without looking. I don't teach that method to kids nowadays, but it sure worked for me.

Against Duke in 1959 in the Dixie Classic, I made 21-of-21 free throws in a single game. That record still stands. The funny thing is that the year before, as a sophomore, I didn't have a great free-throw shooting year. My free-throw percentage wasn't much better than my field-goal percentage. I said, "You know what? I'm going to try something else."

And so one time I tried shooting as quickly as I got the ball, and that worked, and so I kept doing it. All of a sudden my free-throw percentage was in the 80s. Opposing players would give me some heat about it. They would often not even be set up for the rebound, and I'd already have launched it.

This particular game was in Raleigh, where it seemed in those days we'd play more often than we'd play in Chapel Hill back at Woollen Gym. We'd

20

York Larese once went 21-for-21 from the free-throw line in a single game, setting both Tar Heels and ACC records for marksmanship that still stand.

have the Dixie Classic there in Raleigh before the ACC season started. And then we'd play a game at N.C. State, and then the ACC tournament, too.

I had not been shooting very well coming into the game, but Coach McGuire had confidence in me and told me it was just a matter of time.

I started off hot in that game. I was in a zone with my jumper. I shot that real quickly, too—I would just stop on a dime and release. I wasn't a very fast player, and that would later hurt me in the pros. But in college I got the ball off so quickly that footspeed didn't matter as much. There was a lot of emphasis on scoring in those days, and I happened to have a pure shot. It was a remarkable asset.

Also, in those days, you could draw a charge relatively easily and then get to shoot a one-on-one on the other side. So that gave me a lot of opportunities. I would leave my man when a guy was driving the baseline, run to where he was going to end up, take the collision, and that was it. Another charge. Two more free throws.

I knew I was having a great free-throw shooting evening, but I didn't know how many I had. We won the game without too much trouble, jumping out to an early lead over Duke and staying in front the whole way [UNC would win 75–53 behind Larese's 37 points]. I ended up with 21 straight free throws. I was in quite a groove. As fast as I was shooting the ball, I can't believe even now all of them went in. Coach McGuire liked to play all his starters almost the whole game, and that gave me some more chances, too. It was definitely a game I'll never forget.

Another game I will never forget—in fact, the most memorable game of my life—came in 1962. I was a teammate of Wilt Chamberlain's the night he scored 100 points in an NBA game in Hershey, Pennsylvania.

Hershey was an unusual place to play. The smell of chocolate was everywhere. You could actually smell it in your clothes for days afterward.

That was my only season in the pros, although I did play in the Eastern League for many years later—it was sort of a minor league compared to the NBA. I usually played only about seven minutes a game.

But the funny thing was that I was in the groove, too, that night in Hershey. I hit four out of five shots the night Wilt scored 100. But somebody else had the better groove on, and I had to stop my groove. I don't regret it. A lot of reporters have asked me the biggest thrill. The biggest thrill of my life was playing in the 100-point game, because that'll go on forever. Kobe Bryant got 81 once in an NBA game, but I don't think anyone will ever get 100 again.

I was able to get the assist when Wilt scored his 97th and 98th points. It really was something to be a part of that. The New York Knicks weren't letting him score late, either. They made Wilt earn everything. They didn't want to be part of a 100-point game.

There was a funny story that season in the NBA about my free-throw shooting, too. There was this NBA referee named Mendy Rudolph, and he was a showboat. He wanted the limelight more than the players.

In those days the referee would hand you the ball for a free throw and really take his time moving out of the way. So one time Mendy Rudolph didn't get out of the way fast enough, and I shot one that skimmed off his head. "Why'd you do that?" he asked. I apologized and said I didn't mean to, but that was just the way I shot free throws. He let me shoot it again, and this time he stood a long way away and just carefully bounced the ball to me.

Once I got out of college, I returned for many years to work at Carolina's basketball camps. Dean Smith and I worked together in the summertime to come up with a fundamental way to teach free-throw shooting. I had a lot of those already but didn't know it. There are just a few basic rules: balance, concentration on the rim, extending your arm after you shoot, and then really following through. All of those things play a specific part in a successful free throw. I don't teach people to shoot it as fast as I did, though.

More than 50 years after being set, York Larese's 21-for-21 free-throw night still stands as a record for perfection from the line at both North Carolina and in the ACC. In all the years since, no UNC player has ever made more than 16 free throws without a miss during a single game (that was Phil Ford in 1976).

Larese was an all-conference guard for three straight seasons and was also a second-team All-American as a senior, which is why his No. 22 jersey hangs from the rafters at the Smith Center.

Larese played a single season in the NBA—playing under Frank McGuire, just as he did in college. After leaving North Carolina under pressure, McGuire coached the Philadelphia Warriors in 1962. But when the team moved to California the next season, Larese decided not to go.

Larese earned his degree from UNC in sociology, and he worked at an institution for troubled kids early in his career. He also worked for many years in sales and promotion for both Converse and Puma, staying close to basketball.

From 2000 to 2004, Larese was a scout for four seasons with the Indiana Pacers, which he said was the best job he has ever had. Larese has four children—two boys and two girls. He and his wife Barbara live in the Boston area, where Larese is brave enough to openly root for the New York Yankees. He has taught shooting at Carolina basketball camps for more than 40 years.

The

SIXTIES

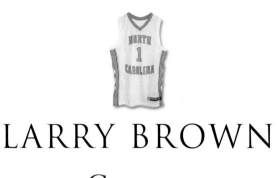

LARRY BROWN

GUARD

1960–1963

I PERSONALLY HAVE BEEN GIVEN A CHALLENGE—a charge, so to speak—to take over for what Coach McGuire and Coach Smith did. If you look at my career, every player from Darrell Elston to Donald Watson to Jimmy Black to Joe Wolf to Dennis Wuycik to Steve Previs to Kevin Salvadori, I either drafted them or signed them or had them because that was what Coach Smith would have expected from me. When assistant coaches got fired—like John Kuester when he lost his job or when Dave Hanners, Phil Ford, and Pat Sullivan lost their jobs—I had them after that.

Here's the perfect example of what I think it is about Chapel Hill. When I was the head coach for the Denver Nuggets, we had the ninth pick in the draft in 1977. That year I already had Bobby Jones, Dan Issel, and David Thompson—a terrific team. And Tommy LaGarde was in the draft. Coach Smith would always call me before the draft and find out where a kid was going to get drafted and ask for my help if a kid wasn't going to get drafted—then either I had to draft him or figure out a way.

So Coach Smith called me and asked me what we were thinking. I told him we had the ninth pick. We were probably going to take Bernard King or Tree Rollins. If Bernard was gone, we'd probably want Tree [the former Clemson star] because we thought Tree could play with Bobby and Dan Issel. Bernard was such a special talent that we thought we could play him at the three position, small forward, where he could be a tremendous rebounder.

Coach said Tommy LaGarde is going to be picked at No. 4—Coach was really proud of that.

Carl Scheer was our general manager at the time and would always ask me what I thought about the draft. I told him what we were thinking. Then, before the draft started, I got a call from Coach Smith. "Tommy LaGarde failed a physical," he said. "He's not going to go at No. 4. You're going to draft Tommy LaGarde."

I said, "Coach, you know Tommy is too much like Dan and Bobby. We're going to draft Bernard or Tree. That makes more sense." But he repeated, "Tommy failed a physical. You're going to draft Tommy LaGarde." I said, "Coach, you know I love you, but I can't do that.'"

So there were five minutes between picks. Bernard went at No. 7. In a few minutes, it's our turn. Carl Scheer turned to me and said, "Okay, we're going to take Tree?" And I said, "Carl, we're going to take Tommy LaGarde."

Yes, we took him. We got a contract exclusion on his knee because he didn't pass the test. If we traded him, there was no exclusion. The contract was guaranteed. So we took Tommy, his knee was not 100 percent, and I traded him to Seattle. That fully funded his contract. He played maybe one season for us, so I did my duty there.

Years later I was teasing Coach. We were playing golf together, and I said, "Coach, we knew Tommy was a little banged up. That was a big draft for us. Why'd you tell me to draft him?"

And Coach said, "I knew you would be all right."

That, to me, is what Coach is all about. I know how much he cares for me. But at the end of the day, he wanted me to be all right, but he also wanted to make sure Tommy LaGarde was all right. I try to tell all our guys that it's just a unique thing.

I've heard so many people tell me that they don't understand Coach Smith, that they don't know him. Outside the Carolina family, I mean. I would tell them he's the finest, most decent man I've ever met, but you guys would never know it because he doesn't have enough time for anybody else. He only has time for the people in our family. And it's not that he's going to disrespect you guys or he doesn't really care about you, he just has so much time in his life, and his only interest—aside from his family and religion—is those kids and those coaches and those people who have been part of that program. Everyone would love him if they had that opportunity.

Little things make you know it's a family. Say you go to watch a practice back when Coach Smith was coaching. I'd bring some people with me—people who were close to me. He'd make them sit up at the top. But if you're a Carolina family guy, you can sit down on the floor.

I go to an NBA All-Star Game now, and all the Carolina guys will be together. And I will watch how the other programs would, in a way, envy that. They would make fun of it, but I know, deep down, they wanted the same thing. Coach McGuire did that, but Dean took it to another level. And I get a little bit upset that a lot of guys have forgotten about what we're about in terms of hiring guys, signing guys, looking out for guys.

Coach Smith had a saying that he lived by: during the season, it was about the team. So if you were a player and you were a little out of whack, didn't get your priorities straight, you weren't going to do anything to affect that team. But when the season's over, it was about the kid. And that's why he pushed guys out to the NBA.

Forget about the team. Just like when he resigned. Coach Smith wasn't sure Bill Guthridge would take the job. He won't admit that, though.

But when he resigned in 1997, he left Bill a phenomenal group. He put them in a position where they couldn't do anything else but hire Bill. And, as a result, Bill did a phenomenal job. He might not have accepted that responsibility had it been the summer.

I've been blessed because a lot of people who have worked with me are now coaching. And that's my greatest thrill, because I'm doing what I'm doing because of Coach McGuire and Coach Smith. The fact that I went to North Carolina has enabled me to do what I love.

I've always been reluctant to ask Coach for anything. But if I had a guy I wanted to help get a job, I figured if you asked Coach Smith to put in a recommendation, it would hold a lot of weight. So every time I've ever asked Coach to please call on behalf of somebody, he'd say, "Well, let me check with…," and he'd go down a list of 15 Carolina guys who might not be working at the time. And then if they were all taken care of, he'd say, "Yeah Larry, I'd be happy to do that."

If you call him up, the first thing Coach says is, "How's Shelly, how's L.J., how's Madison?" That's my wife, son, and daughter. And it's not just me. He's like that with everybody. He remembers.

As for why I went to Carolina in the first place after playing basketball in high school in New York, people don't realize that my high school coach

Larry Brown (with ball) was a good enough point guard to play both for the Tar Heels and the U.S. Olympic team, but he would achieve his greatest success as a Hall of Fame basketball coach.

went to Carolina. His wife went there. He'd tell me about how great it was, how he used to take her to the Arboretum. I didn't know why he'd want to look at plants and flowers, but then I figured it out. You can use your imagination. But he said someday he hoped I'd be good enough to go to Carolina. And I remember one day he came up and said, "Wow, you're good enough." That was a big day. And Coach McGuire…he really recruited my mom. And she told me that was where I was going.

I was Jewish, and I remember when I decided to go to Carolina, some people said I'd see some prejudice, going down South. But I never experienced anything. It never entered my mind.

When I went, we had an unbelievable recruiting class. But Artie Heyman—we grew up together—he left and went to Duke instead [Heyman's stepfather and North Carolina coach Frank McGuire got in an argument one night at the

Carolina Inn, and afterward, Heyman backed out of his commitment]. And we had several other guys who couldn't get into school or it didn't work out. So suddenly my recruiting class was just Dieter Krause, Marty Conlon, and myself. And so my freshman team was awful. My sophomore year, we went on NCAA probation [due to "improper recruiting entertainment," according to the NCAA] and couldn't go to the NCAA tournament. So Coach McGuire said, "Screw it, we ain't playing in the ACC tournament, either." Then I got in a fight [in 1961, when North Carolina played Duke at Cameron Indoor Stadium, Brown and Heyman were part of a major scuffle] and got suspended for the rest of the season. We only had a limited schedule anyway, so I played about 15 games my sophomore year.

Then Coach McGuire left after my sophomore year. I was devastated because I didn't know Coach Smith like I know him now. So in my junior year they cut our schedule to 17 games [because of irregularities under McGuire's watch], and then my senior year, we still only had 21 games—I barely played 50 collegiate games in three years. And my coach left halfway through. And still, I look back on it, and it's still probably the most significant, important time in my life.

After two years of playing basketball with Goodyear [for a team supported by the tire company] and then playing on the 1964 Olympic team, Coach asked me to come back to coach. And those were the two happiest years I've ever had in coaching—my two years as his assistant. At that time there were only two assistants. He made me the coach of the freshman team. He'd watch, but he'd let me make mistakes and learn how to coach. He never allowed me to miss any varsity practices.

To this day, I believe Larry Miller was the most important signing the program ever had, even though Bobby Lewis was phenomenal before that. But Larry was the first phenomenal player in Coach's era who could have gone anywhere but said, "I'm going to Carolina." And then that group of Rusty Clark, Bill Bunting, Dick Grubar, Gerald Tuttle, and Joe Brown—that was the most significant recruiting class ever. That team went to the Final Four three times in a row, from 1967 to 1969. I coached them all as freshmen. And I think from then on it was history. The program kept growing and growing and growing.

The biggest disappointment I think I've ever had is not getting to be the Tar Heels' head coach. Coach Smith called me when he recommended Roy Williams the first time, in 2000. He told me, "The reason I'm recommending

Roy is obviously he's a great coach and he's in college now at Kansas. So he's more in tune with it." But then he said, "If Roy turns it down, I want you."

So Roy turned it down that time. And then Dick Baddour [the UNC athletics director] came to Los Angeles, and I met with him when Roy turned it down. And it was the most bullshit thing. It was just a guy spending an hour with me telling me why I shouldn't have the job, why I shouldn't coach there. It was the most embarrassed I've ever been. I finally told Baddour, "With all due respect to Roy, I think I'm not chopped liver as a coach. I think I can coach."

I told Coach Smith about it later, and he said, "Well, I'm going to go and make sure you're going to get this job." I said, "Coach, Shelly and I talked about it. Why would I want to work for somebody who really didn't want me?" And I don't know if the president really wanted me, either. Coach kept saying no, you should be the coach, and I said, "No, that's okay."

And then when it came about again, the second time in 2003 when it didn't work out with Matt Doherty, Coach Smith told me again, "We want Roy, but if it doesn't work out, we want you."

And again, I wanted so badly to be involved. For one, because I've always loved coaching college. And two, I remember when I was a young coach. In my heart, I wanted to be the next coach at North Carolina. But I realized that meant I would be replacing Coach, and I never wanted him to stop, so that was not a real goal of mine. But when he decided to step down, well, I realized Bill should have been the coach. But when Bill resigned, I thought that based on what I've done, not just as a coach but what I've tried to do to be part of that family—I always thought I honored and respected that charge.

With all that being said, I got to coach Kansas, and there are so many similarities between the two programs. I got to coach UCLA. I've had a pretty charmed life doing this.

I still have Tar Heels everywhere around me in Charlotte, coaching the Bobcats. I have Phil Ford and Dave Hanners here, as well as all the other coaches I've had in the NBA now. They're all family. I did love going to school there, too. Outside of basketball, I made a lot of great friends. But my whole life, I've had a hard time balancing family and coaching. That's something that has always been an issue with me. But I love the program, I love Roy. I talk to him some, and I want to see him do well. I die when I watch Carolina lose, and I have a big smile when I see the accomplishments.

29

I go back to Chapel Hill at least once a year when Roy has his coaching clinic. We bring back everybody—all the coaches—and share ideas and play some golf. We do it around Labor Day each year. But I don't like to get up there for games as much as I do just watching them on TV.

Still, the school means everything to me. My two older daughters went there. My first wife went to Carolina. My two daughters' husbands went to Carolina. My younger daughter wants to go to Carolina. My son wants to go to film school, so he probably won't go there, but we all love North Carolina.

I take a lot of pride in having gone to school there, played there, and coached there. And just think how fortunate I've been—coaching in some way at UCLA, Kansas, and North Carolina.

Coach McGuire did it his way. He was so unique. And then Coach Smith set the bar so high. And it's not even his record, it's everything he's done—how he led his life, how he respected the game, how he helped integrate the school with Charlie Scott.

I'll tell you a Charlie Scott story to finish up: one time in 1966, when I was an assistant, Coach sent me out to see him. He said, "Larry, I heard about this kid from New York who happens to be going to a school in North Carolina. And we can't afford not to look at every North Carolina kid because we can't lose anybody and say we didn't see him. I want you to go down to Laurinburg and see this kid play."

I was in Lebanon, Indiana, at the time, and was there to watch Rick Mount. That day I sat in the stands with Frank Deford, who was doing an article for *Sports Illustrated* on Mount. Rick ended up on the cover of *SI* [in February 1966].

I don't know how many coaches were there—dozens, at least. Mostly they were head coaches, and I was an assistant at the time. I got no time afterward— I got to shake Rick Mount's hand, and that was about it. Zero time. So I called Coach Smith up, and he said. "What did you think?" I said he was all right. He said, "What do you mean? Did he disrespect you? Did he not show you any love?" I said he was a terrific player, but I didn't go all crazy about him.

So then I got on a plane, flew to Raleigh, and drove down to Laurinburg to go to this game. They had a tile floor. I saw this kid running up and down the tile floor about four or five trips, and I went running to find a pay phone. I called Coach and said, "Coach, this kid is a better prospect than Rick Mount."

"Awww, Larry," he said. But I told him he had to believe me—he had to come down there and see him. So he came down the next day. He thought he was pretty special, too. That Charles Scott—let me tell you, he was something.

Larry Brown was the first Tar Heels basketball player to play in the Olympics, winning a gold medal for the U.S. in Tokyo in 1964. He was the leading scorer (16.5 points per game) in Dean Smith's first season as head coach, made All-ACC as a guard, and later served as an assistant for Smith for two years in the mid-1960s.

Later a famously nomadic head coach himself, Brown won an NCAA title at Kansas in 1988 and an NBA title with the Detroit Pistons in 2004. He also has won more than 1,000 professional games (coaching in both the NBA and ABA) and was enshrined into the Naismith Memorial Basketball Hall of Fame in 2002.

Brown now coaches the NBA's Charlotte Bobcats—Michael Jordan hired Brown to do so in 2008 in his role as the Bobcats' managing member of basketball operations. He led the Bobcats to their first-ever playoff appearance in 2010, following his second season as the team's head coach. Brown has also been the head coach of eight other current NBA teams.

Born in 1940, Brown is considered one of the preeminent teachers of the game today. The Bobcats took his "Play the Right Way" mantra and made it the team slogan.

CHARLIE SHAFFER

FORWARD

1961–1964

I'VE HAD A VERY LONG CONNECTION with Chapel Hill, dating back to 1951. My mother and father both went to school there in the 1930s. A lot of my other relatives did, too, including my mother's father, who was named John Wallace Winborne. He was an attorney and ended up being the chief justice of the North Carolina Supreme Court.

My father played football at Carolina. He was a classmate of Jim Tatum, who would later become the football coach. I was born December 21, 1941—two weeks after Pearl Harbor—and we were living in Greensboro in 1950 when the UNC chancellor called Daddy. He wanted my father to become the university's first director of development. He said, "Charlie, have you ever thought about coming back to Chapel Hill?" As the story goes, my father said, "No, not more than once a day." And he'd been out of college 15 years by that time!

So we moved from Greensboro to Chapel Hill in 1951, and Daddy worked at the university. I grew up mostly in Chapel Hill and was so blessed to do that. The whole campus was my playground. I loved all sports. Since my dad knew Coach Tatum, occasionally Coach Tatum would invite us over to his house, and we'd throw the football or watch some film in his den. We lived two blocks from the tennis courts, and so I would go over there and play. I later played tennis for Carolina, too. And then, of course, there was basketball.

I remember a lot of cold Saturday mornings, going down to Woollen Gym when I was about 11 years old, and playing on that main court from about 8:00 AM to noon with my friends until they started putting the bleachers up and turning the lights on for the home games. Then they'd kick us off the court. Coach Frank McGuire came to Chapel Hill in 1952 and was very kind to me. I used to go out there and watch his teams practice in the 1950s. I got to know Coach McGuire and his assistant, Buck Freeman, as well.

Sometimes they'd say, "Come on down here," and I'd get to shoot layups with the varsity as the team warmed up or maybe free throws at the end of practice. People know a lot about McGuire, but Coach Freeman was a real character, too. He was this rough, tough Irishman who was single and lived in the bottom of Woollen Gym. Just a great shooting coach. And he had all these ideas. He thought you needed to eat at least three vegetables every day—two grown on top of the ground and one in the ground, or "two over and one under," as he would put it. He also thought that the backspin on your free throws should make the ball rotate backward no more than three and a half times when you shot them—more rotations than that, and the ball would come off the rim too strongly. Things like that.

One spring in 1955 I went into Woollen Gym and saw Tommy Kearns there. I had had braces on my teeth for about five years and had just gotten them off that morning. I wanted to go shoot. Kearns had just played on the UNC freshman team, and the season was over. This was before his team would win the 1957 national championship and he would jump center against Wilt Chamberlain and all of that. He was just shooting the ball and didn't know me from Adam. But he invited me to play one-on-one with him.

33

They had pulled all the big baskets up, and all that was left were these baskets you could roll around. They were portable and had these steel pipes on the side. He was shooting on one of those. Well, he was beating me easily, but I was loving it, to get to play with someone you knew was a high-school All-American when you were only about 13 or 14 yourself. One time I tried to drive around him, went up for a layup, and came down on one of those steel pipes. Face-first.

It knocked me out. And when I came to, I had knocked out five teeth. I was bleeding all over the place. And here was Kearns, who didn't even know who I was and sure didn't want something like this to happen. But he took me to the training room, they called Daddy, and then they took me to the UNC Dental School. They rushed me right in there and worked on my

34

Charlie Shaffer grew up in Chapel Hill and captained both the basketball and tennis teams at UNC before becoming an attorney and eventually helping secure the 1996 Summer Olympics for Atlanta.

mouth, teeth, and face for five hours—until about 10:00 that night. Tommy Kearns stayed with me the whole time—with a kid he didn't even know who had busted his face up. That really meant so much to me. They ended up giving me false teeth, and I played with them for years. At least they put them in straight, so I didn't need braces again.

I ended up going to Carolina, but the teams I played on weren't that great in terms of their records. These were the real early years for Coach Dean Smith—I played on his first three teams. But we did have some great moments, and I think my favorite was our game at Kentucky during my junior year. Larry Brown was our point guard, Yogi Poteet was our big guard, I was the small forward, and Billy Cunningham was our center.

On December 17, 1962, we went out to play at Kentucky. They had Cotton Nash, who was a preseason All-American. It was on a Monday night. We got there early and saw a little of the freshman game. There were thousands of people already there, and their freshman team was great. It was made up of "Rupp's Runts," who would play for the national championship a few years later. Anyway, the freshman team was winning 48–6 or something like that. We thought, *Holy cow!* The whole situation was a little intimidating.

But when we got in the dressing room, Coach Smith said, "When you look at the other team's jerseys out there, don't see 'Kentucky' on them. Pretend it says, 'Tennessee.'" At that time, Tennessee wasn't very good. And that really helped us. What also helped us is we played a box-and-one on Nash. Yogi Poteet trailed him all over the floor.

When Coach Smith got there that first year, he had taught us tenacious man-to-man defense. If you're one pass away from the ball, you do not let the person you're guarding touch the ball. You have to be between your person and the ball. This was a lot different—Frank McGuire's teams mostly played zone. We worked and worked on man-to-man defense.

And Nash simply could not get the ball. When you watched films of the game, at the end you'd see Nash just standing in a corner on offense. We were on this big stage out in Kentucky, using this defense, and Kentucky didn't know what to do. Coach Smith was 31 years old at the time and was outcoaching one of the greatest coaches in basketball history in Adolph Rupp. That's when I could really see Coach Smith's greatness—that night. That was a remarkable breakthrough for us. To me, it remains the finest game he's ever coached.

I ended up shooting 5-for-5 from the floor that night and 5-for-5 from the free-throw line, too. We won 68–66. Larry Brown was our point guard, and we played what was sort of a version of the "four corners," although we called it the "Kentucky play" at the time. You had to have a great point guard to run it, and Larry Brown was a great one.

It was just one of the most exciting games I've ever played in. I'll never forget toward the end of the game when a ball rolled right in front of Adolph

35

Rupp and I was chasing it and ended up standing right over him. He had this puzzled look on his face, like he didn't know what to do. I thought to myself, *Everybody knows you, but there's a young coach on the other team tonight who's going to be better than you are.*

From 1964 to 1967, I was an assistant coach for the freshman team while I was in law school at Carolina. That was fabulous. I loved playing for Coach Smith, but by coaching a little I got to see the program from the inside. I could sit in on some of the coaches' meetings, see how well he treated all his players, and get involved with the recruiting just a little. There were some great freshmen coming in at that time—Larry Miller, Rusty Clark, Dick Grubar, Bill Bunting, Charlie Scott—guys like that. I started to understand what a great recruiter Coach Smith was then, too. He was never flamboyant. He didn't talk loudly. But he had this incredible knowledge of the game and was so straightforward and sincere.

I have spent most of my adult life in Atlanta since attending Carolina. But I have remained involved with the school because it is so important to me. I was one of the leaders of the "Carolina First" fund-raising campaign, which raised $2.3 billion over a seven-year period. We were fortunate to hold that campaign at the right time, before the economy had its tough times, and we really caught a wave of alumni affection for Carolina. And I have maintained many connections with the school over the years. My mother and daddy lived in the same house at 716 Gimghoul Road for 50 years. My wife, Harriet, and I have two daughters, and they both went to Carolina and played tennis there. It's just such a wonderful place, and I feel so blessed to have been a part of it.

Because of all that, I am so glad I played in the UNC alumni game in February 2010. I wasn't going to play when I first heard about it. I'm 68 years old. I've had a knee transplant and back problems. I just didn't see any way in the world I could run up and down the court. But Billy Harrison, an old teammate, called me about a month before and said, "You're going to play in the game, aren't you? There are a couple of alumni from around the Class of 1942. If they're going to play, you've got to play." So I did, and I'm so glad I did.

That was a great reunion. There were about 230 lettermen who came back, and I think 64 or 65 of them said they would play. They divided us into blue and white teams. In my part of the game, I got lucky and was able to make a layup late. It was so great being out there. They had these four-minute segments and then an interval where Woody Durham would interview somebody or there would be highlights shown on the scoreboard to keep the crowd involved—and it really was a sellout, more than 20,000 people were there.

For one of the final intervals, they lowered the lights and introduced Coach Smith at halfcourt. He stood in the spotlight—reluctantly, of course, trying to drag other people in there with him—and he got at least a five-minute standing ovation. Maybe more. It was one of the most moving things I have ever seen. All of the players who had dressed out ringed the court when it happened. It just brought tears to my eyes. Coach Smith set such a high standard as a coach—and an equally high standard as a man—for all of us. He has always been such a gentleman, whether the ball bounced the right way or not. It was just a wonderful evening, and it just made me so proud and honored to be a letterman at Carolina.

Charlie Shaffer lives in Atlanta, Georgia. He was a Morehead Scholar at Carolina and graduated Phil Beta Kappa. He also earned a law degree from UNC. He was a captain for both the basketball and tennis teams, earning six letters, and would have been the varsity football team's quarterback, too, if not for a serious knee injury he suffered while playing quarterback for UNC's freshman football team. As Dean Smith once noted in an interview, "Charlie really came to UNC as a football player first. [Coach Jim] Tatum thought he'd be one of the great quarterbacks of all time."

Shaffer didn't do badly at basketball, either, averaging 11.1 points and 6.3 rebounds in his three seasons for Smith.

"What a résumé Charlie Shaffer had by the time he finished here," Smith said. "Multisport leader, all sorts of academic honors, involved in student government—we didn't do anything there. That was all him. He did so many great things here that people were forecasting him to be the future governor of North Carolina by the time he was finished here."

Shaffer (rhymes with "laugher") now looks a bit like the late actor Gregory Peck. He was a trial lawyer with an Atlanta law firm for 37 years. A renowned civic leader in Atlanta, he was instrumental in Atlanta's bid to host the 1996 Summer Olympics, which was successful against all odds. He also helped on the city's successful efforts to lure the 2000 Super Bowl and the 2007 Final Four to Atlanta.

After leaving his law practice, Shaffer served for four and a half years as president and CEO of the Marcus Institute, a resource center for children with developmental disabilities. He now serves as the executive vice president for institutional advancement at the Westminster Schools in Atlanta—a private Christian school in northwest Atlanta that serves grades K through 12.

Shaffer and his wife, Harriet, have three children—Charles III graduated from Princeton, and Caroline and Emi both graduated from Carolina. They also have eight grandchildren—Charles IV, Andrew, Ada, David, Dylan, Daniel, Houston, and Henry.

BILLY CUNNINGHAM
FORWARD/CENTER
1962–1965

W HEN I THINK OF CAROLINA and what it means to be a Tar Heel, I think
of two words before anything else: Dean Smith. Of course, there's a
lot more to it than that, but Dean was such a wonderful complement to the
University. He and the school just seemed to go together so perfectly.

I tell people now that—in the instant-gratification society we live in—
Dean might never have survived those first three or four years he had in the
early 1960s. Because we weren't very good, and we weren't making the
NCAA tournament, and who puts up with three or four years like that now?
Shoot, people get mad at Roy Williams now if he loses a couple of games in
a row, and he won two NCAA championships in five years. But luckily we
had a chancellor at Carolina then in William Aycock who had hired Dean,
who believed in what Dean was doing, and who knew that it just took time.
Dean was able to build a foundation for us, and it just took off from there.

I was Frank McGuire's final recruit at Carolina, but he never ended up
coaching me there. He was gone to Philadelphia to coach the NBA's
Philadelphia Warriors by the time I was able to play any basketball. In New
York City, when I was growing up, you started school in either February or
September, depending on your birthdate. So I started in February and then
graduated in February, too, in 1961. I actually went down to Carolina for
three or four months after that, but my true freshman year started in the fall
of 1961. By that time, Frank was gone.

Now McGuire was different than Dean. When McGuire walked into a room, you could sense it. He just had this presence. It's a gift that some people have, and Dean didn't have it. He's not that way. But Dean also made you feel like a person, not just a basketball player. He cared about you long after you left school, and that was whether you were the 12th man or the star. He helped you find jobs and helped you through life—the kind of things you appreciate more once you're out of school.

But I didn't know Dean well when I was in high school. I came to North Carolina because of Frank. Frank's sister lived around the block from us. I delivered the newspaper to her. So I was one of the easiest recruits he ever had. My father said I needed to go to either a Catholic college or down to play for "Uncle Frank." I had lived in the same house for 18 years, and I was ready to get down to a place that looked like Carolina, so that was a no-brainer.

I grew up in a little row house in Brooklyn. Guys were jealous of me because we actually had a tree in our yard—most people didn't. Basketball was my first love. For my fifth birthday, I got a basketball from my father—he was the assistant fire chief for all of New York City. I loved that basketball. I took it out to the schoolyard that day and fell in love with the game.

The thing was that I wasn't sure I wanted to stay at Carolina once McGuire was gone. A lot of schools started pursuing me again, wanting me to transfer once they heard he was out. Dean was taking over, and I had to make a decision whether to stay there with this unknown coach.

Why did I stay? I guess the simplest way to say it is that I felt comfortable more than anything. That might be oversimplifying the thought process a little, but that was really it. I told my dad I wanted to stay there, and so I did.

We weren't very good for most of my years there. We never played in the NCAA tournament. The most famous story from that time is when some students hung Coach Smith in effigy and we ripped it down. We were coming back on the bus from Wake Forest—this was in 1965, and we had lost another one badly, by 22 points.

We pulled up in front of Woollen Gym, and this thing was hanging there on a tree. The truth was that we weren't sure what the devil it was. Then someone said, "They're hanging Coach Smith in effigy!" And we didn't understand why. We knew we were the ones who lost the game, not Dean Smith. We took that very personally, and several of us jumped off the bus and took turns ripping it down. [Smith has said many times since that he

Billy Cunningham, known as "the Kangaroo Kid" at North Carolina, still holds numerous school records for rebounding and would later win NBA championships both as a player and a coach.

knew it was supposed to be him because of the big nose, and that he was glad the students "settled for hanging a dummy" instead of the real thing. Smith was also hanged in effigy on campus a second time a week later after a loss to N.C. State—that incident attracted little media notice, and Cunningham and the other players were mostly not aware of it until years later.]

What I remember more than anything about those days are not the games. Those fade away. What I remember are the relationships and the friendships that came out of that time. We got to go back for the 100th anniversary of Carolina basketball in February 2010, and I can't tell you how excited my wife and I were about that. A few years before that, we had a reunion of the first five teams that Dean Smith coached. Once we got there, it seemed just like yesterday that we had been on that campus. You picked right up where you were 40 years ago. It was just wonderful seeing these people. And here's an interesting fact—nearly 70 percent of the players in those first five years ended up going on to graduate school. Forget just getting your diploma—everyone did that. Seventy percent kept on going. There were so many lawyers in that room, it was scary!

There is still a big connection among those old teams, even though not all of us won that often. Not that long ago I went to Denver for a dinner honoring Doug Moe. Larry Brown was there, and so was George Karl and some other Carolina guys, right in the middle of the NBA season. All that sort of thing goes back to Dean Smith, he's the foundation of it. And I'm sure there are better stories from the guys after me, once Dean had a lot of success. I was there when it was as bad as it got for him. But do you know what? The game after they hung him in effigy, we beat Duke. We needed to make a statement as a group, to show our loyalty to him, and we did that.

That's something I got from Coach Smith—loyalty and friendship. If a friend needs you, you don't ask what for. You just go.

In my senior year at Carolina, our two biggest wins were beating Duke twice. I also remember going up to dunk once against N.C. State—we were playing them in Chapel Hill—and instead I hit my forearms on the rim and missed. The ball ended up in the stands. When we went to Raleigh later that year, and they had some cute signs saying, "Try to dunk again, Billy," and stuff like that.

When I was a senior, Bobby Lewis was a sophomore and just starting to come into his own. He grew more and more as a young man. He got down on himself early in his career, but that boy could jump out of the gym. It was close between us as to who could jump higher. He was a good guy and the first real recruit Dean Smith had after the probation was lifted. And then the key was really Larry Miller. He could have gone anywhere and came to play for Carolina and Dean, and that really helped turn the whole place around. By then, of course, I was gone and playing in the NBA.

I had an interesting NBA career. At first, I didn't know if I was going to make it. Then I made it, and I wanted to play a lot. Then I wanted to start. Then I wanted to play in an All-Star Game and win a championship. I was fortunately able to do all that. My game was mostly going to the basket—that was my strength—but eventually I became a better-than-average jump shooter.

I played seven years with the Philadelphia 76ers and then jumped to the ABA's Carolina Cougars for two seasons—that move was purely for the money. The Cougars were going to pay me $300,000, and they wouldn't even pay me $90,000 in Philly.

When I coached in the NBA, I was fortunate to have some Carolina guys. Bobby Jones was one of my favorites. You cannot believe the love and respect his teammates in Philadelphia had for him. He really should be in the Basketball Hall of Fame—what an unselfish, wonderful player. He only got mad at me one time that I know of when I was coaching him—I instituted a "wear a sports jacket" rule on the road, and he didn't like that.

When I was still coaching Philadelphia, I would come down some to Chapel Hill. Dean and I would look at each others' film and critique everything about each others' teams. It was a good, healthy relationship.

Once I was watching a practice before the 1982 season began and saw Michael Jordan play for the first time—they called him Mike Jordan then. I told Dean after the practice that Jordan would be the greatest player to ever come out of here.

Dean got mad at me. He was asking me how I could say that? I tried to calm him down, saying, "Coach, it isn't brain surgery. Look at him." Dean didn't like that, though. To him, everybody was equal. But Jordan—well, he had no equal.

We've lived in the same place now in Philadelphia for more than 35 years. Most of our house burned down a few years ago. Fortunately, no one was hurt—that's all that really matters. My two daughters were very upset, though, and they were here in a heartbeat. It's fascinating when something like that happens—what becomes important to you. We were going through the rubble later, and you know what we were looking for? Pictures. Memories. That's what became important to us.

That's the same way that Carolina is. We weren't that good when I was there. But the friendships I have from that time, I would never give those up for anything.

Billy Cunningham still holds the Carolina record for most rebounds per game, and it is likely a record that will never be surpassed. Cunningham averaged 15.4 rebounds per game—nearly five higher than the next UNC career average (Doug Moe at 10.6).

Nicknamed "the Kangaroo Kid" for his jumping ability, Cunningham was a two-time All-American at UNC. He averaged 24.8 points per game during his

Tar Heels career as a 6'6" inside player. He holds the NCAA record with 40 straight double-doubles in points and rebounding. Once, Cunningham had 48 points and 25 rebounds in a single game against Tulane.

A first-round NBA draft pick in 1965, Cunningham won NBA titles as both a player (in 1967) and as a coach (1983)—in both cases, with the Philadelphia 76ers. Cunningham averaged 20.8 points per game in his NBA career and made the Naismith Memorial Basketball Hall of Fame as a player in 1986. Later, the NBA would name him as one of its 50 greatest NBA players of all time.

Cunningham left coaching in 1985 while in his mid-forties and, despite some opportunities to go back, never did. In the years since, he helped lure an NBA expansion franchise to Miami as a part-owner (he later sold his share of the team) and did some TV announcing for NBA games. Now he keeps busy with charitable endeavors, including heavy involvement with a learning center for children in Philadelphia and raising money for a statue of his former NBA teammate Wilt Chamberlain. Cunningham also still plays squash and works out three to four times per week.

CHARLIE SCOTT
GUARD/FORWARD
1967–1970

Playing at Carolina was a great and exhilarating experience for me. The biggest thing about sports is the camaraderie that builds as you go along in a season. It's an us-against-them mentality. You really gain 10 other brothers. It's hard to duplicate and hard for athletes to give up. It's very special.

I almost didn't end up at Carolina at all. I came very close to going to Davidson. Lefty Driesell had a gregarious personality, was very friendly, and really recruited me hard. Coach Smith had a parental demeanor with me. Lefty had a best-friend demeanor. When you're young, you want the friend.

I'll tell you that story, but first you need to know where I came from. I grew up in Harlem and went to junior high there. My father was a cabdriver in New York. He and my mother separated when I was 11, and I lived with him. I had three older sisters. We were poor. My father died when I was 14 years old. He was not really an athlete at all, but I was, and I also practiced very hard. I pushed myself as hard as I could. I was never satisfied. I never liked mediocrity. I modeled myself after Elgin Baylor back then.

I got a scholarship to Laurinburg Institute in North Carolina and so went down there for high school. It was a school where some friends of mine had gone, and it was known to have a good basketball program. You would compare it to an Oak Hill in Virginia today. I knew my family wouldn't be able to afford me going to college, but I wanted to go, and so a scholarship was going to have to be my ticket to college.

I went down there to Laurinburg and played three years, and the first person to really give me recognition was Lefty, who was at Davidson. I went up to Davidson for a summer camp. He was the first college coach to recruit me and offer me a scholarship. I applied for early admission to Davidson and was accepted. I wasn't going to have a problem getting in as far as grades—I was my high school valedictorian. When I finished a test, I always wanted the teacher to grade it right away so I could see how I did. I was always like that.

Back then you could go on visits to a campus as many times as you wanted to. I'd go to Davidson on a lot of weekends and stay at this motel in Charlotte. This one movie theater across the street was always playing *The Sound of Music*. I loved going to the movies, and I saw *The Sound of Music* about 100-something times. Literally. I sang in the choir for three years at Laurinburg, so all that "Do Re Mi" stuff—we had learned to do that. I loved that movie.

Lefty used to let me come visit and help show a guy around whenever he was hosting a recruit. He wanted to let me see if I wanted to play with the guy. When you're 17 years old and the coach says pick the other four guys you want, that makes you feel important. It ended up, though, that instead of picking my teammates, I picked the guys who I played against.

I made a verbal commitment to go to Davidson and would have just ended up there if not for a man named Frank McDuffie, who was everything at Laurinburg. He was the president, the basketball coach, and the band director—and a father figure to me. He wouldn't let me sign any letter of intent right away—he wanted me to investigate the possibilities more.

On one of our trips to Davidson, we had something bad happen. I was with Coach McDuffie and his wife, and we went by the Davidson basketball office. They told us Lefty was out to eat, so we went to the restaurant and found him. My coach's wife saw Lefty's lima beans and she said, "Oh, they look good!" Lefty told her to have some—for us to sit down, join him, and eat.

The waitress took the order, but then the owner came back a few minutes later and said they weren't going to serve us the food in the main dining room because we were black. We never did get any food. We left instead, and Lefty got up and left, too. It embarrassed him, and I know it was a circumstance he wished he had never got caught in. It did have an effect on me, and I know it had an effect on my high school coach. That made it very vivid to me, what the times were like in the 1960s.

But that didn't turn me away from Davidson by itself. I also had a great recruiting trip to Carolina in the spring of my senior year. The Temptations and Smokey Robinson & the Miracles both were performing that weekend in Chapel Hill at an event called "Jubilee." That had a lot to do with it, honestly. Davidson was all-male then, and UNC was coed. That helped, too. I also got to know a lot of players that weekend like Dick Grubar and Larry Miller, and they were really nice to me. So were all the assistants. I was really intrigued by Larry Brown, who was recruiting me at the time. He grew up in New York, and I was a New Yorker. We had a lot of things in common. He has a very charming personality. And Coach Smith took me to church with him—I liked that. He was the only coach recruiting me who ever invited me to do that.

Frank McDuffie made a lot of difference. Deep down inside, I think he believed it was more important for me to go to the state university rather than to a private school. He was looking more at the significance to the state. That's not what I was looking at so much.

So I decided to go to Carolina. My mother didn't like it at all. She was stuck on the fact I was going back on my word. There was a lot of tumult around all of this.

Lefty made one last try. The story everyone tells is that he jumped out of some bushes to talk to me. It wasn't quite like that. I had called him to tell him I was going to Carolina, but I had only talked to his wife. He came to see me one more time to see if he could change my mind. He got a friend of mine to take a walk with me to this place off campus, and then he did come out from behind some bushes to talk to me. I listened, but I was going to Carolina.

47

I could have gone somewhere up North, but I made a conscious decision to be the first black scholarship athlete at Carolina. It was the late 1960s. A lot of blacks, including me, knew we had responsibilities. I wanted to do something. I wanted to break the color barrier. I was realistic, accepting that some bad things were going to happen. And they did, especially on the road at places like South Carolina or Clemson. But on campus, I really didn't feel bias or bigotry. I never felt unwanted.

I played right away once I was eligible as a sophomore—you couldn't play as a freshman back then. Early in my career I got voted as the tournament MVP at this tournament where we were playing in Oregon. But after Larry Miller scored a lot of points in the second half of the final, Coach Smith asked the voters to reconsider and vote for Miller instead of me.

I felt a little angry that Coach Smith took an MVP away from me, but I also didn't feel like I could say anything about it. I knew Jackie Robinson's story, and I felt a little symmetry—not that I went through anything like

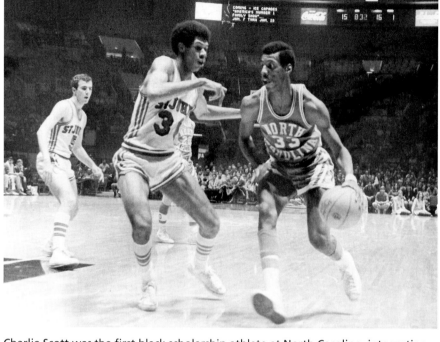

Charlie Scott was the first black scholarship athlete at North Carolina, integrating the program with the help of coach Dean Smith during the tumultuous 1960s.

48

what he did. But for the first two years at UNC when I was playing, I felt like I couldn't say anything derogatory.

We beat Davidson to get to the Final Four my sophomore year and then got all the way to the NCAA Final, which we lost to a great UCLA team by a lot [78–55]. We had been expected to win that game against Davidson and Lefty in 1968. The next year against Davidson, it was different, and that game still stands as one of the highlights of my college career.

It was an Elite Eight game again—the winner would go to the 1969 Final Four. I had thought I was the best player in the ACC that year, but I lost the media vote to South Carolina's John Roche. I thought it was racism. I thought about not playing in the NCAA tournament to protest. Being young, my first reaction was, *I'm going to show them, I'm just not going to play.* That vote had been like a pin in my balloon. It pricked me. I thought it would be a good form of protest. But it would have been the wrong thing to do. Assistant coach John Lotz—who was a friend and the person I could talk to the most on the staff—talked me out of it. We drove around for a while, and he let me vent, and then he said if I sat out, it would really hurt the team. And I didn't want to do that.

So I suited up against Davidson again. I always wanted to play well in front of Lefty Driesell because he was the first guy who really recruited me. I guess I thought of it as validation—I wanted to show him that he was right to pursue me. So playing against Davidson was very fulfilling for me.

A week before this game, we had lost Dick Grubar, our starting point guard, in the 1969 ACC tournament final against Duke. That was another big game for me, too—I had 40 points in that one, and 28 in the second half. Beating Duke is always a highlight, especially back then when the tournament meant everything.

But now we were facing life without Grubar again. That handicapped us. We were a ship running with a new captain, and that was tough. With us losing a star player like Grubar, people were probably expecting them to beat us. And Davidson was very good that year. I knew all of their guys, because I had helped recruit most of them to Davidson back when I was going there. We were No. 2 in the country, and Davidson was No. 5.

It was such a back-and-forth game. We were so competitive and so evenly matched. Eddie Fogler subbed in at point guard and did as well as he could for us, but he was about six inches shorter than Dick. It was one of those games that, when you were playing in it, you just knew it was going down to the wire. And it did. We were down 85–83, and I hit a jumper to tie it with a little under two minutes left. Then Gerald Tuttle made a huge play—he drew a charge on Davidson's Jerry Kroll. That was big. So we held it for about a minute in the "four corners"—this was before the shot clock—and called timeout with 13 seconds left.

Coach Smith then made a speech during that timeout. He told me that they'd come to me when I got the ball so somebody would be open. But when I got the ball from Jim Delany with about eight seconds to go, there was no way I was going to pass. We were going to lose or win, and it was going to be with me. I got the ball and started to the left, which was the way I liked to go when I was going to shoot. But I heard guys on the Davidson bench yelling, "Force him right! Force him right!" So I gave them what they wanted: a couple of hard dribbles to the right, and then I pulled up and shot.

The shot gets longer through the years when people tell the story. They'll talk about 27 feet or 30 feet. Really, it was about 18 feet. And it swished. The team went crazy. And we won. I played a lot of games in the pros—big games. But there was no single game like that for me, no do–or–die circumstance quite like that. That was my best highlight.

The next year we weren't as good and didn't make the NCAA tournament.

I was one of Coach Smith's first players to do well in the NBA. Billy Cunningham had done very well, but most of the other guys hadn't. The best team I was on was the 1975–1976 Boston Celtics team, which won the NBA championship. We really thought we were the best. We had Don Nelson, John Havlicek, Jo Jo White, Paul Silas—they were intelligent players and great players. We really felt we had no weakness.

More than 40 years after it happened, people still talk to me about that Davidson game and that shot. I know one thing. It may have been karma, it may have been my high school coach, or it may have been me, but I made a really fortunate choice when I decided to go to UNC.

Charlie Scott was a signature player at UNC. Roy Williams—a student at Carolina during the early 1970s—named his only son "Scott" in honor of Charlie Scott.

Scott, in turn, would give one of his sons the middle name "Dean," in honor of Dean Smith. He was the first black scholarship athlete at North Carolina and averaged 22.1 points per game at UNC.

Frank Barrows of the *Charlotte Observer* once wrote during Scott's collegiate career that Scott was "the third-favorite topic of conversation in Chapel Hill, ranking behind only coeds and beer."

Of the 1969 shot that Scott hit to beat Davidson, Driesell said at the time, "He hit the money shot. He's fabulous.... The greatest defensive player in the world couldn't have stopped him on that one." That two-point loss to UNC turned out to be the last game Driesell would coach at Davidson. He took the head-coaching job at Maryland the next day.

Scott won a gold medal in the 1968 Olympics while still in college and was a two-time, first-team All-American while a Tar Heel. He ranks sixth all-time in scoring at UNC with 2,007 points. He played 10 seasons in the ABA and NBA, winning an NBA title with Boston in 1976. Scott's No. 33 was honored at UNC. Antawn Jamison later retired it.

Scott now lives in the Atlanta area with his wife, Trudy. They have three children, and Scott has done some coaching of AAU basketball teams in the area so he could coach his own kids. For much of his post-basketball life, he has worked in sports marketing.

The

SEVENTIES

DAVID CHADWICK

FORWARD/CENTER

1968–1971

So many of us were impressionable, wide-eyed 18-year-olds when we first walked onto the Carolina campus as students. That's the way I was back in the late 1960s. There was a lot of history to Carolina basketball then, but not like it is today. I remember Coach Smith saying right away when I got there, "If you ever need me, call me." At that time in my life, though, I didn't understand the significance of a statement like that. I was sort of thinking, *Yeah, I appreciate it, but where's the gym?*

But Coach Smith wanted you to know right away that he was there for us and that he wanted to make us into good people more than into good players. My life principles and moral standards were already fairly well-established, because I had two excellent parents. But in a situation like mine, Coach Smith would reinforce what your parents taught you. He would cement it.

I remember so much about my time at Carolina. I remember the first time I walked into Carmichael Auditorium, it had that smell that's unmistakably Carmichael. That smell is still there today. I remember the first three-on-three game I got into as a freshman. I took a shot, Bill Bunting blocked it, and I quickly had to reevaluate how good I was.

I remember the friendships. There were five of us who came in together on the freshman team. And when we had the 100-year reunion of Carolina basketball in February 2010, those other four guys—Lee Dedmon, Don

Eggleston, Dale Gipple, and Richard Tuttle—were four of the first guys I saw. It's that Carolina family thing. We're all a part of it. Coach Smith is kind of the surrogate godfather of the family, so we all know each other through him even though the different generations of players may not know each other directly. There's a great commonality of experience.

When I played, freshmen were still ineligible, but those freshman games would sometimes attract crowds as big as those for the varsity. Our freshman team was really good. We went 12–4. Duke had the top recruiting class in the country, but we beat Duke two out of three times. In my sophomore year, I was probably the ninth or 10th man. I didn't play that much. That was a really good team, though. That was the team where Charlie Scott hit those amazing shots against Duquesne and Davidson—the one against Davidson is the one that more people remember—to get us to the 1969 Final Four. Then Rick Mount and Purdue shot us up there. That was the most successful team I played on at Carolina.

In my junior year, I started four games and averaged about 5.5 points per game. I had one 19-point game against Maryland that I remember. That was the year where Charlie Scott really became something of a one-man team for us, when he averaged about 27 points per game. That was the only season Coach Smith didn't win at least 20 games in the last 30 years he coached at Carolina. If Charlie played well, we won. If he didn't, we didn't win. We weren't quite a team that year. My senior season, 1970–1971, was a good year for me. I started 11 games, had a 30-point game against Clemson, and a lot of other double-figure games. We lost a heartbreaker to South Carolina in the ACC final, so we didn't make the NCAA tournament, but we won four straight in the NIT to win that championship. We just blew through that tournament, beating a Massachusetts team with Julius Erving on it and then also beating Duke and Georgia Tech.

After college, I was one of the first Carolina basketball players to play basketball overseas. Then I needed to find out what to do with my life. I felt an overwhelming call to join the ministry, which I did. My father was a minister, as well, and we moved several times when I was a kid as he followed his call.

I've been in Charlotte since 1980 as the senior pastor at Forest Hill. We started with about 150 people coming on Sundays and now have close to 5,000. We use contemporary styles and forms as a way of communicating the message. We use video and contemporary Christian music. The fancy way to

53

David Chadwick had a solid career as a post player for the Tar Heels before becoming a pastor and also penning a well-received book about the leadership principles of coach Dean Smith.

say it is that we contextualize the Gospel. But we don't change the message—the message is always the same. God loves us all, unconditionally.

So much of what I learned about leadership I learned from Dean Smith. One day I was thinking that I sure would like my own kids to know the principles that Coach Smith lived and led. I thought maybe I would write some of it down. My wife, Marilynn, said she thought maybe I should try to get it published.

I wrote two chapters and thought, *This is really interesting. I'm enjoying doing this.* I showed them to Rick Ray at Raycom Sports in Charlotte. He took a red pen and marked it up some, but then he said it could be something that could be published. And so we talked about it, and he underwrote me being able to travel all over the country to meet with some other former players and talk to them about Dean Smith. I talked with James Worthy, Roy Williams, and Matt Doherty, among others. I talked not just to Tar Heels but to other basketball greats like Jerry West and Mitch Kupchak. About the only person I couldn't get to was Michael Jordan—I tried, but it just didn't happen. Then after all that research, I came up with 12 basic principles as to who Coach Smith was as a leader and a person. I took this to him and said, "I would like to write about you."

The first thing he said to me was, "Don't deify me." I said I wouldn't— that my respect for his methods would shine through but that I wouldn't deify him. One of the principles, for instance, is called "Making Failure Your Friend."

Then the second thing he said was this, after he read through the principles. He quizzically raised his head and said, "Where did you get all these principles, anyway?"

I don't think Coach Smith even knows those principles are there because they are so embedded in him as a person, from what his own mother and father taught him. But it's what he does. The reciprocal law of loyalty—I'll be loyal to you, you be loyal to me. The power of positive words. Focusing on the process, not the outcome. Not caring so much about immediate gratification. That's the way he is.

In the book, I divided the 12 principles into three overarching core values. The first one is that people are your most important product. Above everything else, you need to have a commitment to care about the people above the winning, and that's what really drove him.

The second is that the team is more important than the individual, and he lived by that. When the first two values collide, he would always choose the team. It has to be team-first.

The third value is simply him being a man of such deep character and integrity. Telling the truth. Being on time. Leaving the cupboard full for Coach Guthridge when he retired. Being the same man on the inside as he was on the outside. Words matching deeds. All that kind of stuff is what made people instinctively want to follow him.

Those three overarching core values—those are the leadership practices I try to have to this day. I try to make people my most important product. I try to make the team more important than any individual—pointing to the person who gave you the pass, so to speak. I've tried to operate as a leader of integrity in my life and in our ministry at Forest Hill.

It was so nice to see Coach Smith at the 100-year anniversary reunion in 2010. I think all of us just felt privileged to be there. The alumni game was at 8:00 PM on a Friday, and my first response was that I wasn't going to play in it. But Bill Chamberlain talked me into it. So I did, and we had a great time. We all played against other Carolina guys from our same era. They had uniforms with our names on them, Carolina blue basketball shoes, the whole bit. Plus, 20,000 people were there.

When it was our turn to play, I saw Lee Dedmon on the other team and I thought, *Okay, this is fine. We can probably guard each other.* And then Bobby Jones walks onto the court, looking exactly the way he did when he played except that he doesn't have as much hair. He's one of the greatest defensive players in the history of the game. He said, "I've got Chadwick," and I thought, *Oh, no.* I did get Bobby to foul me one time, and I made a free throw. So I got into the boxscore, I guess. That was a lot of fun. We all had a great time. I think a lot of the guys in the stands wished they had been out there by the end. When Coach Smith came out, that place went crazy.

To just know I'm a part of that heritage, that legacy—it means a lot to me. Carolina means a lot to me. The Old Well. Avery and Ehringhaus dorms, where I lived. The Bell Tower. I'm just so thankful to be part of the heritage. I don't know why God allowed me to do that, but I'm so thankful.

David Chadwick has been the senior pastor at Forest Hill church in Charlotte since 1980. Born in 1949 in Winston-Salem, North Carolina, Chadwick, a 6'8" post player for the Tar Heels, graduated from UNC in 1971. He played three years in the European professional leagues. He later received two degrees from the Columbia Theological Seminary in Decatur, Georgia, in 1980.

Chadwick's book *The 12 Leadership Principles of Dean Smith* was published in 1999. It sold more than 40,000 copies. Chadwick has written several other books and also has hosted a weekly faith-based radio program on WBT-AM in Charlotte for many years.

Chadwick and his wife, Marilynn, have three children, Bethany, David Banner, and Michael. David Banner was a highly-recruited basketball player in high school and is currently a scholarship player at Rice.

BILL CHAMBERLAIN

FORWARD

1969–1972

IDIDN'T KNOW A WHOLE LOT ABOUT THE CAROLINA PROGRAM before I got to Chapel Hill from New York City. I was the second African American scholarship player in UNC history, after Charlie Scott. My first contact with the university came with John Lotz, who was one of the assistant coaches at the time.

John was a great guy—a true gentleman and a smart fellow. I also used to admonish him a bit because he was a clotheshorse—a very dapper guy. I first saw him in the Bronx when I was playing in a tournament. He had this dark green silk suit on and alligator shoes. In New York, you didn't see white guys dressed like that. The guy looked like he was in the mob.

Years later I had a chance to introduce Coach Lotz for a Fellowship of Christian Athletes function, and I told that same story. Everybody laughed. But he really did look like he was in the Mafia. Once he got to talking, though, he really impressed me, my high school coach, and my parents. Now there were a lot of other coaches talking to me, too. By my senior year, I had more than 120 scholarship offers. But Coach Lotz got me indoctrinated a little bit, and then I met Coach Guthridge and finally Coach Smith. All three were really consistent—great guys and true gentlemen. Still, I looked around. I visited Duke. I visited Davidson. I thought about Syracuse, Marquette, St. John's, and Princeton. But ultimately I picked Carolina, and I'm so glad I did.

Bill Chamberlain was a second-team All-American at UNC and played a big role on the Tar Heels' 1972 Final Four team.

58

I never would have had the opportunity in the first place to go to Carolina if not for Rev. Ed Visscher, who had a huge role in my life. He, his wife, and their five children took me in during high school. I lived with them five days out of the week and then went home to Harlem to stay with my parents on the weekends. Rev. Visscher was the school principal at Long Island Lutheran, as well as a minister and the head basketball coach. So he knew everything. This school was way out on Long Island, but close to C.W. Post, where I had an older brother playing college basketball.

For me, the experience of going there was a total culture shock. There were kids my age who drove to school. There was one girl who would ride her horse to school. These kids lived in a wonderland, although a lot of them didn't realize it. I was astounded that this was part of New York, too—a part I never knew about. It was a great opportunity for me. I had had difficulty in junior high, academically and socially, but I really straightened out at Lutheran. Rev. Visscher really walked the walk as well as talked the talk— not too many people are going to bring a teenaged black kid into their house and let him sleep in one of the bedrooms five days a week. I loved the Visscher family for that.

About 98 percent of my high school was white, and so that's where I really learned to get along with everyone. These were the 1960s, remember. You could follow the teachings of Malcolm X or you could follow Martin Luther King Jr. I chose Martin Luther King. I didn't think all white people were evil, although that's what some people would try to have you believe back then. My parents were Christian people. We went to church regularly, and our church was integrated. The priests were white and black. The summer camp I went to up in Connecticut was integrated, too.

Our high school started winning a lot. In my senior year, we were ranked as the No. 1 team in New York State. We beat a team with Len Elmore on it. When I chose Carolina, it was for a number of reasons. I liked the coaches. I liked the climate. The people were very friendly. There were a lot of stories about bigotry and racism in the South that I had heard, but I didn't experience a lot of that. I understood the way that Coach Smith wanted you to play—hustling and playing defense. So I was a natural for the way Carolina played. And I could also run—I was a 6′6″ center in high school, but I also ran track. When I got to Carolina, I played more of the two forward positions. We had a really great class of guys—Steve Previs, Bill Chambers, Dennis Wuycik, Kim Huband, and Craig Corson.

In my freshman year, before I even got on the varsity, I became involved in the Black Student Movement. The South was different than what I was used to back then because the culture was more about separation and segregation. Coach Smith didn't think that was right, and that was huge to me. He didn't play around. What I didn't know but learned shortly after I got there was that his father had helped integrate Kansas high school basketball. And then he had integrated UNC athletics with Charlie Scott.

Charlie was not so active in the BSM, but I really got involved. We found out that the black workers on UNC's campus—the maids, the grounds crew, the kitchen staff—did not have the same compensation package that the white workers had. They weren't getting benefits like they should have. Once we found that out, the BSM decided to close down the cafeterias. There was a lot of unrest at that time. Jesse Helms did an editorial that was partly about me on TV—it was very negative.

We had a petition going about trying to get the black workers fair treatment. I went right to Coach Smith, told him the story about the black workers, and asked him to sign the petition. He said he'd be the first one to sign it, and he'd ask everyone else in the office if they wanted to sign it, too. One time the UNC chancellor was in Coach Smith's office during the height of all this. I came in and asked to see Coach Smith. He sent the chancellor out in the middle of their conversation and asked me to come in. The chancellor had to wait while we talked. Coach Smith always took care of his players.

I was only playing on the freshman team at the time. We were pretty good, though. We won the Big Four freshman tournament. Roy Williams was on that team, you know, as a reserve. He was fast as a greyhound. Great quickness. But Roy was really small—maybe 135 to 140 pounds. We were all skinny in those days—I don't think kids ate as well or lifted weights as often as they do today.

When I was a sophomore—my first year on the varsity—I started. That was very encouraging for me. Some people had trouble playing with Charlie Scott, who was a senior at the time. He was so fast. I didn't. When he took off with the ball, I was fast enough to run the wing next to them. He'd hit some guys in the head with passes, though. I produced pretty well that season, but we didn't win that much. I gave Charlie a lot of grief that season, because he shot the ball all the time. I got hurt that season, too—I was in a cast for three weeks from my thigh to my ankle. And we only won 18 games. That was the last time a Carolina team didn't win 20 until Coach Smith retired in 1997.

The culture was changing then. There were racial problems in both Columbia when we played South Carolina and in Raleigh when we played N.C. State. We went on to lose both in the opening round in the ACC that year and then in the opening round of the NIT to Manhattan. That's what I give Charlie grief about, really—Manhattan had a guy who just ate Charlie's butt up. Charlie is really my main man, though. I just tease him.

My junior year, we were galvanized by a couple of strange circumstances. We had lost Charlie, Eddie Fogler, and Jim Delany, and we were picked to finish seventh in an eight-team conference. But Coach Smith worked us really hard. The good thing about Coach Smith's philosophy was that he had 11 guys who played a lot. We had a blue team. Those guys would come in and win their part of the game, and then we'd come back in as starters and would run people out of the gym. We were very energetic. We ran everywhere—to the bench, to the free-throw line, whatever.

That was the year we lost to South Carolina in the ACC final when South Carolina stole a tip at the end, but then we won the NIT. That was big for me. The whole thing was played in Madison Square Garden back then. I was home in New York. My folks were there. My friends were there. We beat Julius Erving and Massachusetts in the first round, 90–49. It was a tremendously balanced team—no one person was "the man." We just ran people to death in that NIT tournament, and I ended up as the tournament MVP.

The next year we got Bobby Jones—he was a sophomore—and then Bob McAdoo came in as our first junior-college transfer. I was a senior and ended up as a second-team All-American. That was really quite a team. We got all the way to the Final Four and should have beaten Florida State there. But that was partly my fault. I was late to the training table in the hotel for the team meal and didn't start that Final Four game in Los Angeles. I was technically late. I actually showed up on time, but I didn't have on my Carolina blazer and tie like I should have. They said, "You've got to go to the room and get your blazer on." I did that and rushed back down, but by then I was too late.

In the first half of that Florida State game, while I was waiting to go in, my brother had a seat just behind our bench. He was about 6'8", 240 pounds and kept yelling to Coach Smith, "Put Bill in! Put Bill in!" That probably didn't help. We got pretty far down in that game—it reminded me a little of the 2008 Final Four, when Carolina got so far down to Kansas in the first half. They kept beating our press and getting layups, and we lost. No question we should have won and played UCLA in the final, but we were looking past Florida State. We lost that opportunity.

I've stayed in North Carolina since then. I made this state my home for a number of reasons. To me, you can't find a better place to live in the country.

61

I've had some great times here and some hard times. I raised two sons here. When my wife had our second son in 1988 in Raleigh, we were so happy. And then something awful occurred—my wife passed away five weeks after our son was born, of a cerebral aneurysm. It was a very difficult time. I only made it through by the grace of God and through friends like Dean Smith and David Chadwick, another teammate of mine who became a pastor in Charlotte and has been a dear friend for many years. David has just been a rock for me. My wife's passing happened more than 15 years after I left Carolina, and they were there for me. My teammates. My coaches. They were so great during this time. I don't even remember everyone who was at the funeral, it was such a blur to me. But I know many of them were.

What doesn't kill you makes you stronger. My faith galvanized during that time, and by the grace of God, our family made it through. My son William Jr. lives in Charlotte now and has two children. My son Carlton is an assistant manager of a furniture store in downtown Raleigh and is just a great young man, as well. I did remarry in 2007 to Ernelle Eaton Chamberlain—a retired teacher who spent 33 years teaching music. She's just a great woman. I work for the state of North Carolina and live in Durham. We are very happy, and I consider it an honor to have played for Carolina all those years ago.

Bill Chamberlain's No. 31 jersey hangs in the Smith Center rafters at North Carolina due to his selection as a second-team All-American for the 1971–1972 season. Chamberlain had a brief professional career following his time as a Tar Heel, playing in 78 total games in the NBA and ABA.

Later, Chamberlain worked as a basketball coach and a teacher at Laurinburg (N.C.) Institute. He now lives in Durham and works for the State of North Carolina, in the department of crime control and public safety. Chamberlain's specific job involves emergency management. He helps the state plan for all sorts of potential manmade and natural disasters, from large-scale fires to plane crashes to train derailments or gas spills. "You have to be ready for something like this to occur," Chamberlain said, "even though you hope it never does."

GEORGE KARL

GUARD

1969–1973

WHEN YOU MEET SOMEONE—even if it's just for 15 minutes—there's something there if you both played for UNC. A brotherhood. An automatic respect. It's the greatest fraternity of sportsmen in the world. I'm convinced of that. And most of that is due to one man—Dean Smith.

We Carolina guys can only go so long without a Carolina fix. We have to talk to somebody or something. I don't watch every game or anything. I see so much basketball that I try to get away from basketball when I'm at home. Don't get me wrong—if Carolina is playing Duke, I'm watching. If Carolina is playing UNC-Asheville, I don't think so.

But I always keep up with the program. Now that I'm the coach of the Denver Nuggets, I don't physically get to North Carolina as much as I'd like. But when I do, there's a harmony, a karma, to being there. There's a tingle. There's an enjoyment in being around Michael Jordan, Roy Williams, Larry Brown, David Chadwick, and all the other guys who are in the state and/or in the Charlotte area, which we go through each season with the Nuggets. There are always some guys who have good memories and, as you get older, you like those memories. They're fun to be a part of, and it's a very proud fraternity. It's a fraternity that has not only developed great basketball players, but also great people and great leaders.

We all love Carolina. Those years Matt [Doherty] had it—when the program was losing a lot—that hurt us. We would have all done anything to make it better. Fortunately, Roy decided to take it [in 2003], and now we can be our cocky, egotistical selves once again.

Deciding to go to Carolina was the best decision of my life. Carolina didn't really start recruiting me until April of my high school senior year, following the Dapper Dan all-star game. I was a high-school All-American from Pennsylvania who was used to taking a lot of shots and scoring a lot of points. I came in a little cocky. My teammates would tell you that. Too cocky, really. I had back surgery as a freshman. My career didn't start well. But they turned me from a cocky guy into a total team guy.

Coach Bill Guthridge was very instrumental in my career, along with Coach Smith. As a freshman, I had a back injury and missed a lot of the season. But Coach Guthridge thought I could be a pretty good player. And he allowed me to watch film with the coaches for much of the time I was hurt. Sitting in the film room with them, listening, watching what they watched— it was invaluable. That was really the beginning of my coaching career.

I've always considered myself kind of an "energy and hustle" guy who probably had a little more talent than people thought I did. Steve Previs and I were both point guards, and we both shared those responsibilities.

We were two of those "all he does is take charges, get loose balls, and play defense" kind of guys. But we were better than people thought we were. Our character was to be tougher than the other team.

With us both being from Pittsburgh, there was a toughness factor, a pride that we could outwork anybody. Steve was a harder worker than I was. I knew it, and I had to live with it every day. He would amaze me on a weekly basis. He'd say, "Let's go and work out at 6:00 AM." And I never could say no to him, because I'd think, *I've got to be as hard a worker as him.*

Also, his dad had this saying: PMA. He'd give out hats, shirts, pencils— they'd all have that on it. It stood for "Positive Mental Attitude." I really made that the focus of my attitude, and it's had a big effect on me since then, along with Coach Smith's teachings. I'm a big believer in positive motivation. Two things that I have kind of based my career on: talent means something, but it doesn't mean as much as attitude; and you wake up every morning trying to turn whatever you have into something better. Steve and his father were both very important to me in that respect.

Steve was one of these totally selfless team players. He had no desire for the spotlight, no desire for the glory. All he wanted to do was play and win. There are so few of those in our game today. It's fun to see a college or a pro team

George Karl was a floppy-haired guard for the Tar Heels in the early 1970s long before he won more than 900 games as an NBA head coach.

have a guy like that. Bruce Bowen in San Antonio was like that in the NBA. I had Nate McMillan when I was coaching Seattle—he was a selfless player like that. Those guys are so important for championship teams but don't ever get the glory or the credit. And Steve Previs on this team was probably that guy.

The best weekend of my college career came in 1972. That was my junior year, when we went to the Final Four. To get there, we had to win two games in Morgantown, West Virginia. That was a special weekend. Three days of Carolina, all shared with my family. And then we got to go to the Final Four to sustain our dreams a little longer.

This was a great weekend for me. A lot of my family was there since it was so close to my hometown. And in the first game, we played South Carolina, who had beaten us the year before in the ACC tournament. I had missed two free throws in that game that I still feel bad about. And we just killed South Carolina [92–69] to set up the game with Penn.

Penn had this huge lineup—everybody was 6'5" or bigger. And Chuck Daly was coaching them, too, and he had been at Duke. So there were all types of little motivators.

I started the game very well. I made four shots in a row in about four minutes. I was energized. I was hot. And it was the only time I ever gave the tired signal to Coach Smith. And he looked at me and said, "Why do you want to come out?"

They came back and, I think, tied the game or took the lead. I got into some foul trouble, although my recollection is that I never worried about foul trouble with Coach Smith on the bench. I knew he could always manage it. I had a really strong game going, sat down in the second half, and ultimately came back during the spurt that won the game. Even though we ended up winning 73–59, it was a very well-played game by both teams. And the glory and joyousness of that getting you to the Final Four—that's a special feeling. You get to carry your celebration further when your dreams somewhat come true.

I'll always remember that '72 team. It was a team that was very talented. The front court always had much more prestige and talent. Bob McAdoo was there, and he was a great player. But Steve and I always had a pride about how we did things and always prided ourselves on being winners. I don't think anyone was ever going to give us the "Most Talented Backcourt" award. But the Final Four was like Hollywood—that year it was actually near Hollywood, in L.A., and we got to go. I had never been to Los Angeles at the time. Unfortunately, we didn't play very well against Florida State in that Final Four. But before that, we got those few days of glory.

I wish we could have gone further, but Florida State was very underrated that season. In my entire UNC career, we never played a more athletic team. Honestly, we probably overlooked FSU and looked ahead to UCLA. But FSU was so fast. They had two point guards whom I simply couldn't guard. I was chasing their backs for a lot of that game.

I ended up becoming an NBA coach and, oddly enough, I had a son who made it to play some in the NBA, too. Coby, my son, is a better scorer than I was in college. I was more of a gutty, tough guy. Coby is more of an athlete—

a shooter, a clever player. I don't think I'd ever be called clever. His courage is in a different way. His courage is in overcoming his genes, as Doug Moe would say, his own genes. And also his cancer. He overcame a scare there. And I think he's going to have a career in the NBA. For me to say that, after all he's been through—that's something.

George Karl has won more than 900 games as an NBA head coach with Milwaukee, Seattle, Golden State, Cleveland, and the Denver Nuggets. Karl also has coached in the CBA and in Spain before becoming one of the most respected NBA coaches in the business.

He played three seasons as a guard for the Tar Heels, helping them win the 1971 NIT and advance to the Final Four in 1972. He also played five seasons professionally, splitting his time between the NBA and the ABA, before beginning the coaching career he has never left. Although Karl's name was mentioned as a possible candidate for the Tar Heels head-coaching job in 2000, his employer at the time (the Milwaukee Bucks) wouldn't allow him to pursue the job, and Karl had no escape clause in his contract. Matt Doherty got the head-coaching job instead.

It's hard to believe now, given Karl's baldness, but as a player, he had blond, floppy hair and was thought of by some opposing fans as a showoff. Said Bobby Jones, who was one of Karl's Tar Heels teammates, "George was such an outgoing guy back then with a lot of personality, and was seen by many as a hot dog. When we played Duke, they'd always throw frankfurters out on the court near him. I think it was just the way he carried himself, probably. I didn't consider him cocky on the court. I just considered him a hustler. He was the best at diving on the floor I've ever seen."

In February 2010 Karl discovered a lump on his neck. A biopsy determined it was a form of neck and throat cancer that was treatable. (He had already had a bout with prostate cancer in 2005.) Karl began an intense program of radiation and chemotherapy and had to temporarily give up coaching the Nuggets during the latter part of the 2009–2010 NBA season, but still planned to resume his coaching duties with Denver as of this writing.

"Cancer is a vicious opponent," Karl said at the press conference announcing the cancer. "Even the ones that are treatable, you never get a 100 percent guaranteed contract."

BOB McADOO

FORWARD/CENTER

1971–1972

I'VE BEEN IN THE NBA FOR A LONG TIME NOW—first as a player, now as an assistant coach for the Miami Heat. And I can tell you that still, after all those years I've been gone from Carolina, it's like a family. I'll see guys in the league from different decades who went to Carolina, and they'll come over and speak to me. That's unique.

Usually, there's a disconnect at any school between the younger and older players. You wouldn't normally see a McAdoo and a Brendan Haywood talking before the game just because they went to the same school. But with Carolina, the bond is so strong that we'll recognize each other and make the connection.

We played the Boston Celtics not long ago, and I saw Rasheed Wallace. Then we went to Sacramento, and I saw Sean May. He's a recent Carolina guy, but he still comes over to talk. Vince Carter. Jerry Stackhouse. Larry Brown—one of the few guys in the league who actually went to Carolina before I did! It's just a family situation. Everyone recognizes each other, and it seems like there's someone in every city. The other players from other teams see it and recognize it, too, as a special thing.

Dean Smith is the one who put all that in place, and now Roy Williams is following right in his footsteps. He fosters that. He tries to remember the older guys. We had a function up there in 2007 that celebrated the Carolina guys who have made it into the Basketball Hall of Fame. I got to see Billy

Cunningham there, and James Worthy and Dean. It was a nice thing. Another nice thing is that all my boys have gone to basketball camp there. We still have connections with the university in that respect. They started there at nine and 10 years old. Now I've got my grandsons going there, too—I have six children and three great-grandchildren.

The way I got to Carolina was roundabout, even though the school was only 47 miles from where I grew up in Greensboro. My mother was 6′1″, and my father was 6′6″, but I didn't go into basketball right away. My first loves were football and baseball. I didn't really gravitate to basketball until I was about 14 or 15, when I kept getting so tall, and it became my main sport.

I had to go to junior college because of grades, and so I went out to Vincennes, Indiana. I'd originally planned to go to UCLA after a year—UCLA was taking junior transfers back then sometimes and helping themselves immediately. But that didn't happen. I needed a 3.0 grade-point average to transfer after one year but had a 2.9. I think some of the mail I was getting from the UCLA coaches got lost, too—I still don't know what happened with that. We won the national junior-college championship in my freshman year, 1970, and I stayed, and we tried to win it again my sophomore year. We came up just short, but in my sophomore year, UNC came into the recruiting picture. It was the first time the Tar Heels had ever gone after a juco player.

I started thinking about it. My mother and father were getting up in age, and it was going to be a lot easier for them to make the drive from Greensboro to Chapel Hill to see me play than to get on a plane and fly to Los Angeles. North Carolina had won the NIT the year before I got there, and I knew a good team was coming back. I thought I might be able to slide right in there with them, in the spot where Lee Dedmon had graduated, and that we could be a contender.

When I went on my visit, though, there was really nobody on campus. So I didn't see too much—just the gym, and Granville Towers, where the players lived. It was basically a basketball decision to come. I liked Dean Smith, and assistant coach John Lotz, who was doing most of the recruiting, and Bill Chamberlain, who took me around on my visit.

That one year I was there, 1971–1972, we really had a good team. We had Bobby Jones coming up from the freshman team, and I knew him from high school, and knew he could play. We had Bill Chamberlain and Dennis Wuycik.

Nobody thought too much of me at first—I was just the little juco player. What they didn't realize was that the team that I was on in Vincennes had

Bob McAdoo played only one year for the Tar Heels, in 1971–1972, but helped the team to the Final Four before becoming the first UNC player to leave early for the NBA.

about 12 high school All-Americans on it. It was more talented than our Final Four UNC team. Nobody believes this, but that team would have beaten our Carolina team. My roommate there was Clarence "Foots" Walker, and he went on to an NBA career of 10 years. There were several other guys who would play at Division I schools. Believe me, I was ready for Carolina basketball when I got there.

I think a lot of people questioned Dean and wondered what he was doing when he signed me. But like I said, UCLA had been doing it. Carolina has barely done it at all, though, before or since. When I first got there, I heard some rumblings of discontent. There was a depth chart, and suddenly I was pushing people down it, and that caused the rumblings.

I played both the power forward and center positions—the four and the five. Dean was into mobile big guys, and Bobby Jones and I could switch off at those positions.

There were a couple of games that year I remember very well. One came against St. Joseph's, early in the season at the Sugar Bowl tournament in New

Orleans. We saw their team at a pregame banquet for all the teams, and I remember that well. They had a team full of brothers—just about all of them were black—and they were snickering over there like, "We're going to dust you guys." And then we absolutely smoked them [93–77]. The joke was on them.

We didn't have that many black guys—just me and Bill Chamberlain on that team—but we sure could play. St. Joseph's had a kind of air of superiority, though, or arrogance, that really fueled me. I saw that a lot in my one year at Carolina. First, I saw it from my own team, in the "c'mon, this is just a juco guy" sort of attitude. I didn't say anything about it. I just played. The press kept asking me, "How are you going to fit in?" But I wasn't worried. I knew how good my junior-college team was.

Another big game came in the NCAA tournament when we played South Carolina. I grew up watching South Carolina play North Carolina in the ACC—those games were always very heated. And there was some racial stuff going on down in Columbia. I remember about all the names Charlie Scott was called when he went down to play at Columbia when he was the first black player for the Tar Heels, and I just hated South Carolina for that. I so upset when the Gamecocks pulled out of the ACC and became an independent—my one season at North Carolina was the same year they did that. I had really wanted to play South Carolina, because their fans and their team were so offensive to me, and then I ended up getting the chance in the NCAA tournament. We beat them by a lot [92–69], and that was a significant game for us.

In the Final Four, we played Florida State, which wasn't in the ACC at the time like it is today. I fouled out with close to 10 minutes to go—a couple of my fouls were very bogus, too—and we ended up losing a close one [79–75]. I was going good, too—I had 24 points and 15 rebounds at the time.

College basketball was a lot different back then in terms of contact, by the way. You see a college game now, shoot, it's more physical than the NBA. Back then, though, if you blew on somebody, it was a foul.

Then after that one year I had a decision to make. A handful of players—but not many—had gone to the NBA early at that time. But no one from Carolina. This was way before James Worthy and Michael Jordan would leave a year early. Back at this time, it was really frowned upon to leave. We had just made the Final Four, and a lot of people wanted me to stay and make a run at the championship the next year.

71

I found out I was going to be picked high, what they would now call a lottery pick. I would probably make about $100,000 in my first season—that sounds like peanuts today when you're talking about the NBA, but back then it was huge money.

There was a real split in my family about it—quite a division. My mother, Vandalia, was a schoolteacher and valued education above everything. She basically told me, "You are not going." My father was a carpenter—he was very talented with his hands. He could do brickmasonry, carpentry, plastering—everything.

My father pulled me to the side and showed me a piece of paper that showed me how much money he had made the year before: $10,000. He said, "It would take me 10 years to earn what you can earn in one if you go." And that conversation basically made up my mind for me.

Some people at Carolina were mad at me for leaving early, but not Coach Smith. He gave the idea his stamp of approval. He said if I could get $100,000 a year, I should go. That was very big to me and calmed down some of the uproar. [Smith wrote in his 1999 autobiography that he "heartily approved" of McAdoo's decision. The coach noted that, in the early 1970s, Smith himself was only making $18,000 a year.]

But it was still a hostile environment there for me for a while. I was the guinea pig on the "leaving early" thing at Carolina, and it was hard in some ways. I never did go back and get my degree there. I tried once, but it just didn't work out. And at the time I didn't feel too much like people wanted me back there. I got a few nasty notes, things like that.

But you know, over the years things are forgotten. It helps that I had a great professional career. I became the Rookie of the Year and won three scoring championships. By my third year, I was the Most Valuable Player of the NBA at a time when Kareem Abdul-Jabbar, Tiny Archibald, Wes Unseld, Rick Barry, and a lot of other greats were playing. And I made the Basketball Hall of Fame.

Early in my career, I wanted to validate myself as a player. Then I began to realize that you have to have a lot of talent if you're going to win a championship, and my goals became more team-oriented. I won two NBA championships as a player once I got on the L.A. Lakers. Then I won some European and Italian League championships when I went overseas in my thirties, and I won another NBA championship as an assistant coach for Miami the year that Dwyane Wade went berserk in the NBA Finals in 2006.

I haven't done anything to embarrass the university, either—I've kept my nose clean. So now it seems like all is forgiven between me and Carolina. Which is great. I'm happy with what I'm doing now. I'm into being happy. I don't worry about things too much.

My main responsibility with the Miami Heat is to work with the big guys. And I do personnel reports on all the other teams—strengths, weaknesses, things like that. I don't play basketball anymore, but I still play some tennis. And I remember my year at Carolina very fondly now, and all the connections and memories it provided.

Bob McAdoo was the first-ever junior-college player to play for Dean Smith at UNC. Smith had lost a recruiting war for Tom McMillen, who had said he would go to Carolina but ended up at Maryland, and badly needed another big man. In his one season as a Tar Heel, McAdoo averaged team highs of 19.5 points and 10.1 rebounds for the 1971–1972 Final Four team. The UNC students started a chant that season that went: "We know what Dean can do, but what can Mc-a-Doo?"

McAdoo left Chapel Hill after one season and was picked No. 2 overall by the Buffalo Braves. He won NBA championships as a sixth man for the L.A. Lakers in 1982 and '85. McAdoo was elected to the Naismith Memorial Basketball Hall of Fame in 2000—one of nine players or coaches with Tar Heels ties to have received that ultimate honor. A 6'9" forward who averaged 22.1 points and 9.4 rebounds in his NBA career, McAdoo led the NBA in scoring for three straight years in the mid-1970s and was renowned for being able to score inside or outside.

McAdoo has been an assistant coach with the Miami Heat since 1995, working primarily with the team's big men. He was part of the coaching staff for the Heat team that won the NBA championship in 2006. Although he was the first high-profile Tar Heels basketball player to leave school with eligibility remaining, he was far from the last. Since McAdoo, 17 other UNC players have gone pro before their senior season—the highest number of "early entries" into the NBA from any college program.

BOBBY JONES
FORWARD/CENTER
1971–1974

IN 1972, WHEN I PLAYED ON THE U.S. OLYMPIC TEAM, I felt like I represented the entire United States. When I played for the Tar Heels, I felt the same way—that I was representing the entire state. Not just the students or the alumni—the whole state. It was an honor, a responsibility, and a motivator to show that you have pride and a desire to bring honor to your institution and your state. I was very privileged to be a part of it.

Although I live in Charlotte now and mostly grew up in Charlotte, too, I wasn't actually born in North Carolina. I was born in Akron, Ohio, in 1951. My dad worked for Goodyear Tire. We lived in New Orleans; Texas; Goldsboro, North Carolina; and Winston-Salem before we moved to Charlotte when I was starting sixth grade. So Charlotte in the mid-1960s—that's mostly what I remember from childhood.

Back then Charlotte was big basketball country. I liked three teams—Davidson, Duke, and Carolina. My dad was big into basketball—he was 6′4″ and had played basketball at Oklahoma. Growing up, I was naturally left-handed, but my dad switched me over when he was showing me how to play. The court where I grew up shooting was a dirt court. The right-hand side was washed away, so we could only go to our left-hand side. So I got pretty good at going to my left.

My brother Kirby was two years older than me and played at Oklahoma, just like my dad. My dad would take my brother and me to college games at the old Charlotte Coliseum. Davidson was really strong, with Mike Maloy and Fred Hetzel. Davidson had some nationally ranked teams. And of course Carolina and Duke were good. I remember watching Art Heyman. And there was this Duke player I really liked named Hack Tison—he was tall and thin, like me. I was real uncoordinated and gangly. But Carolina—I liked the way that whole team played. I remember watching Larry Miller, Rusty Clark, Dick Grubar, and those guys. I was a Carolina fan before I was recruited by Carolina.

My coordination took a while to catch up to me. I played varsity as a sophomore at South Mecklenburg High in Charlotte, but my brother was the star of that team. I started getting recruited as a junior when my coordination came along. I was eventually a high-school All-American, but recruiting was different back then. I mostly just got recruited by schools in the Southeast. I visited Florida. I was not a very good shooter in high school. There were questions about my offensive ability. But Carolina wanted me, and that was my first choice by far.

John Lotz was Carolina's main recruiter then, and he and I had a lot of good steak dinners in Charlotte at places like the Epicurean. I picked UNC because of the coaches—I felt there was a real sincerity to the whole staff.

In high school, Bob McAdoo and I had some running battles. In my sophomore year, I won the state high-jump championship. I jumped 6′5″, something like that. The next year, my junior year, McAdoo started high-jumping. It was his senior year, and he beat me. Then he graduated and went onto UNC, and my senior year I won it again when he was gone. We also met in the state playoffs my junior year. His team beat us in the state semifinals. And I had about 28 points, the most I'd ever scored in my life. Bob had a little less. But all during our pro careers, he never would admit I outscored him to any of his friends. So I was always ticked about that—I'm kidding!

Coach Smith has been a big influence on my life. During my freshman year, he brought me into his office and asked me, "Bobby, are you the kind of player who needs to be yelled at in practice to get motivated or to correct something you're not doing right?"

First of all, I was stunned he would ask me. I said, "You know, Coach, I really don't like to be yelled at." He said okay, and he never yelled at me for four years. Some other guys were different. He recognized people were different and need to be treated differently, but everyone needs to be treated fairly.

Bobby Jones—one of the best defensive players in UNC history—shoots over N.C. State's David Thompson. Jones and Thompson would later become pro teammates and close friends.

One of the things Coach Smith would always do—and we hated this as players—was to point out our mistakes in a unique way. After a game, we'd watch film the next day on one of those old 16-mm projectors. He had a rewind button. You'd make a bad play—not box out or something—and he wouldn't say anything. He'd just rewind it a few times. You'd just be sitting there and everybody would be cutting their eyes at you. It would be total silence. That's all he really needed to say. Then, at the next practice, you'd do a drill on whatever it was for 10 minutes.

What I loved about Coach Smith was the way he never showed any nervousness or apprehension in the huddle. He always projected, "Hey, we can do this." We never thought we lost, we just thought we ran out of time. You know who else always projected that? Frank McGuire. I only played for him once in an all-star game, but he was the same way.

I enjoyed our practices—they were so organized. Once every week or two, though, Coach Smith would allow some visiting coaches to watch practices. We would always cringe when we saw them, because we knew we were in for a lot of running that day. I'm not sure if he wanted them to see how hard we worked or what.

The best team I played on at Carolina was my sophomore year. We made the NCAA tournament that season—the only time I got there. That was also the year I met my wife, Tess. We got serious while we were in college, and I wanted us to get engaged by the time my senior year rolled around. But her comment to me was, "I don't know if I can marry somebody if I don't know they are a committed Christian."

Now I had been to church all my life. In the South, that's part of the culture. I knew the Bible, but I didn't understand that I had to yield to Christ on a daily basis. I didn't want to do that. My skewed perception of Christianity at the time was that Christians were either weak people or not aggressive or they were missionaries in Africa or something. I wanted to play pro basketball. I didn't understand God had his best plan for us, not his worst.

After Tess said that, it kind of shook me up. I went away and went to my room and thought about what it meant to be a committed Christian. Is it going to church? Doing good things? No, it's committing your life to Jesus Christ. I had not done that. So I got on my knees and asked Jesus to forgive me of my sins, to be my savior, but also to be Lord of my life every day. I can really say there was a change in my life after that.

Coach Smith knew I was exploring Christianity in college and gave me a couple of books on it. He didn't really push it, he just said, "You might want to look into this." I really appreciated that.

In terms of basketball, most Carolina players probably remember a win as their most significant moment on the court. For me, though, it was a loss.

The ACC tournament was so important back in those days. Everything depended on it, because you couldn't go to the NCAA tournament back then without winning it. I remember we would stay in Tanglewood—on the west side of Winston-Salem in a town called Clemmons—to avoid all the media and everyone at school for the tournament. It was like a little retreat, basically.

In 1973 we were going to play Wake Forest in first round of the tournament. We had beaten them twice in the regular season. But we had also lost Bob McAdoo from our Final Four team the year before. My recruiting year had been described as a mediocre recruiting year, and we were considered by North Carolina standards an average team. We weren't world-beaters, although by national standards we still ranked pretty high.

I don't remember much about the game itself—the aftermath was what was important to me. But I do remember the last couple of plays. I had a tip-in with one second left to put us up two points in regulation. Then Wake threw a pass the length of the floor to a guy named Lee Foye. It went right over our fingertips, the guy caught it and knocked the shot down to send it into overtime.

Then in overtime, we were tied but we had the ball and were holding it for a last-second shot. George Karl took a shot, Eddie Payne got a quick rebound for Wake, and they threw two quick passes and a layup at the buzzer. They won. Both of those plays were just perfectly executed by Wake, and we lost.

As we were walking off the court, and all that was going through my mind was, *This is our season. We're done.* There was the NIT, but that wasn't much consolation at the time. Everybody felt bad. We went straight to the locker room, and Coach Smith headed toward the media room off to the right.

But before I got to the locker room, Coach Smith just grabbed my arm and pulled me aside. You could just see it in his face, how worn out and devastated he was. And he said, "Bobby, I just wanted to tell you how much I appreciated the way you played today."

And if you know Coach Smith, you know that was rare. Usually, whenever you met with Coach Smith, you'd go up to his office and you'd always come out a little bit shorter. If he had something good to say to you, he would say it. But there was always something where he'd knock you down a couple of pegs, too. Keep you humble. That's just the way he was. So when he told me that after the game, the sincerity really came through. It was like we just came through a battle together. We were shot up, but he was saying, "Thanks for helping me." To me, as a player, I really appreciated that.

Later, for me as a coach, I came to value the importance of encouragement. My dad—he knew basketball, but he would never criticize my play. He felt like that was the coach's job. And it is. So after any game, even if I played poorly, he would find something positive to say. I actually think about the Wake Forest game now more as a moment of encouragement for me.

What Coach Smith said that day helped form me as a coach. I can certainly criticize but also I can encourage and not deflate somebody and what he's trying to do. So I've always thought of that. When I think of Coach Smith, I think of the fun it was playing for him and the confidence he instilled in you. That moment meant a lot to me. I've always appreciated it.

I also had some really fun wins at Carolina, of course. Two were against Duke. One of them came at Cameron Indoor Stadium in Durham. I stole a pass right at the end of the game—the guy had put a lot of air under it—and went in for a left-handed layup just before the buzzer and just kept on running into our locker room. That was one time when being a natural lefty really helped.

I was also fortunate to be a part of the eight-points-in-17-seconds win against Duke in 1974. Walter Davis finished that comeback with that incredible shot. I started it with a couple of free throws, and that was rare for me back then, because I wasn't a very good free-throw shooter.

79

After Carolina, I was fortunate to have a much better pro career than I thought I would. I wasn't a very confident person, and I didn't think I could play in the NBA until I made the '72 Olympic team. Making that team was a mixed blessing. I understood then that sports was just a business. It wasn't our controversial loss to the Russians in the gold-medal game so much as the terrorists' massacre of the Israeli athletes at those Olympics. When that happened, all of us on the team thought, *Well, surely the Olympics will be canceled.* Yet they weren't. If I could do it again, I would do it. It didn't turn out the way I wanted it to, but it was a great honor to play for my country, in much the same way as it was to play for Carolina.

I had hoped to play pro basketball for seven years, but I was able to play for 12. The most special pro season was when we were able to win a championship in 1983 with the Philadelphia 76ers, with another Carolina guy in Billy Cunningham as the head coach. I was a pretty good defensive player—I got good at baiting people—and I could jump and was somewhat quick. I was able to dunk from the free-throw line when I played in Denver, like Julius Erving could. David Thompson and I played together and became good friends in the pros. He was more of an explosive vertical jumper—I was kind of a glider.

I remember we were playing in Denver one night, and someone from our team took a shot. My man boxed me out, and the ball hit the back of the rim and bounced way out. David was in the foul line area, and suddenly I felt his knees on my back. He caught the ball, fell over both of us, and dunked it. I'm 6'9", so that was pretty good elevation. That was the weirdest feeling—to have someone's knees on your back while you were standing up.

When I was in the NBA, I actually took my Carolina letter jacket as my only coat for my first five years out of college. It was a typical letter jacket with little snaps on the front. Dark blue. The sleeves were dark blue leather, the body was dark blue felt. I just loved it. I took the block "NC" off, but every time someone asked about the coat, I loved to tell them I was actually wearing my college letter jacket.

I retired in 1986 and came back to Charlotte. I took a year off and then started volunteering at Charlotte Christian School as a coach. I was there for 15 years as a coach. All three of our kids—we have two boys and a girl—went through there and graduated. I've been involved in some ministry work, as well. My Christian walk is still daily. I still mess up. I go to church. That doesn't get me to heaven, but I know I'm going there.

I occasionally still play basketball, but I'll be sore for a day and a half afterward. I play more tennis than anything else.

I don't get back to Chapel Hill as much as I used to—maybe once a year now. But I still feel a commonality with the program and with everyone who either went to school there or simply follows the school closely.

Bobby Jones played for the Tar Heels from 1971 to 1974 and was first-team All-America. He won a controversial silver medal with the U.S. Olympic team in 1972 and an NBA championship with the Philadelphia 76ers in 1983.

Known as one of the best defensive players in NBA history, he earned All-Defensive First Team honors for eight straight years in the NBA. He is a past finalist for the Naismith Memorial Basketball Hall of Fame, and his jersey is honored in the rafters at the Smith Center. Jones now lives in Charlotte, where he does some speaking at banquets and athletic events, runs his own basketball camps, does ministry work, and coaches a middle-school basketball team.

WALTER DAVIS

FORWARD

1973–1977

EIGHT POINTS IN 17 SECONDS. That's what people remember about me being a Tar Heel more than anything else, and I guess it's not a bad thing to be remembered for. It means a lot to me. I still remember that comeback game against Duke very well—1974, in Chapel Hill, when I was a freshman.

What most people don't know about that comeback is that my final shot from way, way out—which tied the game and sent it into overtime—was supposed to be a swish. That's what I was going for. Instead, it banked in, even though I had a bad angle to bank a shot in from there.

So many people had left Carmichael Auditorium at that point, thinking we were going to lose, that a lot of people actually missed the shot. I understand now that after they heard the roar from those who had stayed, they started coming back in. When I come back home to North Carolina, I always get somebody coming up and saying, "I'm sorry to tell you I didn't see the shot. But I did come back in and see the overtime."

I live in Denver, where I'm a community ambassador for the Denver Nuggets. Although most of my NBA career was spent in Phoenix, I also played several years in Denver and have made a home here. A lot of Carolina guys are in the NBA, of course. So when they are in town playing the Nuggets, I try to visit them. Plus we've got George Karl as our coach and Ty Lawson as one of our point guards, so we have a very good Carolina connection here. I still stay in touch with Coach Smith and with Phil Ford, who was my teammate at Carolina.

I learned to share early, so I understood the team concept Coach Smith preached. I grew up in the Charlotte area, the youngest of 13 children. Yes, 13. My mom and dad were married for 52 years—they are both deceased now. I'm so proud of our family. Of the 13 kids, nine of us went to college and got our degrees. I had a wonderful childhood. We were far from rich. My mom did domestic work, and my dad had two jobs. But it was a good life. I was probably a little bit spoiled as the youngest, but I like to think that I wasn't.

My family was so big that there was always someone to hang out with, be around, and learn from. You probably know the name of one of my nephews, too. My brother, Hubert Sr., had a son, Hubert Jr., and Hubert Jr. played for the Tar Heels, finishing his career there in 1992, and now does a lot of college basketball analysis for ESPN.

I played in high school at South Mecklenburg in Charlotte. Bobby Jones and I both went through South Meck, but he was a little older than me, and we didn't play together. South Meck won the state championship three years in a row while I was there. Bobby's team did it when he was a senior, and then we won it the next two years. We only lost three games over a three-year span. And in my senior year, the starting five all got Division I scholarships. We pretty much ruled Charlotte there for a while.

When I got to Carolina in 1973, I was a little skinny and was just a freshman, feeling my way. I was the first freshman starter under Dean Smith—freshmen had only recently become eligible. That eight-points-in-17-seconds game changed me. I became more aggressive after that. More confident.

Our game against Duke in 1974 was going to be Bobby Jones' final appearance at Carmichael—he was a popular senior, and we were finally getting to play together after going to the same high school and not doing so. That was the most important thing going in. We wanted to win it for Bobby and the seniors. Of course, Duke didn't want to cooperate.

We had much better talent than Duke that year, and this game really shouldn't have been that close. But it's such a rivalry. Duke played really well for almost the whole game, and I remember being down about that. We were down eight with 17 seconds to go, as everyone knows, with Bobby Jones going to the free-throw line for two shots.

There was a timeout right before he shot them, and Coach Smith was very positive. He said, "This is what we're going to do. Bobby will make the free throws, we'll steal the ball, score, and then call timeout." He was smiling, and that seemed to take all the frustration away for us. We all concentrated.

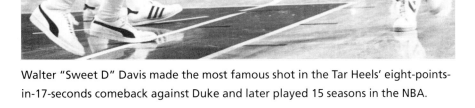

Walter "Sweet D" Davis made the most famous shot in the Tar Heels' eight-points-in-17-seconds comeback against Duke and later played 15 seasons in the NBA.

And it pretty much came true just like he said. Bobby hit the free throws. We stole the ball, and John Kuester hit a layup. Instead of 86–78, it was 86–82. There were 13 seconds left. We called another timeout, set up the defense, and Duke made another turnover. Bobby scored again—this time after an offensive rebound—and we had cut it to two with six seconds to go. We called timeout again.

Duke still could have won, of course, with just one free throw. There was no three-point line back then, and so we wouldn't be able to catch them. Coach Smith said, "We've done it twice in a row, let's steal it again." But this time we couldn't. They got it in successfully, and we fouled right away. Their guy [Pete Kramer] had a one-and-one with four seconds left. He missed, Ed Stahl got the rebound, and we called our final timeout with three seconds to go.

Coach Smith said, "Let's go 513, but skip the 1. Walter, you'll have time—get as close to the basket as you can and get a good shot."

What all that meant was our "5" man, Mitch Kupchak, would inbound the ball. Usually, he would throw a short pass to the "1," our point guard, but there wasn't enough time. I was the "3," the small forward.

We thought they would think we'd throw it long to Bobby, so he took off toward the basket. I would curl back to get the ball at around halfcourt. Sure enough, when Bobby took off, about three Duke guys went with him. Nobody was on me after John Kuester set a nice screen. Coach Smith would later say he thought I came back too far to get the pass. But Mitch threw a great one. I caught it at halfcourt, dribbled three times, and just put it up from the right side. The angle was bad for a bank, like I mentioned, so I was going for the swish. I had a clear look at the basket—a Duke guy came in right at the end, but he wasn't really close.

And so it banked in, and the people left in Carmichael went absolutely crazy. It was like an explosion of sound. I think I was the last one to really react to it. You literally couldn't hear in there—Carmichael was like that in the best of times. And finally, I realized what I had done.

It's not like football, where there are yard lines on the court, so no one knows exactly how far that shot was. Some people say 28. Some say 32. I say about 40 feet. Hey, I shot it, after all—who are you going to believe?

We still had an overtime to go at that point. People were streaming back into Carmichael, wondering what they had missed. I didn't know this at the time, but Coach Smith was very confident we'd win it—so confident, in fact, that he told Bill Guthridge he could go ahead and leave. Coach Guthridge had to take a plane to get to Arkansas to interview for its head-coaching job, although luckily he would end up staying with us. I didn't even notice he was gone at the time. I just found out about that later.

The overtime wasn't that easy, either—people forget we were down in it, too, for a while. But we were finally, finally able to get ahead there and win it 96–92. Even now, more than 30 years later, that banked shot is the most memorable one of my career.

The next day in practice Coach Smith smiled and said, "I want to see you hit that shot again." We set it up the same way. Kupchak threw it to me. I took three long dribbles and shot…an airball. The guys killed me about it. But when I got to the NBA, I came back to Carolina basketball camp one year. Mitch was there, too, and some folks started talking about the shot. So we reenacted it one more time, in front of all the campers. And this time, I made it. Hey, I just need an audience! No sense in wasting a shot if hardly anyone is there to see it!

In my college career, I'm proud of the fact we only lost to Duke once in four years. I'm also proud that we won a gold medal for the U.S. Olympic team in 1976—Coach Smith was the U.S. coach, and Phil Ford, Tommy LaGarde, Kupchak, and I were all on the team. Our best season at Carolina came when I was a senior in 1977. LaGarde tore up his knee during the season, and someone sent some flowers to the basketball office. There was a note attached that read: "With sympathy, because your season is over." It was a nasty trick. I remember the seniors called a team meeting. We all just went down the line and talked about what we had to do to save our season.

We ended up winning 15 games in a row that season and got to the 1977 Final Four and then to the national final against Marquette. We lost that one 67–59. I played the whole NCAA tournament with a broken right index finger I got in the ACC tournament. I went in for a shot, a guy tried to draw a charge, and I came down awkwardly. My finger didn't hurt until the next play down the court. I caught the ball and was getting ready to shoot, and it felt so strange, I thought something was wrong with the ball. I called timeout and went to the bench. I finished that game and had surgery right after we beat Virginia in the tournament final.

In the NCAA tournament, I taped my index finger to my middle finger and actually shot the ball better. My shooting percentage went up! But I couldn't handle the ball very well at all. It was a shame that we weren't healthier for that final against Marquette—Phil Ford had an elbow injury by then, and of course LaGarde had his knee injury.

When I went to the pros, I caught everyone by surprise at first. In college, I wasn't supposed to look for my shot that much, because we were focused on getting the ball inside. In the pros, they saw I could shoot and gave me the green light. I was Rookie of the Year and second-team All-NBA.

I had a good, long career, mostly in Phoenix and Denver. Now I work for the Nuggets. Right now, myself and two other former Nuggets—Calvin Natt and Mark Randall—make a lot of appearances. We go to elementary and middle schools and talk to them about getting a good education. All these kids today think they're going to be pro athletes. We try to tell the kids that even if they do become a pro basketball player, the average is only three or four years for a career, because either you get hurt or someone is better. You can't just concentrate strictly on sports. We get into more than 100 schools during the basketball season. Then we schmooze a lot with corporate people on game nights. We play a lot of golf and do some corporate outings for charity in the summers.

I've been out West a long time now—ever since I graduated. But I still remember those days in Chapel Hill fondly. And whenever I get back there, someone always asks me about eight points in 17 seconds.

Walter Davis blasted into the NBA in 1978 when he was named Rookie of the Year at Phoenix and averaged 24.2 points per game. It wasn't a fluke—Davis would average 18.9 points per game in his 15-year NBA career and shoot a career 51.1 percent—an almost unheard-of percentage for a small forward in the NBA these days.

Known as "Sir Walter" or "Sweet D," Davis was one of the purest shooters in Carolina history and was particularly adept at the baseline jumper. He played 11 of his 15 NBA seasons in Phoenix and participated in six NBA All-Star Games. Phoenix so appreciated him that the Suns retired his No. 6 jersey.

Davis's career had one major blemish. In the 1980s he struggled with cocaine and alcohol, and his time at Phoenix ended because of his involvement in one of the drug controversies that haunted the NBA that decade. He told the NBA he needed treatment the day after scoring a career-high 47 points in a Phoenix victory. He has now been clean for more than two decades but does not like to talk much about that dark time in his life.

"I believe everyone's recovery is their own personal thing," Davis said. "It's not an issue with me anymore."

One of the most well-known stories about the eight-points-in-17-seconds game was that in Rocky Mount, North Carolina, high school star Phil Ford was so disgusted with the game that he turned off the TV and went outside to wash the family's car. Ford would later play in a number of games like this himself and would end up as UNC's all-time leading scorer for more than 30 years, but at the time he still wasn't fully vested in the Carolina mystique.

"That's true," Ford said many years later when asked whether he missed one of Carolina's fantastic finishes. "I missed the comeback, but I saw some of the overtime. I walked back inside after washing the car, and the game was still on. My dad was still in the chair, watching the overtime, which was about over. He said, 'Son, you just missed something special.'"

JOHN KUESTER

GUARD

1973–1977

WHEN I THINK OF NORTH CAROLINA, I think of family and the group of people I was associated with on the basketball team, as well as the basketball staff. It was such a special experience for me. I'm fortunate enough to meet a lot of people in my job, and anytime you talk about North Carolina basketball, there's just this special gleam in people's eyes. There's this tone that they use. There's a connection there, and I don't care if you played on the basketball team or not. Anybody who went to Carolina can connect with anybody else who also went there.

For the players, one thing that made it very different is how much we cared about our coach. Not everyone likes their coaches as much as we did. I was fortunate enough to play and now to coach in the NBA, and a lot of times you hear from other players, and a common theme is what went wrong somewhere, in college or in the pros. How a certain situation didn't go as well as the player wanted it to. Of course, we didn't win every game at Carolina when I was there, and certain things didn't go the way I would have liked them to. That's always going to happen. But it was a privilege to play there.

I was born and raised in Richmond, Virginia. My father was a candy salesman—he worked for Russell Stover. He passed away in 2010 at age 89 and was such a sweetheart. He was more of a football player, really. I played baseball and basketball growing up and knew I was a pretty good athlete.

But then I went to Benedictine High School and played for a legendary high school coach—Warren Rutledge. I really think I went from the best high school coach in the country to the best college coach in the country in Dean Smith, so I was very fortunate.

In high school, I learned what it was to be in great shape. I also found out the type of work you have to do to be a college athlete. I got a head start on some of the things that Coach Smith taught, and I knew North Carolina would be the right place for me because it was a place that would appreciate the things I did as a basketball player. I was a guard, and I really put a premium on effort, on defending, on sharing the basketball, and on playing the right way. I could have gone almost anywhere in the ACC—the only school that didn't recruit me was Wake Forest—but I chose Carolina.

I played in a lot of great games at Carolina, but when I think of my favorite memories, I mostly think of my teammates and how fortunate I was to have a great group of guys over the four years to play with. To have so many other people around you who had a passion for the game—that was priceless.

I really liked Coach Smith's style as a coach. I'd describe it as firm but fair. Always under control. Getting the maximum potential out of every player.

After Carolina, I played for three years in the NBA. I was with the Kansas City Kings in the late 1970s, and Phil Ford was our first pick, but he was sitting out and showed up to camp a couple of weeks late. Cotton Fitzsimmons was our coach. Phil came in and was behind because he had missed some time. Cotton said, "John, make sure you teach Phil all the plays." Sure enough, I taught Phil all the plays, and right after that I got waived. I still tease Phil about that.

I also had the privilege of playing half a season in Denver for Larry Brown, who has been instrumental in my coaching career. Even while I was playing for all those years, I was thinking about becoming a coach. Even way back in about eighth grade, I knew that might be something I wanted to do. I started coaching in college in 1980 and have been in college or in the pros most ever since.

In terms of my profession, the Carolina connection has opened doors for me that never would have opened otherwise. I've been very fortunate to work with a lot of great people, to be a head coach both in college and in the

John Kuester, shown here running the Tar Heels' "four corners" offense, later became a head coach in both college and the NBA.

NBA and, most of all, to be able to wake up and look forward to going to work every day. A lot of people don't have that luxury.

And I owe a lot of what I've been able to do to Carolina. I just feel so passionately about the place. I don't know about you, but I've never met somebody who didn't enjoy their experience at college there. That sort of thing is so rare.

As a player, John Kuester was voted North Carolina's top defensive player in both 1976 and '77. He played on the Tar Heels team that advanced to the Final Four in 1977 before losing to Marquette in the championship game. Kuester was the MVP of both the 1977 ACC tournament and East Regional for the Tar Heels. Selected in the third round of the 1977 NBA Draft, Kuester played three seasons in the NBA for three different squads.

Nicknamed "Kue" (pronounced "Q"), Kuester has been a basketball coach for the past 30-plus years, coaching such players as LeBron James and Allen Iverson during his tenure. He became the head coach of the NBA's Detroit Pistons in 2009 after serving 14 years as an NBA assistant for six different teams.

Prior to joining the NBA, Kuester was the head coach at George Washington from 1985 to 1990 and at Boston University before that (where he succeeded Rick Pitino). For much of his tenure in the NBA, he worked under fellow Carolina alumnus Larry Brown. Kuester served on Brown's staff when the 2003–2004 Detroit Pistons won an NBA championship.

Kuester and his wife, Tricia, have two children, John and Katie. Both attended St. Joseph's University in Philadelphia. John graduated from St. Joe's, and Katie is currently a member of the school's women's basketball team.

PHIL FORD

GUARD

1974–1978

I WAS VERY LUCKY THAT I HAD THE OPPORTUNITY to live a boyhood dream in going to North Carolina. I think all of the boys who grew up in North Carolina in my generation and who played basketball would have loved to have the opportunity to go to UNC and play for Coach Smith.

They didn't have to do a lot of recruiting to get me to come to Chapel Hill. I grew up in Rocky Mount, just about 85 miles away. My parents were both schoolteachers. They called my father "Big Phil" and me "Little Phil," and he was the one who kept up with my basketball. My mom didn't go to many of my games—it made her too nervous.

The first time Dean Smith ever came to visit me at our home, basketball didn't come up for the first 45 minutes. We talked about race relations. We talked about being a good student. My brother was in medical school at the time, and we talked about that. We finally got into basketball a little bit. Then we walked Coach Smith to his car, and my mom told my dad, "Big Phil, wasn't that nice of North Carolina to send a dean down here to call on Little Phil?" She was a little confused about what sort of dean he was.

People ask me pretty often what my favorite moments as a student-athlete at Carolina were. It's hard to pick, because my entire experience was just unbelievable. All the losses hurt. When we won, we were tickled pink.

But I will tell you that one game—my last one in Carmichael Auditorium in my senior year—stands out. My mom and dad were both there for Senior

Phil Ford and Dean Smith formed one of the most famous player-and-coach basketball combinations of the 1970s, and Smith would later employ Ford as one of his own assistant coaches at UNC.

Day, and we were playing Duke. I had missed the game before because I had sprained my wrist badly in a game against Virginia. I still have problems with that wrist today. There's a bump on it, and I get arthritis in it. So I missed that N.C. State game—the only game I missed in my career—and we lost. Then we were going to play Duke, and there was no way I was going to miss that one. I remember I had a bet with Walter Davis before the game that I wouldn't cry. I lost the bet.

Duke games were always emotional for me, but this one was really special. For most of the time I was in school, it was N.C. State more than Duke that was our main rival. But by 1978, that was switching over. Duke was getting very good, and this game meant a lot for us. We really wanted to win the ACC, and whoever won the game would win the regular-season title.

I knew it was going to be my last time playing in Carmichael Auditorium with some people I had grown very close to. More so than how I played, I remember this one because it was my last game there. I think people kind of remember firsts and lasts in their lives. I'm still trying to forget my first game in a Carolina uniform—that was when a guy wrote the article headlined "This Ford's an Edsel." That's how bad I was playing!

So Senior Day was a sad and a happy time for me. I loved playing for North Carolina, and I knew I'd never be playing in Carmichael again, and that I'd be graduating in a couple of months. It was very emotional.

There were three seniors that year who they recognized in the pregame—Tom Zaliagiris, Geoff Crompton, and myself. Believe it or not, both those other guys are dead now. The three of us were standing at halfcourt, and they gave us a standing ovation, and the players clapped. My parents were there with my younger sister. My brother had graduated medical school the year before and was doing an internship in St. Louis, so he couldn't come. I remember that I started crying in the pregame. It was really tough, but it was a good feeling, too.

How we won that game, I don't know. Duke was really good. Duke would end up in the national championship game that year, losing to Kentucky. But everyone played well. And Carmichael? Oh, it was loud that day.

Let me try to explain to you how loud it was in there for games like this. I remember breaking the huddle one time at a timeout. I was behind Walter Davis. I can remember Coach Smith, calling me back. He grabbed me and told me something and said, "Now go tell Walter."

Walter was only five or six feet away, but he had his back to me. I was screaming at the top of my voice for him to turn around—I mean *screaming*—and he couldn't hear me. I had to go around and get in his face to tell him what Coach Smith said. That's how loud it was.

I never went into any game for us saying, "I've got to score," or, "I've got to pass." Now I did always think I had to play defense, because if you didn't play defense for Coach Smith, you didn't play. So the 34 points that day just happened—I happened to score my career high in my final game in Carmichael. The shots were going in, and we needed them all.

With six seconds left, I remember we were up by two. Duke fouled me, and it was a one-and-one. Boy, I remember that first free throw—it hit the rim. Then it went in, and I was like, *Whew!* The second one, when I shot it, I knew that one was in. When it was over, I was so happy. I remember jumping in Mike O'Koren's arms, just the sheer joy of it. That was such a great win for us.

As a player, if you compared me to someone like Ty Lawson, there's no way I was that fast over the entire court. In a 40-yard dash, lots of people could beat me. But in a five-yard dash—just from me to you—I was world class.

We didn't win a national championship while I was playing, and that hurts. I will say that, as I get older, winning a gold medal at the 1976 Olympics means more. When you're a player, you just look at it as another tournament. But looking back on it, standing on that podium with the "Star-Spangled Banner" playing and a gold medal around your neck, with the Cold War going on, that was pretty neat.

When my career ended in 1978, when we lost in the NCAA tournament to San Francisco, I didn't want to take off my uniform. That was so hard. I kept the tape on my ankles for a couple of days. Walked around in it. I didn't want to cut it off. I just didn't want it to end.

I was a pretty tough player—not the prettiest player, but it was hard to keep me out of a game. Once in 1976 in the ACC tournament we were playing Clemson. Stan Rome elbowed me in the mouth and knocked one of my teeth out. I kept my dribble alive, got the tooth, handed it to our trainer, and kept on playing. Coach Smith used to always use that as an example to the players who came behind me. He told the story a lot, I guess, and it would get a little exaggerated. I remember I was an assistant coach at Carolina when J.R. Reid said once to Coach Smith, "Hey, Coach, can you tell the story again about Coach Ford jumping on the bomb on-court, getting his arm blown off, and still playing?"

I couldn't dunk, either. Never did it in my life—well, not in a game. Once at a pep rally in Rocky Mount back in my hometown, I sort of half-dunked. But since that's the only time I got up that high, I'm counting it.

I battled alcohol for years. By the grace of God, I didn't kill anyone, and I didn't kill myself, and I didn't have to go to prison. It could have been a lot worse. Alcohol has a way of showing you that if you ever think you've got it licked—that you "graduated" from your problem—you're wrong. I drink cranberry juice or orange juice now when I'm at a function where alcohol is served. Sobriety is very important to me.

I spent 12 years as a Tar Heels assistant coach under Coach Smith and then Coach Bill Guthridge, and those were some great years. Seeing people improve—I really enjoyed that. I remember as a freshman coming to North Carolina and thinking I was a pretty good player and not thinking about how much I didn't know and had to learn. To see the new players come in and get better and then keep their cool under pressure—that was an unbelievable feeling.

I still bleed Carolina blue even though now I coach in the NBA for the Charlotte Bobcats under Larry Brown—another Carolina guy. I'd love to be a head coach one day. I'm in position to be a better coach than I've ever been in my life because of all the hardships I've gone through. I guess I just had to go through certain things for me to be where I am now.

Although I'm still on a basketball court a lot with practice and games, I haven't played in a real basketball game of any type since 1991. I dribbled and held up four fingers at the UNC alumni game in 2010, but that's about all I really did. It's a young man's sport. I've heard too many horror stories about old men playing basketball. I've finally got two good hips, now that I've had two hip replacements, and I plan on keeping them.

As Dean Smith said many times, "No one is more faithful to Carolina than Phil Ford."

Ford's No. 12 jersey has been retired at Carolina. The image of him holding up four fingers with his left hand to signal for the Tar Heels' famed "four corners" offense while dribbling the ball with his right hand is one of the most famous in UNC lore. In the days before the shot clock, giving the ball to Ford with a lead late in the second half was tantamount to passing out victory cigars to everyone wearing Carolina blue.

Ford was the National Player of the Year in 1978 and still ranks No. 2 in scoring all-time (behind Tyler Hansbrough) with 2,290 points. He was first-team All-America in 1976, '77, and '78, and led the Tar Heels to the national title game in 1977, which UNC lost to Marquette.

Ford won a gold medal with the 1976 U.S. Olympic team coached by Dean Smith. He played seven years in the NBA and was the league's Rookie of the Year in 1979 with the Kansas City Kings.

In 1981 a player named World B. Free accidentally stuck his thumb in Ford's eye while trying to pass the ball. It was a serious injury—Ford still occasionally has double vision in that eye. And for a point guard whose vision was one of his most special qualities, it was devastating. Ford played four more seasons, but he was never quite the same as a player.

Ford spent 12 years as an assistant coach at UNC, helping the Tar Heels get to six Final Fours and win one national title, in 1993. He is now an assistant coach with the NBA's Charlotte Bobcats, working under fellow Tar Heels alum Larry Brown.

The
EIGHTIES

JAMES WORTHY

FORWARD

1979–1982

CAROLINA IS MORE THAN JUST A BASKETBALL TEAM. It's a family. It's also a formula. It's special. Coach Smith had a platform at Carolina, but he didn't just use it for basketball. Basketball was just his way to get to people, to make them pay attention. If your parents started something good for you, as mine did for me, he just took that and enhanced it. And not just for NBA-caliber people. For everyone, whether you were Michael Jordan or Chuck Duckett, who was one of our managers. Coach Smith taught you how to submit to authority without losing your integrity, and he taught you how to be a great team player. He prepared you for the real world.

The 1982 season was my last, and it was my favorite year in college. That Georgetown game for the championship—that was unforgettable. Oh, I wanted that last shot. I wanted it so badly. I wanted the win or loss on my shoulders. But Michael stole my glory (laughs).

That game was important to me in a lot of ways, including the fact that I played one of my high school rivals and friends in the game—Sleepy Floyd. My parents, Ervin and Gladys Worthy, raised me in Gastonia, North Carolina. That's about 15 minutes from Charlotte. My parents knew all about Charlie Scott and how he was the first black athlete at Carolina, and because of that, they loved North Carolina.

They passed that love down to me, sending me to basketball camps at Chapel Hill. I was a diehard fan. I idolized Phil Ford. Dudley Bradley was a good friend of mine. I admired Bob McAdoo and Charlie Scott and all the rest. I remember crying many a night after the Tar Heels lost. I remember the loss to Marquette in the 1977 championship game. I remember the loss to San Francisco [in the 1978 NCAA tournament in Ford's senior year]. So I kind of knew where my heart was all through the recruiting process.

We went to Tabernacle Baptist Church in Gastonia, and so did the Floyd family. Sleepy and I went to rival high schools in Gastonia. We dominated them every year until they beat us on a last-second shot in the state playoffs. We had the right guy taking the shot for them—I would have thought Stevie Wonder had a better chance to make it than he did. But he did make it, so I never won a state championship in high school.

My first two seasons at UNC weren't as good as they could have been because of injury. I broke my ankle as a freshman and only played about half the season. In my sophomore season, I played on that ankle, but it had a long rod in it, and my explosiveness was limited. It also hurt, especially on rainy days. We still made it to the NCAA final that season in 1981—we had a really good team. We were to play Indiana. The game was delayed because of an assassination attempt on President Reagan, and then Isiah Thomas basically beat us in the second half. Jimmy Black and I both fouled out in the final. That was a tough experience, to lose in the final. I felt terrible for Al Wood, because it was his last chance. I was determined to get back there. Jimmy Black, myself, Sam Perkins—we were so eager to get back. We had several team meetings throughout the next season, talking about how we had to get it done.

We had four starters coming back from that team—myself, Jimmy, Perkins, and Matt Doherty—and then we added Michael Jordan as a freshman as the fifth starter. I remember Jordan's recruiting trip. He came in one weekend, got off the elevator, and all you could hear was, "Yackety yak yak yak." He was like, "This is going to be my dorm. This is going to be my team. I can kick your butt." He wasn't exactly arrogant, he was just really sure of himself.

Michael would seek me out because he knew I was the best player on the team. He'd want to play me one-on-one. [Worthy said he played Jordan three times over the course of the season, beat him twice, and then wouldn't play him in one-on-one ever again, which has irritated Jordan for the past 30 years.] If Michael lost in anything—backgammon, Ping-Pong, cards—he was irate. I knew he was going to be good. I knew he was going to be a pro player and an All-Star. But I had no idea he would take off like he did. Now someone will see me in the airport and say, "Wait, wait! I know you! Didn't you play basketball with Michael Jordan?"

Coach Williams was an assistant coach back then. He drove this ugly, Carolina blue Mustang that we called the blue goose, and lived out in this two-bedroom apartment on Highway 54. His wife, Wanda, tutored me one summer. I could talk to him. Coach Smith was so busy. Coach Williams was someone you could go lay your head down and talk to him. He was really close to my father and to my mom. And when he was in Kansas, he'd write them every month. He would also call my dad, who was a jokester, any time he needed a joke.

To get to the Final Four, we won a couple of games in Raleigh over Villanova and Alabama. We cut down the nets after that, but I didn't participate in that. The Final Four was going to be played in New Orleans, and the nets I wanted were there.

After we beat Houston in the semifinal, I knew we were going to be in for a fight in the final against Georgetown. They played eight or nine guys and were incredibly talented, especially Patrick Ewing. He was one of the meanest, toughest guys you were ever going to see, and he was a freshman. We played six guys, tops. It was going to be mind over matter for us in that 40-minute game.

And there were so many little stories as part of the big story: Sleepy Floyd and me being from the same hometown. John Thompson being Coach Smith's assistant on the 1976 Olympic team and them being such good friends. For me, I knew it was going to be the biggest game I ever played in.

Georgetown was just an awesome team. And it was a tough game right from the start. There was a lot of anxiety. A lot of jitters. Getting used to playing in a dome that size was a little tough. I couldn't see my parents in the stands, they were so far away. It felt weird. And then John Thompson had obviously instructed Patrick Ewing to play the intimidation card early by blocking anything he could, even if it was goaltending. He actually goaltended our first four baskets. I don't think Ewing or Thompson thought they could intimidate me, but maybe they thought they could intimidate either Sam or maybe Michael, since he was a freshman. Anyway, it didn't work.

But they were strong. And they just kept running fresh guys at you. At halftime, we were dog-tired and we were still down a point [32–31]. I thought to myself, *How are we going to redo everything we had just done—but even better—and we're already this tired?*

After scoring 28 points in the 1982 national title game and making the decisive steal against Georgetown, James Worthy wore the game net around his neck as he celebrated with his parents in the locker room.

But in the second half, Jordan really emerged. Everybody talks about the big shot he made at the end, but he had an almost impossible left-handed layup shortly before that, over Ewing, that was just a huge basket. On another possession earlier, I had thrown a long pass to Jimmy Black, and he missed a tough layup, but Michael followed it and scored. We started to realize Georgetown was a little frustrated, too, in the second half. Michael's play gave us some momentum and encouragement. Sam was playing Patrick Ewing well. I remember he picked up a big foul on Ewing, and that allowed me to go inside some more.

So they saw we weren't going anywhere. They weren't going anywhere, either. But I remember distinctly Jimmy Black saying in a huddle, "We're right there. We're in this. We're going to get this." What a great leader Jimmy was. Coach Smith had been there so many times, he just couldn't lose another one. He would never allow us to feel that pressure, and he never said a thing about it, but we could see it. Not on Coach Smith's face, but on Coach Williams' face. He never could hide his emotions like Coach Smith could.

Then they got up 63–62 on Sleepy Floyd's jumper. That was a scary moment. We called timeout [with 32 seconds left], and I'll tell you this: the biggest highlight of my college career was that timeout. I had never seen Coach Smith so calm. I couldn't believe he was so calm. He looked at us with a slight smile, and there was nothing to smile about. I've heard Roy Williams talking about that moment, too—that when he heard Coach Smith talking, he had to fake a cough and then look up at the scoreboard because he thought we were down one point. But he wanted to make sure, because Coach Smith sounded like we were up 20.

Had it not been for Coach Smith's calm nature, I might not have been able to play the rest of the game very well. I'll be honest—I had just about lost it. I was thinking, *Here we are, about to lose the national title game again. That will be twice in a row. And how are we ever going to get back here a third time?*

But the way Coach Smith presented it was that we were in control of the game. We had the ball, after all. We were down one point, but we were going to get a good shot. We wanted to go inside, of course. I was the first option, Sam was the second, but I kind of knew it would be tough for them to get the ball to me. We knew they wouldn't come out of tough zone. Every time I flashed through that zone, three of them ran to me, and one of them was Ewing.

I don't remember the next part, because I was already back on the court, but Coach Smith said to Michael in a very calm way, "If it comes to you, knock it down."

The other four of us had already gone back on the floor. As Matt Doherty has said, not too many people would have taken the shot at that point. There was still plenty of time—about 15 seconds—and Michael could have passed it back to Jimmy or Matt. I didn't really think he was going to shoot it, either. But when he did, I was in perfect rebounding position. So was Sam. But there was no need to rebound.

When a big shot like that goes down, for a moment, you're in shock. You're like, *What's going on? What do I do? Am I supposed to get back on defense or something?*

Meanwhile, your legs are working—you just hope they're carrying you the right way. Georgetown had a timeout, and I'm surprised they didn't call it. But Coach Thompson didn't want us to have a chance to get set. The man I was guarding was Ed Spriggs, and I knew Spriggs wasn't going to shoot the last shot. He was a role player. He never shot the ball. So I was trying to sag back a little bit, find where Patrick Ewing was. But then I saw Sleepy Floyd coming off a pick, and I thought maybe I'd have a chance to intercept this.

At the same time, Fred Brown, their guard, picked up his dribble. That's like the biggest no-no in sports. So the count was on, and Brown started to panic. When he pump-faked in my direction, I jumped so far out into the passing lane, I guess in his panic, he thought I was on his team. For a half-second there, I was absolutely horrified. I was so far out of position! What if my man got a basket or a tip-in because of that? But instead, Fred Brown threw it right to me.

It was actually the worst defensive play I had ever made, if you want to know the truth. And then it turned into "Right place, right time." So I started dribbling downcourt. I saw Michael running on the wing, but I didn't want to risk the turnover, so I tried to dribble out the clock. They fouled me instead with two seconds left, calling it an intentional foul, so I'd have two free throws. And everyone went crazy. Sam and I jumped into each other's arms—we were about four feet in the air. I kind of lost focus, honestly. That's why I think I missed the free throws—both of them! Coach Smith was telling us all, "Calm down, calm down!" but we weren't really calm. After I missed the second one, Georgetown got it to Sleepy Floyd just short of midcourt. His shot was on target but about six feet short, and we had won the national championship.

103

That turned out to be my last collegiate game. I went pro after my junior year. I probably would have stayed for my senior year if Coach Smith had leaned on me the other way. But we thought it was the right time. I was the No. 1 pick of the 1982 draft, by the L.A. Lakers. And I had a great NBA career. Coach Smith said, "Just promise me you will graduate." And even though I was 27 hours short of graduation when I left school, I came back and I did. That 1982 championship was so important to me, too. Since I never won a title in high school, that was my first real championship. And until I won something, I always felt, *What am I? What have I really contributed?* So winning in 1982, that set the tone for me.

Nicknamed "Big Game James" for his uncanny knack of performing well in the biggest basketball games, Worthy was inducted into the Naismith Memorial Basketball Hall of Fame in 2003. The 6'9" forward was a seven-time NBA All-Star and won three NBA championships with the L.A. Lakers in the 1980s. When Worthy retired from the NBA in 1994, former teammate Magic Johnson lauded him by saying that Worthy was one of the top five "playoff players" in NBA history.

Worthy has been named as one of the 50 greatest NBA and ACC players at different times in his career. His No. 52 jersey is retired at UNC, and the Lakers retired his No. 42 jersey from the pros. At both locations, he was known for his one-handed, swooping dunks.

He scored 28 points on 13-of-17 shooting in the 1982 title game against Georgetown. His best game as a pro may have been in Game 7 of the 1988 NBA Finals, when he had 36 points, 16 rebounds, and 10 assists against Detroit. It was the first triple-double of Worthy's career and led to him being named the NBA Finals MVP.

Worthy still lives in Los Angeles but gets back to Gastonia, North Carolina, and the greater North Carolina area frequently. He has his own charitable foundation (www.JamesWorthyFoundation.org). Worthy also does some work as a TV analyst in L.A. for Lakers games and also has several entrepreneurial interests. He lives two blocks from the UCLA campus.

"I have to educate all those UCLA people about where the real basketball school is," Worthy laughed. He remains close to his former teammates and to coach Dean Smith.

JIMMY BRADDOCK

GUARD

1979–1983

I LOVED BEING A TAR HEEL WHEN I WAS PLAYING, but I'm even prouder to have been one now that I'm older. Being a Tar Heel means being a winner and being around classy people on and off the court. It's a lifelong adventure, and it started the first day I set foot on that campus. It really evolved into an unending love affair with the school. I think everyone who went to Carolina—basketball player or not—knows what I'm talking about.

I grew up in Chattanooga, Tennessee, the youngest of four kids. Basketball definitely ran in the family. My one brother played high school ball. My father had been offered a basketball scholarship to Georgia Tech out of high school but ended up going into the military. I went to high school at a place called Baylor School. I played on some pretty good teams, but we really didn't have any big guys, so I was asked to do a lot of scoring. I ended up averaging about 36 points per game my senior year. My whole family liked basketball, and I would go to high school games or games at UT-Chattanooga, or sometimes we'd venture off to Knoxville and watch Tennessee play.

I didn't pick teams to follow, I picked players. Pretty much, I picked guards like me. I was a fan of every good guard who ever played. Phil Ford, Earl Monroe, Jerry West, Walt Frazier, Ernie DiGregorio, Gail Goodrich—all of them. Since I was a basketball junkie, I tried to pick up something from everybody.

Jimmy Braddock played both guard positions at UNC in the early 1980s and was one of the first Tar Heels to capitalize on the then-experimental three-point shot.

I loved the ABA because it had the three-point line. I loved the up-and-down game. I was a big fan of the long jumper. But at the time, I never thought a shot clock and a three-point line could even exist in college basketball.

I was known as a good offensive player coming out of high school and had a chance to go to a number of places. I ended up choosing UNC because of the people. I met guys like Jimmy Black and Chris Brust on my visit and could just tell what type of people they were. They had their priorities straight. They weren't there just to play ball and party.

I was awestruck when I came to Carolina's campus for the first time. But what really got me was the current players and the coaching staff being genuine, not making promises, telling you that playing time would be determined in practice and not saying, "You're going to average 20," or something like that. The Carolina coaches didn't sugarcoat the truth like so many other programs did. Even as a kid, you know when you're being conned.

James Worthy and I were the same year in school—we entered Carolina in 1979 together. I knew all about him when he was coming out of high school. People thought he might be the next Magic Johnson. When I was being recruited, Coach Smith told me that they had signed Worthy. He was such a good ball handler, I was a little worried they would try to make him a point guard, but Coach said, "No, he's going to be our power forward. He's not playing guard."

That helped seal it for me, because I wanted to go where someone of Worthy's ability was going. I had grown up a UCLA fan, but then I knew we really did have a good chance of winning the national championship. In our 1982 championship season, James was really "the Man."

But in our freshman year, he wasn't a great defensive player and didn't like running all the sprints we did, either. He'd be saying stuff under his breath when we ran. But it paid off. He buckled down, and that made us all better.

107

I so much wish there had been a three-point shot for all of my college career instead of just for one season. One of my clearest memories is that 1982 ACC championship game when we played Virginia and the final score was 47–45. We slowed it down in the second half, and then they didn't come out to guard us.

A lot of the players in that game could have scored 40 by themselves—Ralph Sampson, Michael Jordan, James Worthy, Sam Perkins. It was just not the way I imagined college basketball at the top should be—a methodical game where you're basically trying not to lose. I would have loved to have seen that game end up 115–112 with all that talent on the floor.

I didn't play a whole lot my first three years at Carolina. As a junior going into the 1981–1982 season in which we would ultimately win a championship, there was some question if I would start over Michael in the season opener against Kansas. I had a good preseason. Obviously, though, at 6′1″, it was going to be tough playing shooting guard in the ACC. Offensively I was enough of a threat, but guarding the other team's "2" guard would be my weakness.

In that preseason, Michael spent about the first three weeks trying to learn the system. That hindered him. Like everyone at the beginning, he was thinking too much. But he was a quick learner, and 10 days before the opening game, once he got really familiar with it, you could tell he was playing so much better in practice. All kids want to play, of course. But realistically by then, I knew we'd be a better team with him starting and me coming off the bench to sub in for both guard positions. And that's what I did the year we won the national championship.

The next year was my senior season. We lost our first two games, then won the Rainbow Classic in Hawaii, and then we played Rutgers in Greensboro. That remains a very special game for me, because it was the first one a UNC team ever played in when the three-point shot was available. We were going to use it on an experimental basis in the conference that season. [The three-point shot didn't get instituted permanently until 1986–1987 in college basketball, and then the distance was 19′9″. The ACC's "experimental" three-pointer of 1982–1983 was only 17′9″ and actually cut through the top of the key.]

If both coaches agreed in a nonconference game to use it kind of as a test drive, you could do that, too. So Coach Smith and the Rutgers coach said we should give it a try, and we did. The weird thing about that whole year was we all had to prepare for playing games both with and without the three-pointer. It was obviously a challenge to players and coaches. I remember going into that game very excited. We were all talking about it. We had six or seven guys on the team who could hit it. I thought it was long overdue, and of course it played to my strengths. It would make me more valuable and guards more valuable, in general.

I had thought it was time for a three-pointer in college basketball, and I'm still proud to say I played in the first game in which UNC got to shoot three-pointers. We had so many guys who could shoot that shot on the 1982–1983 team—myself, Michael Jordan, Matt Doherty, Sam Perkins, Steve Hale, and Buzz Peterson off the bench. Brad Daugherty could shoot it, too, but Coach Smith wouldn't let him.

This was our first game back from the Rainbow Classic in Hawaii, where we were playing really well. Coach Smith had told us that, for games with the three-pointer, taking an open three-pointer after just one pass wasn't a bad shot—it would have been if it were worth only two points—and I remember my first three of the game.

It was our first possession, and I came down off the secondary break. Nobody picked me up. I got the pass and shot from the top of the key. Generally, Coach didn't want his point guard just pulling up in that situation, but the three-pointer changed his mentality. It opened him up a little. Thank goodness I hit it. After that, we just started jacking them up, and our percentage stayed good.

As the game progressed, everybody started getting involved. Buzz Peterson had some three-pointers [four of them]. Matt Doherty had a couple. This game was kind of a glimpse of the future, with the 30-second shot clock and the three-point line.

Rutgers had a nice team and made a lot of threes, too. But Rutgers also sat back in a packed zone and just let us shoot over the top. That had worked some on us the year before, when coaches set their teams back in a packed zone and just begged our guards to shoot. That's when the games started getting really slow. But we got in control of this one early and stayed in control pretty much all the way.

I know what Coach Smith was probably thinking on the bench as we kept shooting those threes. I can hear him saying it: "Those shots are good as long as you're open, but don't forget to go inside." He was thinking that we had just opened up a can of worms. But it was so exciting, knowing you could always shoot your way back into a game. Defenses had to guard everybody again instead of triple-teaming in the paint. I knew once we played that game that the three-pointer wasn't just an experiment, that one day it was going to be here to stay in college basketball.

Whether we actually knew we were doing it or not, with that experimental three-point line in 1983, a lot of history was being made.

While I was at Carolina, I realized even at the time how fortunate I was to be on a team that could contend for the national championship. When I came out of high school, I had a ton of individual accolades, but I never got to the state championship game.

When I was there, I knew I had made the right decision. And as time has gone by, I've realized it even more. Like Coach Smith and now Coach Williams have preached, this is a family. Coach Williams is the perfect guy to lead the program right now. He's doing everything he can to embrace the former players and make everyone feel special. He's all about including the former players in the current players' successes. We all celebrated when the 2005 and 2009 teams won national titles, because that's what a family does.

Following his graduation from UNC in 1983, Jimmy Braddock played overseas for several years, including one stint in Ecuador, where he played alongside former UNC teammate Chris Brust. "I got into coaching when I was playing overseas," Braddock said. "That was part of the gig. I coached some youth teams. I started realizing that when I threw my basketball shoes away, this was what I was going to do."

Brust's first post-basketball job was in the mortgage business in Jacksonville, Florida. "But I didn't like the office," said Braddock, who has never married. "I needed to be around kids and basketball."

So Braddock coached high school basketball for close to 10 years in Jacksonville before moving to Columbia, South Carolina, where he was a teacher and basketball coach at Hammond, a private school, for another decade. He let all of his teams shoot a good many three-pointers, as you might guess. Braddock has coached a half-dozen college scholarship players in his career, including Alex English Jr., the son of the former South Carolina and NBA star. He also won a South Carolina state title at Hammond.

In 2009 Braddock took some time off from coaching to be an independent distributor for health-related products, such as vitamin supplements and water purifiers. But he plans to resume his high school coaching career at some point.

MATT DOHERTY

FORWARD

1981–1984

COACH

2000–2003

M Y TIME AS A STUDENT-ATHLETE AND AS A COACH at North Carolina—I treat those as two separate events. I think Carolina is probably the best place in the country to be a student-athlete. You can't find a prettier campus. The mix of that campus, the climate, the athletic and academic reputation, the state of North Carolina—it's unique. The fun, the frat parties, the football games, the beaches in one direction, and the mountains in the other— it's something else. There's a pride you have as a student and a graduate of North Carolina. I was on a plane the other day talking to someone about it. You find that at a place like Carolina or Notre Dame—just a few special places like that.

I loved my experience as a player at UNC—and as a coach. To this day, though, I don't like the way things went down at the end of my three years coaching at Carolina. I wasn't treated like family. I wasn't treated the way you would treat a brother or a son, despite the way we preach the family atmosphere. But I've moved on. I'm the head coach at SMU now, and I think it's a great time to be here. I really think we're headed in the right direction.

I grew up in New York. We were big sports fans of the New York teams—my dad had season tickets for the New York Giants for a long time. When it was time for me to be recruited, I visited Duke, Virginia, and UNC. I just felt I fit better at UNC. I had a better feel for the campus and the student body. I remember coming home from the visit, and my mom met me at LaGuardia Airport and just knew I was going there. As soon as I walked through security, she knew.

I called that Wednesday and told them I was coming. Clarke Bynum, who ended up going to Clemson, was coming there to visit UNC the next weekend. We were very similar players. I thought to myself, *He will have to come there, knowing I'm going there.* I'm not sure I would have gone there, actually, if Clarke had committed to UNC first.

I remember my days as a player at Carolina very well. We won the national championship in 1982, but I think our team in 1984 actually was a better team. It was one of the most talented teams in the history of college basketball. Some of the UCLA teams with Lew Alcindor (later Kareem Abdul-Jabbar) were probably the most talented, but we were close. I know we didn't have James Worthy anymore. But listen to this lineup: Michael Jordan. Sam Perkins. Brad Daugherty. Kenny Smith. Those are four very good to very great pros right there. Then you have Joe Wolf and Dave Popson, both of whom made it to the NBA. And Steve Hale—one of the smartest players you'll ever have on the basketball floor. And me. And then we also had the best coach to ever coach sports. Not just college basketball—*sports*. We really should have won the title again that season.

As for the 1982 season, a smile comes across my face whenever I think of it. It was a proud year for UNC for everyone involved—we all came together for a common goal and accomplished it. It was so rewarding.

I still remember those final seconds in the Georgetown game, with us down a point. We called timeout. Coach Smith would make you feel comfortable in those situations by speaking with such great confidence. He had this special gift—making everybody feel like they could make the last shot. So they came out in a zone designed to keep us from getting it inside to Worthy or Perkins. We swung the ball around...and then Michael took The Shot.

It still sort of blows my mind that he took it as a freshman. There were 60,000 people there. He caught it with 17 seconds to go. He could have faked the shot. He could have passed. No one would have said anything about that. He was pretty open, but not that open. But he caught the ball

Matt Doherty was prized for his versatility on the Tar Heels' 1982 national title team and later coached UNC for three tumultuous years, from 2000 to 2003.

and shot it like he was in practice with no one else around, and that's still fascinating to me.

I've got a picture of it in my office at SMU even now. His calmness in that situation—well, it was an omen of things to come. Then, Worthy got so far out of position when Georgetown brought the ball back down, it was almost like he was standing at halfcourt going, *Ooh, I blew this one.* And then Freddie Brown threw it right to him. And we won.

We'll never really understand why Freddie Brown threw that ball to Worthy, or why Chris Webber called timeout in a similar situation 11 years later, or why a baseball once went through Bill Buckner's legs at a crucial moment. Sometimes the adrenaline just gets going. That's just sports.

That 1982 title game was personally very memorable for all of us. Another game I remember with great fondness was against Duke on my Senior Day, in 1984. What a fun, dramatic game that was. It was Senior Day, as well as my last game at Carmichael Auditorium.

Now I'm a New York Yankees fan, but Carmichael was like Fenway Park. It wasn't a beautiful building from an architectural standpoint. But it had a low roof, and, with 10,000 fans packed in there, the bleachers just made tremendous noise when you started stomping on them. It was hot. It had this small doorway—probably not more than 5′10″—that you had to run out of from the locker room. Everyone complained that the visitors' locker room was extremely hot. It was just this unique building with great tradition. It was a very intimate place and special to Carolina players for a long time.

We were undefeated in the ACC at that point. Duke was just coming out of hitting bottom and starting to turn it around. They had Johnny Dawkins, Mark Alarie, Jay Bilas, Tommy Amaker—really a fine team. Just young. But we had a great team.

One of the few problems with Senior Day is you're distracted. The family, the tickets, the pageantry—you don't focus on the game as much as you should. My whole family was there and some other friends, too—probably a crew of 10 to 15 people. There was no doubt we felt we were going to win this game. We had handled them in the past, we were playing at home, and they were mostly freshmen and sophomores.

But they were good. It was very close throughout, and so it was really noisy in Carmichael. There were moments in games in that place where a play would occur—maybe you'd score or make a good play that led to a score and then run back on defense—and you couldn't hear yourself think. You were separated from the crowd. It was almost an out-of-body experience.

It was like a drug, honestly. I'm getting goose bumps talking about it. I think that's why a lot of people coach. You don't get that in the business world. The closest you come to it as a coach is being on the floor when great plays are being made.

We had three seniors—Cecil Exum, Sam Perkins, and myself. And the three of us scored the first three baskets of the game.

You know it must have been Senior Day if I got to take 14 shots. I can't believe I took that many. That was a rarity. But the one that I still remember, of course, was the shot to send it into overtime.

There were only nine seconds to go, and Danny Meagher was shooting a foul shot, the front end of a one-and-one. We were down by two. I was on the foul lane, with my back to our bench, and I looked up and saw a lot of fans leaving. It was kind of a weird feeling.

Meagher missed, though, and we got the rebound and took timeout with seven seconds to go. Down by a basket, obviously the play was to go to Michael. Sam Perkins was going to inbound it to me, and then I was supposed to go to MJ. But as I looked at MJ, three Duke defenders ran right at him. Only Meagher was on me, and I thought I had a chance to beat Meagher and get off a shot. I started dribbling. Toward the end of my drive, I lost the ball for a second. I think he got a finger on it. Then I picked it up and was lucky to hit a shot, a runner.

I remember running to the bench, guys jumping up and down and falling on top of me. It was one of those magical moments as an athlete that you really dream about, the shot to win the game or the one to send it into overtime.

How long was the shot? [Most newspaper accounts put it at 14 to 15 feet.] By now, it's got to be at least a 25-footer. To heck with the facts. To heck with the videotape. Let's say I beat the whole team and hit a beautiful 25-footer.

115

Then we won it in double overtime. In the second overtime we got rolling, and we ended up winning by 13 points—kind of an anomaly for an overtime game. I remember coming out of the game for the final time with about 30 seconds left—shaking hands with the coaches, high-fiving Jordan. It was just a great day.

That season ended badly, though. I still have a hard time talking about our loss to Indiana in the 1984 NCAA tournament. You felt cheated. You felt robbed. Sitting in the Omni in Atlanta afterward, I remember Woody Durham came over to interview me, and I couldn't talk. I was crying like a baby. To have to take that uniform off for the last time—I've actually got it in a frame now, my wife gave it to me, and it's in my office—it was a really empty feeling in my heart.

Losing to Indiana was ridiculous, frankly. We trapped them too much in that game. We jumped on them early—we were better than them at every single position. Their eyes got big. They were scared. But then they got into a rhythm, Coach Knight suckered our trap. They would swing it to Steve Alford, and he'd get open jumpers and was a very good shooter. It was one of most disappointing games ever in my life. There are times even now when I'm driving, or it's late at night, and I'll think about that game. There are times when I lose sleep over it, even now. We were the best team in the country. Georgetown was good [the Hoyas would eventually win the 1984 national title], but we were better. You can argue with me all you want, but it's true.

Then my playing career ended pretty quickly after that. It's a tough thing to deal with in athletics, when you reach your peak at age 21. What does an athlete have at that point if he doesn't have balance in his life? As a college athlete, you can be starting on one of the best teams in the nation one day and then boom! It's like a free fall. You're looking to grab hold of a branch or a windowsill to avoid hitting the pavement. Guys like Jordan or Perkins, they could easily transition to play in the NBA. For a guy like me, though, that was an emotional deal.

I remember going to the Portsmouth Invitational camp for prospective NBA draft choices. All of a sudden there's this guy named John Stockton there from Gonzaga. I don't even know where Gonzaga is, but this guy is the MVP of the camp. I'm thinking, *I've got to be better than John Stockton, I started at North Carolina! Gonzaga? Where the heck is that?* But just because you're on a great team doesn't mean you're a great player.

I got out of basketball for several years and worked on Wall Street. But I wanted to get back into basketball—coaching this time—and I did. I eventually became Carolina's coach, and I know now that I tried to change too much too quickly, but that's a long story that we don't need to go into in great depth. I will say I should have kept Phil Ford as an assistant coach when I came there in 2000—I know that now. But I'm at SMU now, and I think we've got a great commitment to the program here. Dallas feels like a big Charlotte to our family, and that's a good thing. We hope to set down deep roots here.

I will say that as a result of those three years coaching at Carolina, I grew from that. I try to turn those negatives into a positive. I still come back to Carolina. I still feel welcome there. And there were a lot of benefits to that experience—I'm a better coach, father, and husband. I'm closer to God. I'm a little more balanced in my life. And I'm blessed. I'm really blessed.

Matt Doherty remains one of the most polarizing figures in North Carolina basketball. Some folks think he got a raw deal at UNC as a head coach. After all, he recruited the nucleus of the Tar Heels' 2005 national championship team in Raymond Felton, Sean May, and Rashad McCants. And in his first season with the Tar Heels, 2000–2001, he won national Coach of the Year honors from the Associated Press.

Others think Doherty brought the untimely end of his coaching career at UNC on himself because he was so demanding with his players—several of whom at least threatened a revolt and/or mass transfer—and because he changed a lot of traditions very quickly when he arrived in 2000. Doherty fired Bill Guthridge's entire coaching staff so he could bring in his own, for instance—he now says that was a mistake.

As a player, though, most everyone liked Doherty. He was a jack-of-all-trades for the Tar Heels in the early 1980s—willing to let others score. He would rebound, defend, and pass the ball with precision.

Doherty's coaching career included stops at Davidson and Kansas as an assistant coach until he became the head coach at Notre Dame for one year and then Carolina. In three seasons his teams went 26–7, 8–20, and 19–16.

After the Tar Heels administration forced Doherty to resign in 2003, he worked as a TV analyst and then became the head coach at Florida Atlantic. After one year there, he earned the head-coaching job at Southern Methodist University in 2006. At SMU he has yet to earn an NCAA bid or have a winning season, but Doherty says he has high hopes for the Mustangs' future.

BUZZ PETERSON

GUARD

1981–1985

As the coach at UNC Wilmington and as a basketball coach for most of my adult life, what I think of first when I think of what it means to be a Tar Heel is on the coaching side of things. I'm very proud to be a part of it. One of the biggest reasons the program has had the success that it has had is the family atmosphere that surrounds it. We take care of one another. Coach Smith always used to bring all of us back in the fall for a coaching clinic and some golf and an exchange of ideas. Coach Williams now continues that same tradition.

Wherever I go, when I travel, a lot of other coaches ask, "What do you do during that time?" They say they'd love to be a fly on the wall when Coach Smith, Coach Williams, Larry Brown, George Karl, Coach Guthridge, and all the rest are in that same room, talking basketball. And it is pretty neat to be part of it.

Now I'm coaching again in the state. And if I call recruits or somebody, the first thing they generally know about me is that I was Michael Jordan's roommate. Or sometimes, that's how I have to describe myself if they don't know me. That's my ID.

I left the Charlotte Bobcats in 2009 to go back to Appalachian State as the head coach. I had a nice job with the Bobcats. I was working for Michael—he had gotten me to come there from the head-coaching job at Coastal Carolina. I was the Bobcats' director of player personnel. But in the afternoon,

I'd start itching for a practice to coach. And there was no practice to coach. I could go home at 4:00 in the afternoon if I wanted to—beat the traffic. And I didn't like that.

Michael wanted to keep me, but he also knew I wanted to coach. I missed it and I loved it. He told me, "If that's what you really want to do, I would never want to hold you back. Life's too short. You've got to do what you love."

I had talked to him about it a lot. I missed it so much. The hardest thing was when I would be going out to scout and would see other guys coach and wish I was doing that. Once you've been in coaching, it gets in your blood—at least it did for me. Michael was fine with it. We still stay in touch a lot—talk about the Bobcats or about college players.

I left Appalachian State in 2010 to take the head-coaching job at UNC Wilmington. It's a great place, and I've always been intrigued by it, but it was really hard to leave Appalachian. My first job as a part-time assistant was at Appalachian from 1987 to 1989. I started out at $6,800 a year, and then I got a raise to $8,200. I thought I was rich. Then I became the head coach here from 1996 to 2000 after spending some time as an assistant at East Tennessee State, N.C. State, and Vanderbilt. Then I left for other head-coaching jobs, and then I came back in 2009.

I grew up in Asheville. The nickname "Buzz" came from my older sister. It was from a cartoon. There was a character on the cartoon called "Brother Buzz" who was a bee, and I would run all over the house, acting like that bee. I loved basketball. Somebody once convinced me that to become a better shooter I should paint 10 stripes on the court and shoot a lot of shots from each one. So I got one of my mom's good paintbrushes and painted 10 green stripes one day.

As I always remind Michael, I was the high school player of the year in North Carolina in 1981 over him. That was a few months before we both got to Chapel Hill.

We played in some all-star games together the year before we went to college. We started to become friends. One of them was in Wichita, Kansas, and I remember we were playing tag with a lot of the other guys in the hotel swimming pool. He jumped in at a spot where the water was about eight feet deep. I looked dead at him and saw his eyes. They were huge! I pushed him in the rear end and got him to the side. I knew then that he swam like a rock. I think when it was time to graduate at UNC—you know you used to have to pass a swim test to graduate—I believe he kept getting sick on that day.

So I had that over Michael, and I also beat him in the 40-yard dash when we were both freshmen. I still tell Michael, "I beat you out for high school player of year, I beat you in the 40-yard dash, and I could always outswim you."

Michael told me later that a lot of people in Wilmington told me he shouldn't go to Chapel Hill because that guy Peterson was going to play in front of him. So every day in practice he thought about one thing, he said, "Be better than Buzz. Be better than Buzz."

That 40-yard dash I beat him in came in the preseason in the year we won the championship, in 1982. The fastest player on our team was James Worthy. Hard to believe, isn't it? But he won. A few years later I remember Michael and me racing Kenny Smith in a three-man race across the Granville Towers parking lot to see who was faster. Kenny was first. Michael was second. I was last.

We both decided to go to Carolina our senior year in high school. This is ironic: going into our senior year that summer, both Michael and I were at Carolina's basketball camp. I was rooming with my high school teammate. Michael was next door. But we never played against each other all week. My high school teammate told me, though, "That guy, Mike, can jump, but he can't shoot."

I had verbally committed to Kentucky around September of my senior year. I thought I could play there. My high school coach got that taken care of, though. He called Roy Williams, and Coach Smith was at my gym the very next day. He told me the people I would have to beat out to play much, and it sounded like it was possible. The main one seemed to be this other incoming freshman from Wilmington. So I felt I had a really good chance to play right away. Little did I know.

After a while, I knew I was going to be in the NBA. So I started studying more of what was going on in practices. I was always intrigued with the way Coach Smith would run practice—the way he would run the "run and jump" and play different defenses to take other teams out of their sets.

Those practices were like a classroom setting. Later, when I was going into coaching, I remember Michael teasing me and saying, "You can't coach because you can't come down on anybody hard enough." But it worked out okay.

The most successful Carolina team I was on was that first team, in 1981–1982. Jimmy Black was the point guard and really the team leader. He would call these late-night meetings in his and Chris Brust's room and go over what we all had to expect for every game. He was like a coach. He'd say, "Big Game James, time to step up. We need you." He'd tell Perkins to be

Buzz Peterson was named high school player of the year over Michael Jordan in North Carolina and still teases Jordan—now one of his best friends—about that fact.

strong on the boards and Michael to act like he'd been there before, and on down the line. My role on that team was to play five or 10 minutes when Michael or Matt Doherty got tired, and I was fine with that. I understood my role.

The chemistry on that team was unbelievable. Every team has at least one great leader, and we turned out to have two on that one—Coach Smith and Jimmy Black.

Worthy was amazing that year. Sam was a very reserved person. He was not crazy about basketball at that time, but he did what he had to do to be successful. He wasn't like a Jim Braddock, who was just going to shoot hundreds and hundreds of shots. Sam was in his own little world, but did what he had to do. Matt Doherty was that role player who did a little of everything—a behind-the-scenes kind of guy.

They do me a favor sometimes these days and show my steal against Georgetown that led to a Worthy dunk in the final. They don't too often show me throwing the ball away or going 0-for-3—I did both of those things, too, in that game. The Superdome was huge, and it was tough to gauge your shot.

122

One time in that game there was a press, and I caught the ball at halfcourt. Patrick Ewing was there, too—I had played against him a little in high school. I thought I could use my speed to outrun him. But when I got to the basket, he was already there, looming. I made sure he didn't block it by putting it up high—so high that it almost hit off the top of the glass and it didn't even hit the rim. Wasn't even close.

Defensively, we were a pretty solid team that year. I think Jimmy was our best defender. Michael got better and better at defense as the years went on, but he wasn't there yet that year. And Sam was a great shot-blocker inside. His arms were just so long.

That year really started with our conditioning, too. I always felt like we were so much better-conditioned than other teams. That started with Coach Williams and his conditioning program—he ran us hard. We were trained to be in great shape at the end, in the final five minutes. That way our minds weren't blurry in the game's most important moments—we had sharp minds.

Michael, back then, was not that great a shooter. He worked on it and worked on it and became a great one, but back then teams would actually stack it up inside, guarding Worthy and Perkins, and dare us to shoot jumpers from the perimeter. That's kind of the ironic thing. Michael hit the national championship shot against Georgetown and yet that's not something he did well back then. But he had a big ol' heart, and he wanted to win the game.

I remember walking with him in the French Quarter after the game, and him asking me how big I thought that shot was that he hit. I said it seemed big now, but over the years it was going to get bigger and bigger. And that was true.

From time to time, I get asked whether I would go to North Carolina if I knew I was going to have to play behind Michael Jordan. I always say yes. It was the overall experience, not just the playing time. And playing basketball led me to coaching, and there was no better place to learn how to coach than in Dean Smith's practices.

I left coaching for a couple of years and now I'm back, but it still feels the same to me. The college excitement, the atmosphere—I enjoy that a lot. Being around the student-athletes. My favorite week would be five days of practice and a scrimmage on Saturday. But we've got to play these games, too, and that's the tough part. I still get butterflies in my stomach for those. Sometimes I think, *I hate this, I hate this.* Because there's so much pressure to win a game.

But I try to enjoy it as much as I can. I enjoy even the bus rides, when some of the players will ask me about basketball or what it was like being Michael Jordan's roommate.

It's hard to enjoy the moment in coaching sometimes. I remember sitting at St. Elmo steakhouse in Indianapolis in 2000. I was sitting with Matt Doherty. He had just gotten the Carolina job. I had just gotten the Tulsa job. I said, "Matt, these are great jobs. We've got to enjoy them. We've got to enjoy the moment." But that was hard for both of us to do, just like it is hard for so many coaches. The pressure can get to you. It got to me at Tennessee [where Peterson was fired after four seasons and no NCAA bids]. The recruiting can be such a beast, so cut-throat. Sometimes you can't be your normal self. I remember when I started at Tennessee that the athletics director told me, "If somebody asks you to speak, whether it's in Johnson City or Memphis, you go." It was almost like you were a politician. Then boom—four years, you're done. I learned a lot from that experience, and one thing was that you have to keep motivating your players. Keep giving your players confidence. If you get down on them, well, they're a part of you. You have to try and have a good relationship with them.

I still keep up with Carolina guys, of course. I talk to Coach Williams some. Since we're both from Asheville, we've done some business deals together, some golf courses. We trade ideas sometimes, talk about families. I want to mention Coach Guthridge, too. He doesn't get a lot of attention, but I tell you what, I think the world of him. He was always there for us. I'd run through a wall for him—a lot of guys would. He's a great man. He just reminds me of my father. I'd do anything in the world for him. At North Carolina, you felt like you were appreciated, that somebody would make a phone call and help you out. I wasn't ever a tremendous player at North Carolina, but I was treated just like the top guys were treated, and I still appreciate that.

Buzz Peterson is the head basketball coach at UNC Wilmington—the fifth school to hire him as a head coach. Peterson finished at North Carolina with a modest 4.3-points-per-game average, although he had a few nice moments, like hitting nine shots in a row once against LSU and scoring 19 in another game against Clemson.

Peterson could have worked for the family business upon graduation. His grandfather began the Sky City department stores, which were akin to Wal-Mart (the Sky City chain no longer exists). Instead, he was determined to become a coach. After several stints as an assistant, he became the head coach at Appalachian, Tulsa, Tennessee, Coastal Carolina, Appalachian again, and now UNC Wilmington.

Peterson and his wife, Jan, have three children. He still considers Michael Jordan—his old college roommate at UNC—as one of his best friends.

BRAD DAUGHERTY

CENTER

1982–1986

I WILL NEVER FORGET WHAT MAGIC JOHNSON once said to me. "What is it about you Carolina guys?" Magic asked me once. "I'm so sick of you. Every time I see one of you, I see another one of you. It doesn't matter how old you are, you're always hanging out."

And it's true. It's a big family. It's also a very successful family, and so I think a lot of people who don't like Carolina are gleeful when we are struggling.

I've known Coach Williams from a lot younger age than most. Since I grew up close to Asheville, I knew him from way back. I had two older brothers who both played for him for a while at Owen High. This is how far back I knew him—Roy Williams was my T-ball coach. Can you believe that?

When I got to Carolina, I think he was extra hard on me because he knew me. Back then, when I was growing up, Coach Williams also did the recreation leagues. He was the director. Every Saturday I'd go down to the gym, and he'd do drills with whoever would show up. His guys in high school—they were like track athletes. When I got to Carolina, and he was there, and Coach Smith told me that Coach Williams was in charge of running, I knew we were in for it. I told him I didn't sign a track scholarship, but he ran our guts out anyway.

Coach Williams really is one of my heroes. I always admired him, even way back as a kid. He's as hard-working and honest as the day is long. And he's a tough rascal. If he tells you something, that's the way it is. And I respect that. It's hard to be like that.

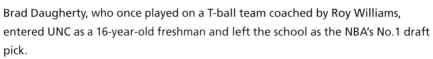

Brad Daugherty, who once played on a T-ball team coached by Roy Williams, entered UNC as a 16-year-old freshman and left the school as the NBA's No.1 draft pick.

When I was young, I was really into auto racing. One of my best buddies as a teenager was Robert Pressley, the driver. His family had such a deep racing heritage. My dad was a race fan, too, and I really enjoyed tinkering with race cars and still do. That's one reason I've been involved in NASCAR for many years and currently work for ESPN on two different NASCAR shows. People sometimes see me as a basketball guy, but I've always been a gearhead, too. I'm just a race nut. I love racing. I love the sights, the sounds, the color, the smell. I just get excited being at the racetrack.

When I was young, I met Richard Petty on several occasions at the racetrack. He was so impressive to me. He took time to speak to me, as he did with everyone, and that just left an indelible impression. A guy like that, put upon a pedestal, who treated his fans so nicely. That's why I chose his number in high school—I was No. 43 in pee wee basketball and in high school, too. And in the pros, as well.

The only time I wasn't No. 43 was in college, because Curtis Hunter had the same number in high school and also wanted it. Coach Smith had us flip a coin to decide who got it, and I lost. That was a bad chapter in the book of 43.

I came to college really early. I placed out of a grade when I was younger, and so I was actually only 16 years old when I entered Chapel Hill. Socially, it was a tremendous challenge, being so young. I had no idea what to do. The academics were one thing—I could handle that because I was a pretty good student. Trying to fit in as a kid on that campus was pretty difficult, though.

But I got used to things, and of course Coach Smith and all the other coaches and players helped me adjust. Socially, I didn't know what to do at a place where my peer group was five times larger than the town I grew up in, but Coach Smith was a huge blessing to me. He said that basketball would take care of itself, and he pushed me academically.

We played all our home games in Carmichael Auditorium, and I just loved that place. Carmichael, in those days, was unbelievable. It was a treat. Packed to the rafters. The crowd was on top of you. And hot?! You were all lathered up before you ever got to play.

I thought Carmichael was better than Cameron Indoor Stadium, I really did. I liked playing there a lot better than at the Smith Center, which was so cavernous.

When you took a charge in Carmichael, though, it hurt. That floor was so hard—it felt like asphalt. You had to really be committed to take a charge. And because the building was small, it seemed like you got to the other side of the floor really quickly. And it smelled like a basketball gym. You heard the sneakers squeaking. The Smith Center was so big, but Carmichael was like playing in a small, hot cave. I loved it.

But for me, it was the same story every year. We had really good teams, but we never quite got there. I didn't play in one Final Four in four years at Carolina. We had some great games, though. One of the best came in my senior year—the season-opener against UCLA. The basket was as big as a barrel for me that day.

It was special, too. You had two of the biggest of the big-time programs hooking up in what was supposed to be the Smith Center opener but wasn't. We ended up not opening that building until a couple of months later, against Duke, because of construction delays.

We knew their young guy, Reggie Miller, could shoot lights out. Our scouting report said he would shoot as soon as he came across halfcourt. We were planning on full-court pressing a lot to keep him from spotting up.

On the second play of the game, Kenny Smith threw me the ball. I turned, shot a jump hook over Jack Haley, and it went in. And that got me started. It seemed like practically every play in the game's first 20 offensive plays for us—everything went through me. I didn't have a bunch of dunks and layups, either. It was a lot of mid-range shots and some on the secondary break.

Everything I threw up there went in. And we were like that as a team. It was like everything we had done in practice in October and November—it all worked. I mean it was a *major* butt-whipping. There was some rumblings from UCLA's coach Walt Hazzard afterward about us running up the score. Hey, don't give me that. We just ran them out of the gym. All the stars lined up for us. It was just a great day for us. I'd much rather have a win like this than a two-pointer—I always wanted to win by 50 if we could.

At the end of the game [UNC sports information director] Rick Brewer came up and said, "You were 11-for-11 from the floor." Then he came back and said, "Actually, it was 13-for-13." I told him, "If they had kept giving me the ball today, I think I could have hit 20 in a row."

I remember afterward sitting on one of those old couches in our lounge and drinking a Gatorade. I was thinking, *You know, this is good and bad. What happens when you achieve perfection in the season-opening game? There's nowhere to go but down.*

Many years later Jack Haley and I would end up on the same team at Cleveland for a while. Jack was a journeyman NBA player, but good enough to stay in the league. He said to me then, "Do you remember just kicking my butt in Chapel Hill one time?" I said, "To be honest, I didn't remember you were there. But son, if you were in the middle of that onslaught, you did get a butt-kicking."

I went into the NBA after that and had a great time playing there. I was lucky, during my time the league had Michael Jordan, Larry Bird, and Magic Johnson. In my opinion, that was really the golden age of the NBA.

Now I don't enjoy the NBA game at all. They don't make open jumpers. They don't make free throws. The ball doesn't move like it used to. I'm the stereotypical retired guy who says the game is not as good as when I played it.

Brad Daugherty was honored at UNC as first-team All-America. He led the ACC in both scoring and rebounding in 1986, and following that season he was the No. 1 pick in the NBA Draft. He went on to a superb NBA career. He was a five-time All-Star and had his number retired by the Cleveland Cavaliers. Daugherty would have played basketball longer, but recurring back problems meant that his final pro game came at age 28. He retired as the Cavaliers' all-time scoring leader—a record since broken by LeBron James.

Daugherty has co-owned race teams at NASCAR's lower levels and in 2007 became a part of ESPN's racing coverage. He still lives in North Carolina—with his wife and their two teenagers—but spends a large part of the year at a racetrack somewhere. If you're ever in a NASCAR garage, he's easy to spot. Daugherty is almost always the only really tall black guy holding a microphone.

Although a self-professed gearhead, Daugherty believes NASCAR's top series is way too long. "It should be 25 races instead of 36," he said.

A friend of NASCAR CEO Brian France, Daugherty cofounded the NASCAR Diversity Council with France. Daugherty can speak passionately about the need to get more Hispanics, blacks, and women involved in the sport to increase NASCAR's fan base. He would like to co-own a team at NASCAR's high level at some point, but knows the costs to do that are huge, even for someone who made millions in the NBA. So for now Daugherty is content getting paid to go to the racetrack instead of the other way around.

STEVE HALE

GUARD

1982–1986

I GREW UP MOSTLY IN OKLAHOMA. My dad, Jerry Hale, was a basketball coach—he was once the head coach at Oral Roberts. I was the ballboy for some of his teams, and all I wanted to do was play basketball. I wanted to play in high school, then in college, and then in the NBA. But it was probably January or February of my senior year at Carolina, in 1986, when I remember thinking, *I don't want to do this anymore. I want to do something else.* The excitement of pursuing basketball was gone.

But I was very excited about medical school. I wanted to challenge my mind. It was kind of a God moment. I have never regretted my decision. There are times in our lives when these moments come, and sometimes we don't realize how important that was until later. For me, that was one of those moments. I had done basketball. I was very, very happy with playing, but I was ready to do something else. So I've never really looked back. I've never really wanted to return to basketball. I've moved on to a different phase in my life.

I'm a pediatrician now in Vermont, and I've been here in the same practice since the mid-1990s. It's intensely rewarding. It's humbling. People entrust me with their most precious possessions—their kids. I take that very seriously. It's a challenge and a reward every single day.

That's not to say I didn't enjoy my time at Carolina. I did—very much so. In fact, I have four children, and the oldest one enrolled at Carolina as a freshman in 2007. And I've stayed somewhat involved in athletics through my kids. All of them play various sports.

The one downside about Vermont is that there seem to be a lot of Duke fans up here and not too many Carolina fans. If I do ever tell a story to those Duke fans, it's about the favorite game of my college career—the first one in the Smith Center, in 1986.

That was something else. It was my senior year and the last time I would play Duke at home. The Smith Center was huge—21,444 seats—compared to Carmichael Auditorium, which was more like 10,000. There were all these hallways. All these doors. Where did everything go? No one was sure.

Both teams came into that game undefeated. We were No. 1 in the country. Duke was No. 3. I think Coach Smith said that no regular-season game had received as much attention in Chapel Hill since Ralph Sampson had used to come there with Virginia.

They had a formal dedication the night before the game, and that did make us understand a little better what a big deal it was. But once the game started, it doesn't matter where you are. It's just basketball then.

Duke was always a big game for us, but this one was even bigger than usual. There was an elephant in the room that no one talked about—how bad it would feel to lose the first game in the Smith Center and always be remembered for that. We'd be a permanent asterisk on the record. We knew that UNC was going to win in there a lot, and we sure didn't want to lose one to start out.

I don't think we really talked about it as a team, how big it was. But we all knew this game would be remembered forever in Carolina history. So there was probably more pressure associated with this game than any other we played, except for those in the NCAA tournament.

Usually, with a home game, everything is so comfortable and familiar. Your locker is in the same place. You do everything the same way. So this was kind of odd. Everything was so new. Everything sounded different. It was almost like having an away game in terms of comfort level—although the showers were a lot better than they were at Carmichael.

We would find out quickly, though, that it took more to get the volume going at the Smith Center. At Carmichael, it would shake your whole body when the crowd got going, and that happened a lot. At the Smith Center, we'd have to score two or three baskets in a row to get the noise up to a similar level. The noise could reach the same pitch, but not as often. It definitely was not as loud as Carmichael on the whole.

131

I scored my career high—28 points—in that game against Duke, but it was all in the flow of the game. Every now and then, you have a game that comes to you like that. Sometimes you feel like when you score a lot of points that you were on fire, that you just couldn't miss. I don't remember feeling that way that night. It just happened to fall that way. I don't remember hitting more than one or two jumpers the whole night. There were just so many backdoor cuts and breakaways. We beat them on the same play all night.

Usually, if you have a really successful night with backdoor cuts, you might get five or six layups split among four players. That night, we probably got five or six of them, but it was me every time. The points really came pretty easily, which is why I shot such a high percentage. We had this regular set play for a backdoor layup that usually works once or twice a game, but Duke played such aggressive defense that we burned them on it.

At halftime, we were up just a little [48–43]. A lot of times that year, we used a big lineup with Brad Daugherty, Warren Martin, and Joe Wolf all in the game. But then sometimes we put Jeff Lebo instead of Warren in there for a different look—really a three-guard look—and that's what we did to start the second half. We would trap a little more out of that. We got a little run going and took a pretty good lead [64–48]. They kind of came back at the end and made it closer, but we held on.

One other funny thing about this game: I fouled out [with 3:37 left]. I still remember that distinctly. I had four fouls and was guarding David Henderson, who was driving baseline and went up for a pull-up jumper. I went straight up with him. No way was I going to foul him—I just wanted to contest it. But then Warren Martin came from behind me to go for the block, and he knocked me straight into David.

Warren just nailed me from behind, and Warren was so big he could really nail you. I couldn't get mad at Warren, because he was just trying to block the shot. I couldn't really complain to the referee, because I obviously ran right into David. So that was that. I sat on the bench the last few minutes and just hoped we could hold on, and we did, 95–92.

We had a really good team that season, but we kind of got disrupted toward the end. We started off really well that season and were undefeated for a long time. Then Warren got hurt a little bit, and I punctured my lung on Len Bias's knee against Maryland. They came back and beat us at our place. I was diving for a loose ball at the Smith Center and landed on Len's knee. I remember thinking, *Man, that really hurt.* I took myself out and then

Steve Hale grew up in a basketball family and scored 28 points in the first-ever UNC game at the Smith Center, but he eventually left the sport behind to become a family doctor in Vermont.

put myself back into the game, just thinking I needed to suck it up. But I ended up sleeping sitting up that night because it hurt to breathe. It turned out to be collapsed—they put a chest tube in, and I stayed a night at the hospital.

I was injured for the second Duke game that year and was in street clothes in Cameron. I remember the Duke students shouting, "In-Hale! Ex-Hale! In-Hale! Ex-Hale!" We lost that one, too. It was the only time in four years at Carolina for me that we lost at Duke. Then in the NCAA tournament we lost to a very good Louisville team. That wasn't a fluke—Louisville went on to win the national championship.

I got accepted to medical school at Carolina, but then I deferred my acceptance for a year and went off to England to play for one season. That was mostly for the cultural experience. Then I came back, went to med school at

Carolina, did my residency in Vermont, joined a practice after that, and I'm still in Vermont all these years later.

Why did I choose pediatrics as opposed to some other specialty? In your third year of residency, you do different rotations. Everything I did I thought was very interesting, but I went through it all and thought, *I don't want to do this.* My last rotation was pediatrics. The first night there I was on call, and there was a baby who needed an IV put in.

I just looked at that baby, about 18 months old, needing help, and it was like an epiphany. *I could do this,* I thought. A light went on. I helped with the IV—there was nothing spectacular about that, it was really pretty routine—but I can point to that moment as the one when I wanted to become a pediatrician. I really have a heart for kids.

The nature of what we do in primary care is build relationships. I'm involved in people's lives in the community. It's not a job that lends itself to moving around. And it gets more rewarding every year.

A 6'4" lefty, Steve Hale was known at Carolina as a smart role player who could defend, rebound, and, if necessary, score. He guarded Michael Jordan much of the time in practice, and Jordan would say years later that Hale was one of the toughest players to ever defend him in college.

Dean Smith routinely put him on the other team's best scoring guard—Hale guarded players like Duke's Johnny Dawkins, Maryland's Len Bias, Georgia Tech's Mark Price, and even Wake Forest's 5'3" Muggsy Bogues during his time at UNC.

In high school Hale was coached at Jenks (Oklahoma) High by Joe Holladay, who many years later would become Roy Williams' assistant at North Carolina. Hale has now been a doctor in Vermont for more than 15 years.

Matt Doherty, who was a teammate of Hale's at Carolina and a similar type of player as a Tar Heel, said that Hale "is the most balanced person I've ever known. He knew he wanted to be a doctor. He gave up basketball. And I don't think he ever looked back."

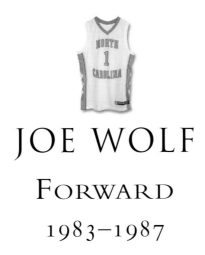

JOE WOLF

FORWARD

1983–1987

I GREW UP IN KOHLER, WISCONSIN—the last of my parents' seven children. Kohler is a town of about 1,600 people. Most people in the town worked at the plant. It's one of the largest family-owned businesses in the world. They make a whole lot of things, but one of the things they are best-known for are toilets, bathtubs, and everything else you can imagine for your bathroom. If you ever look down in a bathroom, you've probably seen the word "Kohler" printed somewhere.

Kohler the town was great. Nobody locked their doors. You could walk in wherever you wanted, ask, "What's for dinner?" and get fed. My father was a truck driver, and my mom was a nurse. They were good parents—very solid people.

My older brother, Jeff, was the first one in the family to play for Coach Smith. He was a forward and played for the Tar Heels in the late 1970s. One of my sisters also went to UNC and played women's basketball for a year.

I had a really good high school career at Kohler High [Wolf, a 6′ 10″ forward, led Kohler High to three state titles, and a 2005 poll conducted by the *Milwaukee Journal Sentinel* named him the greatest basketball player in Wisconsin prep history]. When it came time to choose a college, I narrowed it down to three—Wisconsin, North Carolina, and Marquette, which was then coached by Rick Majerus. He was a great individual and a great coach, but I wanted to get away from home.

Joe Wolf—once voted the greatest high-school basketball player in Wisconsin history—followed his brother Jeff onto the UNC basketball team.

I got to Chapel Hill in 1983, and we had a great team. Michael Jordan was a junior, and we also had Sam Perkins, Kenny Smith, Brad Daugherty, Matt Doherty, and Steve Hale, among others. But we lost to Steve Alford and Indiana in the Sweet 16 in the 1984 NCAA tournament. The next season, as a sophomore, we actually got a step further before losing to Villanova in the final eight. Jordan went hardship before that season and went to the pros a year early. We grew so much as a team that year because we had to.

One of the games I remember the most from my career came at Marquette. Coach Smith always promised players he recruited from far away that he would schedule at least one game near their hometown during their career, and that was mine. I had gone to Marquette's arena in Milwaukee many times as a kid. It was only an hour away.

That was just a remarkable weekend for me—January 18 and 19, 1986. We had opened the Smith Center on Saturday in a huge game against Duke. We had an emotional win and then had to get on a plane right afterward so we could play on the road the next day—that was almost unheard of in college basketball at the time. We got on the plane, got to Milwaukee, and I saw all sorts of family and friends. My teammates were all giving me a hard time about the weather. They knew it was my home game, and I knew that visiting Wisconsin in January isn't necessarily the best time to see it.

137

As for the game, I really didn't score very well or anything [Wolf was 3-for-10 from the field and 4-for-4 from the free-throw line against Marquette. He had 10 points and eight rebounds]. It wasn't memorable for that reason. The first shot I took was a jump hook. That was the shot that basically made me an NBA player—it was my specialty. I was eight feet away, and I shot it about 15 feet. I had a little too much adrenaline going. Plus, Coach Majerus had recruited me, and I know he probably had told his guys to have a little something special for me defensively.

It was a tight game, and Marquette was playing extremely well. We weren't playing that poorly, but they were just playing great.

Finally, with four minutes left, we came out of a timeout and went to a three-guard rotation with Steve Hale, Kenny Smith, and Jeff Lebo. I came out of that huddle and looked at my parents in the stands. I usually don't pay attention to anyone in the stands, but I knew where they were sitting. I smiled at Mom and gave her a wink. She thought I was crazy, I know, but Coach Smith had told us that this is exactly where we wanted to be at this point. I still thought we were going to win.

Right away, the three-guard rotation started to work. We started to pressure their guards more and got two or three turnovers immediately. Jeff got the first one to get it started. We cut into the lead, and then it was a real battle at the end.

During our comeback, I was at the free-throw line, about to shoot, when several things came out of the stands, including a roll of toilet paper that landed almost at my feet. Because of my Kohler background, I considered the toilet-paper roll a personal tribute. That was probably one of my high school friends who threw it.

Finally, it was tied at 64–64, and Kenny Smith got fouled and went to the line with three seconds left. The crowd had been throwing things the past few minutes, and so then they really got it going. Let me tell you, I heard a lot of unpleasant things from my fellow Wisconsin cheeseheads.

Coach Smith would say later he got hit with a penny on the sideline, but Kenny got hit in the side of the head with a quarter while he was at the free-throw line, between his first and second free throw. He put that quarter in his sock and kept it. I'm pretty sure that wasn't an NCAA violation—although you could say he accepted money from a fan! He was so cool—he knocked down both those free throws, and we escaped with the win, 66–64.

It was a great game for the Wolf family. We still remember it today sometimes—the wink I gave Mom when we were down nine with four minutes to go, the comeback, and the fun we had after the game. It was something. We really enjoyed the moment. Everybody knows when another teammate has a home game, and so they really try to get a win for that teammate. They all realized how big that game was for me, which made the drama at the end even more pleasing to me.

That weekend was about as good as it got for us that season. We were 19–0 after that win. But we ended up losing to an incredibly hot Louisville team in the Sweet 16 round of the tournament, and Louisville went on to win it all.

We won a lot while I was at Carolina [Wolf's four teams averaged 29 wins apiece]. But we never made it to the Final Four. Everything has to roll just right when you're in a "one-and-done" tournament. We had some great years while I was there, but we didn't win enough in the tournaments. Still, I have very fond memories of my time at Carolina.

Wolf would go on to be drafted in 1987 in the NBA's first round by the L.A. Clippers and have a solid NBA career. He mostly sat on the bench during his stints with seven different teams, but was regarded as a low-maintenance, high-value substitute and lasted 11 years in the NBA, through 1999. He would play one year overseas in Spain after that. "I really maxed out my potential," Wolf said. "Coach Smith always says about me getting 11 years in the NBA: 'How'd you do that, anyway?'"

Wolf stayed in basketball after his playing days ended. He caught the coaching bug, and that has taken him and his wife, Judy, all over America. He has coached the Idaho Stampede in the NBDL (where one of his players was former Tar Heels star Donald Williams). He was also an assistant at William and Mary in Virginia and was the head coach and general manager of the Colorado 14ers of the NBA's developmental league, called the NBDL.

In 2008 Wolf went back home to Wisconsin, where he is now an assistant coach with the Milwaukee Bucks. He ultimately aspires to be an NBA head coach.

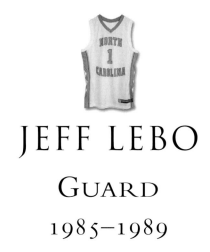

JEFF LEBO

GUARD

1985–1989

IT ELICITS A TREMENDOUS SENSE OF PRIDE to be a Tar Heel, to have played at North Carolina, and to have played for Coach Smith. It's amazing to me how I still get recognized for playing there—and it's been a long time since I played.

That statement to young kids who don't know who you are—"Hey, this guy played at North Carolina"—can make their eyes get big. It can help you in recruiting, I'll tell you that. They may not know that I'm the head coach at East Carolina right away. But when I go into someone's home and tell them about North Carolina basketball—about the tradition, and how much we won, and how it taught me about doing things the right way—all of that helps me a lot when I recruit.

When coaches were visiting me and not the other way around, I lived in Pennsylvania. I played for my father, Dave. I was probably one of the top three or four guys coming out of high school that year, and I had always been an ACC fan even though I lived in Pennsylvania. The ACC was on TV all the time up there, especially North Carolina. And so I was kind of a North Carolina fanatic—although I didn't tell the other coaches who were recruiting me that.

I visited Duke, Kentucky, Maryland, and Virginia, along with Carolina. But Coach Smith had gotten on my good side long before that—I got my first recruiting letter ever from him. That was in ninth grade, and it just

Jeff Lebo could play both guard positions and had one of the sweetest shooting strokes in school history—he shot 42.8 percent from behind the three-point line.

made a tremendous impression on me. So I made some other official visits to make sure that's where I wanted to go, but basically once they decided they were going to offer me a scholarship, my recruitment was over. It was a great decision for me, and not just from a basketball standpoint. My wife went to Carolina, too. She may be a bigger Tar Heel than I am.

The game I remember most in my career at Carolina came in Atlanta—the 1989 ACC championship. We played Duke in that one, and it was the most nasty, physical, and downright hostile environment I had ever been in. You could feel the tension in the air. It was a bloodbath. Some stuff had happened before that game, too. When we had played Duke at Duke and won, some fan had displayed a sign that said, "J.R. Can't Reid," making fun of J.R. Reid. Coach Smith said something after the game about how that sign was racially biased—that it would never have been made if J.R. was white.

Then Duke came and beat us in Chapel Hill. Then, right before the ACC tournament, Coach Smith said that the combined SAT scores of J.R. and Scott Williams were higher than the combined score of Christian Laettner and Danny Ferry.

I've never been in a game quite like that one, and I've been in a lot of them. The opposing head coaches were yelling at each other. Stuff was happening all over the place. Players were hitting the floor and saying things to each other. Really, truly, a bloodbath. And then finally we ended up winning it 77–74 for our first ACC tournament championship since 1982. That was really something.

I have several other great memories at Carolina. One that stands out is that we played Syracuse when they were the No. 1 team in the country in our season-opener in 1987. This was just about seven or eight months after Syracuse had gotten to the national final before losing on a last-second shot to Indiana. We didn't have J.R. Reid or Steve Bucknall in that one—they had been suspended for that game—and yet we managed to find a way to win it.

And Syracuse factors into my biggest heartbreak at Carolina, too. I thought in 1986–1987, my sophomore year, that we were the best team in the country. I know that was the best team I was ever on—we won 32 games. And then we went to play Syracuse in the Meadowlands in New Jersey and we lost. We really thought that was the year that we could run the table.

When I was at North Carolina, I never thought about coaching, to be honest. Like most kids today, I just thought I'd play forever. College, then pros, then who knows what happens after that? But I didn't get drafted out of college, and then I went to San Antonio's training camp but I got cut. I had a chance to go overseas, but I didn't really want to, and it was like, "What's next?"

Some friends of mine had a computer company, and so I used my business degree and worked at that for a while. It was the first time in my life that I didn't have basketball. In those six or eight months working with computers, I thought, *Hey, I need basketball in my life in some way.*

I was still in the Chapel Hill area, and Randy Wiel was coaching the Tar Heels' J-V team. He let me come over there and see what he does. I was able to help him out some as a volunteer assistant—just kind of be around it. It was the first sense I had that coaches have a lot to do that players don't even know goes on. My dad was a coach, too, but back then I was still a player. I guess I didn't understand all the preparation involved.

At East Carolina, we do some things the same way we did them at Carolina. I don't really think the Carolina Way is a system exactly—I think it's a belief in how to play. That's what we have tried to instill in our teams and players, this philosophy of how to play—hard, smart, and unselfishly. How do you do that exactly? You have to change that around due to personnel. My personnel here is always going to be much different than Carolina's personnel, but you can still teach those skills, and they help you not only in basketball but in life.

Jeff Lebo had a relatively meteoric rise through the coaching ranks once he decided that was the avenue he wanted to pursue after his college career ended. He has been a successful collegiate head coach at UT-Chattanooga, Tennessee Tech, Auburn, and now East Carolina.

Lebo took over at Auburn in 2004. Prior to that, he was an assistant coach, primarily for former Tar Heel Eddie Fogler at both Vanderbilt and South Carolina. Auburn fired Lebo after the 2010 season, his sixth at the school, but Lebo was then quickly hired as East Carolina's head coach. Lebo's family has roots in the Greenville, North Carolina, area because of his wife's family—his father-in-law lettered in football at ECU. Lebo and his wife, Melissa, have three children.

While at Carolina, Lebo was known for being able to play both guard positions and for his sweet shooting stroke. Although the three-point line came in only midway through his career, he made 211 threes as a Tar Heel and shot 42.8 percent from beyond the arc. He averaged 11.8 points per game during his UNC career, and the four teams he played on had a combined record of 116–25.

SCOTT WILLIAMS
FORWARD/CENTER
1986–1990

I THINK BEING A TAR HEEL, first and foremost, means a sense of family. Some guys prefer the word "fraternity" for what we have, but I like the word "family" better.

It's a strong, close-knit family, with traditions handed down from generation to generation. We're always able to find common ground no matter our ages—either Coach Smith, Carmichael Auditorium, the Dean Dome, or now Roy Williams, or the people in the basketball office over the years like Linda Woods or Angela Lee or all the good people they've got in place today. We're a strong family, and we've experienced some of the same joys and sorrows as any family has.

As for my own personal story, between my freshman and sophomore seasons I lost my parents. My father killed my mother and then killed himself— it was a murder-suicide. I can't begin to tell you what it would have been like if I was at any other institution when that happened. I don't know if I'd be here today. But my university guided me and consoled me and tried to help me. Obviously, I'm not talking about something that you get over in a short period of time, or really ever get over at all. You go through a tragedy like that, and it's a life-altering event.

I still remember very vividly the morning I found out that it happened. It was October 1987. About 7:00 AM. I was brushing my teeth and about to head out the door for an early class, and my roommate said, "Coach Smith is at the door. He wants to see you." I started thinking to myself, *What have I done wrong?* Because it's not going to be good news if the head coach is at your dorm-room door at 7:00 in the morning.

So he told me what happened, and he hugged me, and he gave me an immediate sense that he'd be there to help support me through the process. And he was. So was Coach Guthridge and the Lee family. Coach Guthridge accompanied me on my flight home. Coach Smith came to the funeral. I thought that was special. They just didn't put me on the plane with a ticket.

I was the baby in my family—somewhat immature back then, very much on the sensitive side. That incident made me grow up. I became a man, maybe a little earlier than I wanted to. But playing basketball was my therapy. I could concentrate on what the coaches wanted me to do and forget about everything else. I liked that.

And since my time at Carolina ended, I hope I've made them all proud of me at the university—Coach Smith and the assistants and everyone else. You can go back and look at my track record—I've never really gotten into any trouble. I've never been in a bad situation. That's the way my mother brought me up and what I learned from the Carolina family, which put me under its wing as soon as I got there and gave me the guidance and tutelage that I needed. I was a young, immature, 18-year-old kid when I got there and a young man of 22 when I left, and now I have two children of my own.

145

I went on campus for my first visit there back in the winter of 1985. So it's been more than 25 years. I live in the Phoenix area now and don't get to a lot of Tar Heels games, but you better believe I'm shaking my blue-and-white pom-poms out here, cheering them on from afar. And I went to the 2009 Final Four and watched UNC win the title there. My good friend and teammate Jeff Denny and I got to sit together. Those friendships, those bonds that you make in college are so special. I feel really lucky to have had that experience.

I had a 15-year career in the NBA and have done a good bit of TV work since I retired. I'm one of two TV analysts for the Phoenix Suns now—Eddie Johnson and I split the duties. I mostly do road games right now. I've done TV work for the Cleveland Cavaliers and the Milwaukee Bucks, too. I also have an audio-video distribution company called Icon Distributing. We serve a lot of housing markets out here—we're a boutique operation, but we hope to grow a little bit larger.

My NBA career probably lasted a lot longer than most people thought it would. I certainly wasn't the most talented Carolina player, but due to Coach

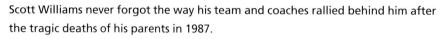

Scott Williams never forgot the way his team and coaches rallied behind him after the tragic deaths of his parents in 1987.

Smith and my own fundamentals and hard work, I made a nice little 15-year career out of it. I was a good Carolina guy in the locker room—a good chemistry guy, and you need some of those. That's an important piece.

I had the rare honor of playing with Michael Jordan at the beginning of my career and LeBron James at the end. I caught both of them near their peak, too—certainly Michael was, and I guess LeBron has gotten a little better, but he was awfully good early in his career, too.

I have three NBA rings thanks to Jordan, and I really appreciate that. The thing about Michael was he could do so many tremendous things in practice. No matter who we played the night before, or where it was, he could still run the hardest and be the best player in practice the next day. Other superstars I've played with, when they play 40 minutes the night before, they are dogging it the next day.

Now LeBron is a lot like Jordan. He plays like Jordan in practice, and the other thing he shares with Jordan is this incredible confidence. They both always expect to win. They expect to be able to do something amazing when they need to so they can get it done. And if they awe you on the way, so much the better.

One of the games I remember the most about my Carolina career was the 1989 ACC tournament final. That's back when the Duke-Carolina rivalry was at one of its peaks of hostility. You had the coaches bickering, the players angry with each other—it was something.

That one came in the same season where some of the Cameron Crazies held up a sign that said "J.R. Can't Reid" when we were playing at Duke. Those fans were just trying to be funny. But when you look at Duke's reputation—the students have a reputation of being a little bit snobby over there—well, it's just not us, let's put it like that. We thought on the team that a sign like that came up more because J.R. was a strong, athletic black man—that it was something of a racial thing.

Then Coach Smith, who had a lot to do with integrating UNC athletics with Charlie Scott, fired back. He said right before the ACC tournament that my SAT score, combined with J.R.'s, was higher than the combined SAT scores of Christian Laettner and Danny Ferry. That kind of stung Duke and Coach K a little bit—kind of put them on the mat. Now let's be honest, that's when Duke was on the rise, too. Duke was starting to be a threat every single year, challenging us more frequently.

Once the game started, of course, most of that stuff was forgotten. We mostly just played the game. I was able to acquire a tape of that game recently, and I'm stunned at how many times I fell down or got knocked down. I was like, *Dang, I was a little soft back then. I needed to toughen up!* We finally won that game, and that was a great feeling. Back in the locker room, a lot of us weren't even to the legal drinking age yet. So we got some cans of Sprite and shook them all over each other, just like it was champagne. That was so much fun—one guy did it, and then we all did it. Sprite got all over the place.

In Arizona, I have my own little version of the Duke–Carolina rivalry. Grant Hill has become a great friend, and his daughter and my son have been in the same elementary-school class for several years. We are always trying to give her Carolina stuff and corrupt her, and they are always trying to sneak Duke stuff into my son Benjamin's bookbag or something. So that's nice— Grant and I always have a chance to trash-talk each other. My son is really into every kind of ball sport; I have a daughter who's the exact opposite. She loves horses and dancing.

I'm always proud of Carolina. I was proud of them in 2009, when I saw them win the national championship in Detroit. But I was also proud of them in 2010, when they struggled the whole season. I thought that team still showed a sense of Carolina tradition and went out there and handled themselves in a classy way, even though they were losing a lot.

I'm a big Carolina fan of all sports. I even watch the Tar Heels football team and am very proud of the job it has done lately under Butch Davis. I don't get to Chapel Hill very much—although I did go to the alumni game in 2009 and drag my big butt up and down the court a few times. That was fun. But no matter where I am, Carolina is always on my mind.

Scott Williams played for 15 years in the NBA after finishing his college career in 1990. He won three NBA championships in his first three years in the NBA— all of them in Chicago during Michael Jordan's prime. Williams now lives in the Phoenix area with his wife, Lisa, and their two children. Williams is a TV broadcaster for the Phoenix Suns, mostly handling the team's road games. He also is the CEO of an audio-video distribution company called Icon Distributing.

The NINETIES

GEORGE LYNCH

FORWARD

1989–1993

THERE'S A SENSE OF ACCOMPLISHMENT in being a Carolina basketball player. A sense of pride. Tradition. Family. Even today I'll be watching Carolina play, and if it's not going well, I get as upset as I did when I was playing. I always feel like somehow I should be able to help, to guide them with my own experiences. There have been so many good leaders through the years now—I'm really proud of the group that won the 2009 championship. I've always been a team player who was able to tell my teammates, "Look, you're good, but we're going after trophies, not individual things." I learned about winning basketball when I was a kid, and I've always understood it.

In 1991 Duke won the national championship. Then in 1992 Duke won it again. You see Duke win it two years in a row, coming out of your own backyard, that really rubs salt in your wounds. In 1993 I was a senior and was going to make sure we were focused. I called a meeting with all of the other players. And we made a pact. We were going to follow curfew, lift weights, and not cut any corners. It was my last year. With a little luck, I knew we had the talent to win a championship.

Eric Montross and I had a funny and productive relationship on that team. Eric was kind of a nice guy until somebody hit him in the head or knocked him around. I would challenge him throughout the game to dunk the ball, not to lay it up—to throw some elbows back at people.

I played hard. I was into working out. I lifted weights. I wouldn't ask someone to do something I wouldn't do. So if I said something to someone, they understood. So sometimes throughout the game if I didn't think Eric was being tough enough, I would go challenge him. It was just one of those situations where we motivated each other, pushed each other, and got the job done.

What I learned at Carolina made me the player that I am and gave me a 12-year NBA career. Although teams do look for superstars on the NBA level, they also look for guys who do the little things for the superstars. I didn't care about scoring, but there are other guys who want to score and score and score. So there's always room for someone like me who's going to keep that guy happy. It wasn't that I was a tough guy. I just knew I was going to play harder than the next man. When I was first in the NBA, I remember James Worthy told me, "Young fella, it ain't about making it to the league, it's about staying in the league." I remember that conversation. You didn't want to be there one or two years, you wanted to play as long as you could. And I did that.

I grew up in Roanoke, Virginia. I was born two months prematurely and only weighed three pounds at birth. I was in an incubator for the first month of my life. My parents were separated early, but I had a stepfather who was a part of my life from age two to high school. My father was still around, too. I had three sisters—one older and two younger.

I grew up in the projects pretty much. At that time I knew they were hard times, but I didn't know how hard they were. I had friends in the neighborhood I could play with all the time, and we'd find stuff to do with just a baseball bat and a tennis ball. And I had a lot of family around—grandmoms, aunts, cousins. We'd have little track meets or football and baseball games where everyone would meet in the middle of the apartments. I learned a lot from my childhood. It shaped me.

For my last two years of high school, I went to Flint Hill in northern Virginia. That helped prepare me for Carolina. Because in my junior year in high school, I pretty much said good-bye to my family and moved in with another family. When I got to college for my freshman year, I didn't get homesick at all. I had already been through it.

At Flint Hill, the competition was stiff every night. It was definitely an experience that I knew I needed. But every Friday I would cry because I wanted to go home. My dad would come and pick me up every other Friday.

It was a three-hour drive back to Roanoke. I lived with the Flint Hill coach at first. That was tough. He wasn't married, didn't have kids, and didn't even have a stove in his house. So we'd go out to eat all the time—there were no home-cooked meals. But it was a great experience. I've been blessed with a lot of people across my path. Later on I lived with the family of a teammate at Flint Hill, and I still keep in touch with that family today. They are great people.

I have a lot of fond memories of Carolina, and some of them don't have much to do with basketball. One time as a team we went to the Canary Islands in 1991 for an exhibition game. We were stopping over on the way to Germany, where we were going to play Henrik Rodl's "home" game. We were walking down the beach and saw these guys wrestling. And so everybody bet me I couldn't beat any of them. It wasn't sumo wrestling exactly, but almost like that. The first person to touch the ground lost. So we were watching first, and then the people saw us. We were all tall. We looked like a basketball team. And the guys were saying, "Go ahead, wrestle," because I was supposed to be the tough guy on the team. And you know as a college student, you don't have any money. And the pot kept getting bigger and bigger, and it was one of those situations where I was like, "Man, if I win, I'm going to be straight for this whole trip."

These guys who were wrestling were about 5′7″. They didn't really speak much English, but they tried to tell me the rules. The first match I lost—my knee hit the ground while I was trying to throw somebody. All our guys said they would double the pot if I would slam the guy. So we kept wrestling. I beat the first guy the second time, but the slam wasn't good enough, they said. There had to be 300 to 400 people on the beach by now in this big old circle. I was looking for my money, and the guys said, "No, you've got to keep going." Then on the other guys' side, the circle parts, and one more guy steps in. I beat that guy. Then came another guy from out of the circle. I beat him. I ended up wrestling, like, seven or eight matches. On the last guy, that was the best of all. I picked him up and drove him into the sand. It seemed funny at the time, but it wasn't funny afterward, because I sort of hurt my shoulder. Coach Smith was mad the next day and said we couldn't do any other extracurricular stuff like that.

I also remember that at a lot of pregame meals, after everybody finished eating, we would take everything that was left over and put it in a pitcher and would see who would drink it. We'd put money out there for whoever

George Lynch (right) left UNC as the school's No. 1 all-time leader in steals and with a championship ring from the 1993 title season.

would. Scott Cherry would take everybody's money every time. I thought things like that brought us closer as a team.

For my senior year, I knew it was my last chance. I knew most of the other guys had another year, but not me. Throughout our training, our whole motivation throughout the summer—with the pickup games and the times when pros would come back and kick our butts—we were trying to get better to win a national championship. So we all challenged each other. Everybody that year had certain things they did, and mine was playing defense and rebounding the ball. I really wasn't a vocal leader. I led by example and saw that it worked. In my first three years, looking at the senior leadership, I felt they let us down a little bit sometimes. I didn't want to do that in my senior year.

And I just loved playing in college. It was better than in the NBA, really. You had it made. It was just great. We traveled well—Coach Smith made sure of that. We always had a lot of fans. If you go into most NBA arenas these days, they are half-empty. I just loved the atmosphere of college games, where you go into a place like Durham and Charlottesville and it's completely full and then you win. That's when the game was pure—when everybody was playing for their university.

One of my favorite games ever came in the Elite Eight in 1993 against Cincinnati. We were really on a mission in 1993. A year before we had gotten a sour taste in our mouths against Ohio State when we lost in the Sweet 16. We knew we had a good enough team to do something special both those years, and we weren't going to fail again.

Coach Smith sold us on believing in each other—the total team effort. And I knew if the game was close, we had the better coach on our sideline. We practiced everything—drills where we pretended like we were down 10 points, traps, zones. Everything.

During the first part of the game, Nick Van Exel just got so hot [Van Exel had 21 first-half points, and Cincinnati took a 15-point lead in the first 13 minutes]. We were out there, seeing what they were trying to do, and he was just shooting threes. Deep threes. We couldn't seem to extend our defense that far. So we just tried to wear them down. Cincinnati had Corie Blount, too. He was so athletic, but still had a lot to learn. They didn't utilize their big men much on that team—their offense was mostly geared around their guards. They probably should have used them more.

After Van Exel just kept burning us, Coach Smith switched Derrick Phelps on him and got Derrick to follow him everywhere. That really helped. We were able to shut him down because Derrick was such a great defender, and we came back. Eric and I were playing pretty well inside. But Cincinnati was tough. The game was tied with just a few seconds left when I had a shot to win it, but the ball rolled off the rim and out of bounds. So then we had a timeout with 0.8 seconds remaining, and Coach Smith drew up this great inbounds play. When I saw it, all I could think of was when Coach Smith drew it up for Rick Fox to get a layup [in the 1990 NCAA tournament], and we upset Oklahoma in a very similar situation. I just knew it was going to work. Coach Smith told Brian [Reese] in the huddle, "You're going to be wide open, but you're not going to have a chance to dunk it. There probably won't be enough time." So everything went according to plan—at first. Derrick threw the ball in to Brian, and what did he try to do? Dunk it.

Brian missed the dunk, and it probably wouldn't have counted anyway because the buzzer was going off, and so we had overtime. But in the OT, we just played great defense and won it going away. Donald Williams made a couple of big threes in the overtime, too. That game pushed us into the Final Four, and it gave us the confidence we needed to win the national championship.

Now that my NBA career is over, I'm living in the Dallas–Fort Worth area with my family and trying to decide if I'm going to go into college or NBA coaching. I helped Matt Doherty out here for a while with the SMU program as a volunteer assistant, but I'm not doing that anymore. I also have a youth program here that is dedicated to youth basketball and keeping kids doing well academically and understanding the recruiting process. My wife and I have three kids—my son is 12 now and is a pretty good athlete, but he's more into football right now.

I want to coach—I think that's what I am meant to do. Just when I was growing up, being on a basketball court eased my mind and relaxed me a little bit. I have a sense of peace when I'm on the court surrounded by kids. That's a nice feeling.

Forward George Lynch averaged a double-double in scoring and rebounding during the Tar Heels' last four games in the NCAA tournament in the 1993 season, leading the team to a national championship. Coach Dean Smith said he was a "jewel" and an "unbelievable leader" for that Tar Heels championship team. Known as a tough guy from his first day on campus, Lynch played in 140 games for the Tar Heels—and missed zero. He graduated with a degree in African American studies.

Lynch went on to the NBA and a 12-year NBA career in which he never averaged more than 9.6 points per game in any season. Lynch stuck around for as long as he did not just through talent, but because he hustled for loose balls, set screens, and kept all the scorers on his team happy by getting them the ball. He eventually retired to the Dallas–Fort Worth area with his wife, Julie. They have three children—an older son and two young daughters.

Lynch has dabbled in a number of business interests in the Dallas area, including real estate and an auto design business that restores old cars. He hopes to enter the coaching field.

ERIC MONTROSS

CENTER

1990–1994

THE CAROLINA FAMILY IS A REAL BROTHERHOOD. I know when I see my teammates from the 1993 national championship team it feels like I only saw them yesterday, even though there may have been several years in between. I'm fortunate to see that Carolina brotherhood up close through my job these days as an analyst on the Tar Heels' radio network, and it is amazing to see the way the family embraces each other, in good times and bad.

One of the best times I ever had on a basketball court was when we made that comeback from 21 points down at the Smith Center against Florida State in 1993, and I'll talk about that game a lot in a little while. I still remember it vividly.

I came from Indiana, and so I count myself very fortunate to have found a home in Carolina for all these years now. Indiana high-school basketball is like Texas high school football—it is huge. It is phenomenal. I signed my first autograph in eighth grade. That was also the grade when I first got a flat-top. I shave my head now, but back in college I had it high and tight, and for whatever reason that kind of became a cult thing on campus.

So the flat-top came about when my dad suggested it in eighth grade. He had played basketball at Michigan before becoming a lawyer. I didn't want to at first, but then I said I would if he would get one, too. So I went in, got mine cut—and then he bailed on me.

I ended up keeping mine, though. That was the age of hairspray and combing and messing with your hair a lot. When I finally got rid of all that, I was like, "That's the best thing I've ever done in my whole life!" I could wash it with a washcloth. I didn't have to get a hairdryer out. Plus, I think it helped me with my aerodynamics (laughs).

I wasn't the most athletic or talented guy. But the work ethic my dad instilled in me made me want to run in the morning before school or get there early and practice for an hour with my coaches before class. My parents never pushed me to the point where I was turned off by basketball, but they gave me a heartfelt, generous chance to get better.

My situation in college was a little bit similar to what Sean May would experience years later. I was a big man from Indiana who was getting recruited everywhere. A lot of people wanted me to stay in-state and play for the Hoosiers. But I loved Carolina. It was just a gut feeling to come here. I just knew it would be the right place for me.

And it was. I met my wife at Carolina, and I made a lot of great friends, and we won that national championship. Everyone remembers the timeout that Chris Webber called in that game. I get a little bit defensive about all that when people say, "Well, that really won it for you guys."

No, that really didn't win it for us. It certainly helped etch it in stone. But that's almost pawning off responsibility to a mistake. Our team had just this magical ability to trust in each other, and not care about which guy got the most accolades. There were no contracts involved. It was just a pure form of basketball where people loved playing and wanted to do it for each other. I've never been on a team that was closer than that one.

The Florida State game at home earlier that season was so important to us winning that 1993 national championship. The year before, in 1992, Florida State's Sam Cassell had said that the Smith Center was a "wine and cheese" crowd. To make matters worse, Florida State beat us twice that season—once at home and once at their place.

So going into that game in 1993, we certainly remembered that comment, although I'd be surprised if anyone thought that was a sole motivating factor. Certainly Sam's comment was more directed to the crowd. It wasn't a direct slam on us, it was a slam on the crowd. But obviously, there was some directive toward us—that was our home court, and he was kind of defacing our home court. Plus, we had lost to them twice the year before, once at home.

They were swaggering. We had a certain amount of pride. It was a "you just can't come in here and do that" sort of feeling.

When you're in a game of the magnitude of the FSU game, and the deck is stacked against you, and you go back to what you know and it works, that's very enabling. We got to see our hard work pay off. All of that goes into making a championship team. I firmly believe you can't just waltz through a season and win it. You have to learn in games like this how to become 100 percent believers in what you're doing.

I can still remember the comeback vividly, and what came before it. There seemed to be a lid on our basket in the first half. Plus, I got three fouls pretty quick [within the first 4:38 of the game] and missed about 15 minutes of the first half. I was sitting over on the bench with my stomach feeling like it was going to rot. Not only had I not helped the team early, I had done the guys a disservice. It was so frustrating.

We were down 21 points midway through the second half, and FSU still had a 20-point lead with just under 10 minutes to go. And then Henrik Rodl made a three-pointer for us, and we called timeout, down 17 points. I remember that image very well. You figure, as a player, it's got to start some-time. We were 0-for-14 from three-point range until Henrik's shot. Maybe the cover was finally going to come off the basket. It was time to move. And if we moved, it was going to hinge off of what we did defensively.

Then we had a couple of other good things happen—a flurry. Suddenly it was down to 13, and FSU called timeout. That timeout told us that their coach was trying to stop the bleeding because somebody's cut. Okay, so the sharks can get in the water. There's blood in the water! And I do remember the crowd being overwhelming at that point. They sensed the run. Now we're all really believing together. There was always a great sense of calm in the huddle, but especially right then.

[On the ESPN telecast, Mike Patrick noted at this point, "Dean Smith has seen his team nearly blown out of his own building, but now he has it back to a manageable 13."]

I remember as a player, a 20-point deficit is a pretty big barrier. But if you can get it to 13, that's not such a barrier. Then Henrik hit another three. We got a steal, and then Pat Kennedy got a technical. That was big. It turned into about four extra points for us. Suddenly, we were right in the middle of the game—we were only down by four points with about six minutes left.

Eric Montross has been involved in three UNC national titles: winning one as a player in 1993 and calling the games for two more, in 2005 and 2009, as the analyst on the Tar Heels' radio network.

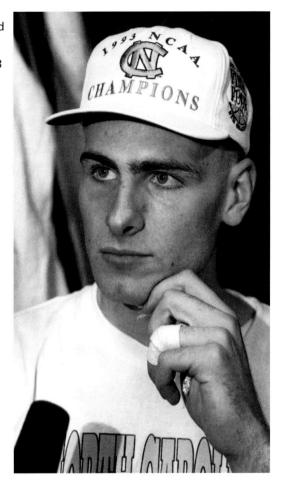

159

[On the telecast after that key technical, Dick Vitale screamed of FSU coach Pat Kennedy, whose mouth has formed a perfect "O" following the technical, "Look at Pat—his mouth is open. He can't believe it! Freeze that! Look at that mouth!"]

All of a sudden, everything was rolling in our favor. We thought every shot was going in. We saw there was a light and drove toward it. There was an inherent belief that this was doable. We had them on their heels. We were rallying. And it was everybody on the court—that was the calling card for our team. It wasn't one player on fire, it was the *team*.

We just kept on coming. They scored a time or two, but we kept coming. We got it to one when I hit a jump hook, and I remember that shot like it was yesterday. That was my bread and butter. If there was ever a time to go to your go-to move, that was it. I was already way into it, but that fueled me even more so.

At this point, the "wine and cheese" comment really came into a play. All of a sudden the fans realized they had a chance to make a resounding impact, and they ran with it. So then we were down 77–76, and George Lynch just made an unbelievable play. We were double-teaming the ball, and Charlie Ward tried to throw it back to Bob Sura. I was always very aware of George and where he was on defense. He and I worked in such tandem. As a play develops, you know where the next defensive guy is going to be. And I knew the only way that pass would have pressure would have been from George. He mustered up the energy to get to that ball, stole it, and dunked it, and it was absolutely deafening.

That did it, really. They didn't score again. Donald Williams hit four free throws at the end, we won by five, and the fans stormed the court. The Carolina crowd is less apt to do that because it's so used to winning. But in these games that bring out this intense emotion, that's what we were looking for. They remember as fans being incited by the comment from Cassell. They, more than us as players, see the revenge factor. To me, revenge elicits raw emotion that can't be harnessed. So the storming of the court was the crowd's final hurrah that night, a "we've been loud, now we're going to make one last statement" sort of thing.

Years later I got to know Sam Cassell when we played together in the NBA. He was an absolute card—a real cut-up. He was always full of smiles and jokes. I never could do that when I played. I had to be serious to concentrate. But you see guys who, for whatever reason, do it the way that Sam does. They just go out there with this energy, this haphazard, happy-go-lucky attitude. Sam could do that and still play really well.

I had a pretty long NBA career—10 years. I'm really positive about it overall. I got to play against Tim Duncan, David Robinson, Shaquille O'Neal, Hakeem Olajuwon, Patrick Ewing, and guys like that. I just wish I could have played more.

My NBA career finally ended because of a baby gate. We were at home in Toronto, where I played then, a couple of hours before a game. We had a baby gate crossing the second or third stair going up to our bedroom. So I stepped over it, as any parent would do instead of taking down the baby gate every time. I didn't trip. I didn't even step incorrectly—it was not a misstep. But when I stepped off my left foot, I felt what I thought was just a foot cramp.

I saw nine different specialists trying to get it fixed. But the analysis is that the step over the baby gate was the straw that broke the camel's back. I retired because of that injury. But I'm still very fortunate to have the career I did and to be able to do what I do now, working with such fine people on the radio network.

The 7', 275-pound Montross, a junior center during that 1993 championship season, graduated from UNC in 1994 with a degree in speech communications. Beside that title game, in which he scored 16 points and had 5 rebounds, he may be most remembered for his "00" uniform and his bloody game against Duke. In that two-point win, Montross scored 12 points, grabbed nine rebounds, and blocked three shots while bleeding from two different cuts on his head.

Duke fans always took Montross personally—in large part because of his success against the Blue Devils. The Duke student newspaper once ran a huge blank space and captioned it: "This big useless white space was put here to remind you of Eric Montross."

Montross became a first-round draft pick for the Boston Celtics. He was a steady and unspectacular NBA big man for the next 10 years, playing mostly off the bench for Boston, Dallas, New Jersey, Philadelphia, Detroit, and Toronto. His career statistics have a certain symmetry—Montross participated in 465 NBA games, averaging 4.5 points and 4.6 rebounds, before foot problems caused him to retire.

Montross has now experienced three NCAA titles for Carolina in an up-close-and-personal way—as a player in '93 and as a radio analyst alongside longtime play-by-play man Woody Durham in 2005 and 2009. Montross is very active in the local community. He and his family live in Chapel Hill.

BRIAN REESE

FORWARD

1990–1994

EVERY TIME I RUN ACROSS SOMEONE who went to Carolina—and not just on the basketball team—I think we have a good connection. Everyone has pride in the university he or she went to, of course, but I'm very biased. I don't think anyone has it as much as Carolina people do. We're a family.

The 100-year anniversary game between the UNC alumni in 2010 showed me that again. It was great. I was on the same team with Bobby Jones, J.R. Reid, Dante Calabria, Pete Chilcutt, and so many others from so many different teams. And we won! I had a great time there, talking to everybody. I feel like I have something in common with the guys who played 60 years ago. I'm a student of the game, and I like talking to everyone about his experience. I loved talking to York Larese. He's another New York guy, and he's up there in the rafters with so many others. The whole weekend was definitely a blessing.

I was raised in the Bronx and was the youngest in my family, with nine—yes, *nine*—older brothers and sisters. I played sports most of the time and so didn't have much time to get into trouble. I was the baby, and everyone wanted to make sure I stayed on the right track. I didn't know too much about the streets because my family sheltered me for so long. I had a couple of brothers who were ministers.

Baseball was my first love—I didn't even play basketball as a young kid. But when I was 12, I grew about four inches. They took me to the park one day—I didn't know how to dribble or anything. They just told me to rebound.

By then I already had a nickname—Baby Blue. That's because my mom dressed me in that light blue color that little boys wear a lot. I liked the color so much that when I was watching the 1982 UNC-Georgetown championship game, I cheered for the Tar Heels just because of their jerseys. Everyone else in my house was cheering for Georgetown that night because one of my brothers was a friend of Fred Brown's, who would make that turnover at the end of the game.

I didn't even understand the rules of basketball when I was 12, but I could really jump. I went out there the whole winter once I got started. It took me no more than four or five months to become one of the best players for my age in our area. I could dunk by the time I was 13. The first recruiting letter I ever received came when I was 15. It was from Kansas. I started playing a lot of basketball, going with traveling teams that would play all over. I always wanted to compete. My mom says that took me away from her at a young age, but it was the best thing for me.

When I came to Carolina, I knew this was where I wanted to be. I've wanted to be here ever since, really—I live in Charlotte now. It's just a great state. I'm trying to get into coaching now, and my dream is one day to be on the bench, coaching at Carolina. I'm starting at the bottom right now, but I'm working my way up.

The year I remember most at Carolina was the 1992–1993 season, when we won the national championship. I was a junior that season, and we really had a strong team. I made the cover of *Sports Illustrated* that season, too.

But the game I remember the most vividly came in my sophomore year, in early 1992, against Wake Forest. We were down 32–10 early and were still down by 20 with about 15 minutes to go in the game.

But when we were down like that, Coach Smith would always keep us calm. He would say, "Let's play these next five minutes the right way, and we should be here. We'll still be down, but it'll be by about 15 instead of 22." We'd work hard and have a plan. We really took pride in being in better shape than our opponent.

Think about it: teams do that to Carolina a lot. They come out and hit all sorts of shots. They're pumped up. They go up 15, even though we're trying as hard as we can. But the adrenaline rush they always have in the first half—they usually can't maintain that. We can come back. Sometimes, they can keep it up, and then, you're going to lose. An example would be the Boston College game [in 1994 when Reese's last UNC squad as a senior was upset early in the NCAA tournament]. But if they don't keep it up, you execute and win.

What we concentrated on against Wake Forest when we were down so far was what we always concentrated on: get a stop on one end, then get a good shot on the other. We had some shooters on that team—it was Hubert Davis, especially, in this game, but we had Donald Williams and a lot of other guys, too. And we had some guys who could crash the boards like me.

So as we crept closer, we got more confident, and they got a little less confident. They kept calling timeout, trying to stop us, but by then we were really into the game. I had a baseline dunk that got us within two points, and finally, we tied it at 78–78 when Pat Sullivan hit a couple of free throws with 38 seconds left. Wake Forest had the ball, but we double-teamed a Wake player, and I managed to knock it off his leg for a turnover.

In this game I got a lot of "isos," which is what we called "isolation plays." Coach Smith was calling my number a lot. He'd tell me, "Just get in the paint. Go to the hole hard. If you have a shot, shoot it. If not, someone's going to be open on the three." Now I was the kind of player who felt like I needed a double-team to stop me—one-on-one just wasn't going to work.

164

So we came out of a timeout with 10 seconds left and the ball, and Coach Smith had called my number again. I was kind of surprised. Usually, in that situation, it would be Donald Williams who would have the chance to do that. But in this game I was being really aggressive and getting into the paint pretty easily. I guess he just had confidence in me.

So I got the ball, made a couple of moves, got into the paint…and missed the shot from about 15 feet! It was short. Front rim. I knew it as soon as I shot it. But the ball came back to where I had a chance to get it. Everyone else went one way, and I went the other. I chased it down, shot it again, and that one went in—the last shot of the game. It came with less than two seconds left. Wake was out of timeouts, so the clock ran out before they could even get the ball in bounds.

After I made it, all I heard was ROAR! It sounded like an animal or something, but it was coming from the crowd. I got so scared, I ran right off the court. I'm not good with people grabbing me. I don't like that. So I ran right into the tunnel. I was so quick, nobody could get to me. The crowd stormed the floor, but I was gone! I was in the locker room. My teammates came in a few minutes later and were saying, "B, where you at?"

Brian Reese was a high-jumping forward on the 1993 national title team and once made the cover of *Sports Illustrated* after a 25-point game against Florida State.

I said, "I didn't want people grabbing me. I didn't want to be underneath the pile. But I'm happy now!" So then I celebrated with my team in the locker room after it had calmed down outside a little. It was just a great feeling.

Our junior year was great, and I stay in touch with all those guys on the 1993 team that won the championship. Then in my senior year I hurt my ankle in the preseason. It was a pretty bad injury, and Coach Smith told me I should redshirt and come back the following year. But I was in a hurry—

too much of a hurry. I played on it the entire year, but my explosiveness was never quite the same. Coach Smith was right. I should have redshirted. I didn't make it to the NBA but had a lot of fun playing all over the world. I played professionally in Japan, Korea, Australia, Austria, and France. I found out early that I had to adopt "No pay, no play" as one of my mottos in foreign countries—you never were quite sure if the next paycheck was coming when it was supposed to.

Now I'm back in North Carolina and getting into coaching. I have coached at the high school level and now in college, at High Point University. I'm just trying to build my résumé now. I think I'm on the right road. Life is really full for me now. I have my wonderful wife, Monica, who went to Carolina also and graduated in 1995. My son from my first marriage, Brian Jr., lives with us, and we have two other children, Taylor and Brooklyn. I'm just trying to work my way up. I think I understand the Carolina Way very well, and I really want to teach it as an assistant at the college level.

In 1990 Brian Reese joined one of the most highly touted recruiting classes in UNC history—a class that also included Eric Montross, Derrick Phelps, and Pat Sullivan. That quartet would all play key roles in the Tar Heels' 1993 championship, when they were juniors.

Reese played basketball overseas for many years after his UNC career ended in 1994, in places as varied as Iceland, Finland, Japan, Taiwan, and Puerto Rico. He is still approached occasionally to sign the *Sports Illustrated* cover he graced after scoring 25 points in a game at Florida State during his junior season at UNC. Reese also is remembered for missing a dunk off a beautiful inbound play against Cincinnati at the buzzer in a 1993 NCAA tournament game—the Tar Heels won the game anyway on their way to the national title.

Reese has worked primarily in the mental health field since retiring from basketball but now is concentrating on coaching. Former UNC guard Scott Cherry—who once roomed with Reese in college—became the coach at High Point (N.C.) University in 2010 and hired Reese onto his staff in June 2010 as an assistant. Reese had previously served as an assistant coach at Wingate.

DONALD WILLIAMS

GUARD

1991–1995

UNLIKE A LOT OF GUYS WHO PLAY for North Carolina, I was local. I grew up about 35 minutes from the Carolina campus, in the town of Garner. So I was very familiar with what Carolina basketball meant to so many people.

While I was close to the Chapel Hill campus, I was physically even closer to N.C. State. That one was only about 10 minutes away. Coach Jim Valvano was the first coach to really show a major interest in me, and my decision ultimately came down between State and Carolina.

My father was a truck driver. My mom was a restaurant cook and sometimes worked at the local farmers' market to make extra money. My father was gone a lot because of his job, so a lot of times it was just me and my mom at home.

In my eighth-grade year, my family moved from the housing projects into a real house. At that house, we had a backyard goal. That was big for me. The surface was straight dirt—that red clay everyone in the Carolinas knows about. The ground was uneven. It wasn't much to dribble on, but that was a *shooting* goal. That's mostly what it was good for, and that's where I learned to shoot. I worked at it for hours, and my father would come out there when he was home and shoot with me. He was a good shot, too. I guess it ran in the family.

At Garner High School, I picked up a nickname. It was "the Show." They let me shoot a lot, and I ended up scoring a whole lot of points. Once, I

Donald Williams was the Most Outstanding Player of the 1993 Final Four after hitting 10-of-14 three-pointers in the two games and scoring 25 points in the national final against Michigan.

scored 55 in one game. At North Carolina, I picked up a less flattering nick‐name. Some of my teammates called me "Sports Illustrated," because they said my jump shot arrived about once a week, just like the magazine did.

That was before the 1993 national championship, though. I just took off that weekend. I was flying. Everything was going my way. Even today, someone asks me about that Final Four almost every day.

When it came down to choosing a college, I had a hard time trying to pick between State and Carolina. I really liked Coach Valvano and had spent a lot of time on that campus, playing pickup basketball. I always played with guys older than me from a young age. But I thought I probably had a better chance to win a championship at Carolina. I was a kid and really didn't know where I wanted to go. So I took the advice of my parents. It was probably more their decision than mine. I just wanted to go somewhere and play.

During my freshman year, I actually thought about transferring. I played out of position a little—I was the backup point guard behind Derrick Phelps. I was frustrated at the time, playing only about five minutes per game. But then Hubert Davis graduated, and there was a spot open at shooting guard. That's what they had recruited me to play to begin with.

We had a really good team that season. Coach Smith knew it, too. Before the season started in October 1992, he had put this doctored photo in all of our lockers that showed a picture of the Louisiana Superdome and read: "Congratulations, North Carolina, 1993 national champions." He wanted to motivate us.

We won 11 games in a row at one point. We lost to Michigan early in the season, though, on a last-second basket by Jalen Rose. Then we got to see them again in the tournament, in the national final.

I don't think many people expected us to win that game but us. Michigan was very talented and had all the "Fab Five" hype. And Michigan had already beaten us at the buzzer in Hawaii earlier that season, too. But we were a team on a mission. Everybody was sacrificing and fitting into their roles. We had come together as a unit. And I had probably the easiest role on that team. Everybody wanted me to shoot the ball. Everybody did a lot of sacrificing and screening to get me a shot.

I remember watching *SportsCenter* on ESPN before the game to see what they were talking about. They just kept talking about Eric Montross and George Lynch as our big threats against Michigan. They didn't talk about me at all, and that fired me up some.

In the game's first five minutes I was really more nervous than anything else. I think within the first couple of minutes I had taken myself out of the game with the "tired" signal. I came out, went back in, and that settled me

169

down. It was one of those games that, even while you were in it, you knew it was just a very well-played game on both sides. The teams knew each other well, and that seemed to make it even better. I felt pretty good after I hit my first three-pointer. I really had felt good shooting the ball for the last two weeks of the tournament. It must have been the spring weather or something—I just felt like I was going to make every one of them.

I think as a team we didn't ever feel we were going to lose that game, no matter how many runs they made. They may have been more talented than we were—to be honest, they probably were—but Coach Smith was the greatest coach in the game in terms of preparation. And preparation was everything. We were really focused, and we didn't know or care how big the stage was after a while. I felt like I was just shooting in my backyard. I really did. The coaching staff and my teammates knew I had it going, and they did a lot of looking for me. This team was the most unselfish one I had ever played on.

In the final moments we were ahead 73–71. Michigan had the ball after Chris Webber got the rebound on a missed free throw. Webber started dribbling upcourt, and then he traveled. It was obvious. Our bench was going crazy. Michigan got very lucky that the officials didn't see that. And then we had our best two defenders suddenly on him, trapping him in front of the Michigan bench—George Lynch and Derrick Phelps. He had nowhere to go. And then Webber called for the timeout and put his hands together in the T symbol. I didn't know they were out of timeouts—I hadn't been paying attention to that—but I sure was relieved when the officials called the technical foul.

Coach Smith started screaming to me to go shoot the free throws, and then I knew it was over. I wasn't going to be missing any free throws. It was just like back in the backyard again, on my dirt court.

As for the way people talk these days—like we would have never won the game if Webber hadn't called the timeout—hey, we were *ahead* at the time when he made the mistake. I guess people just have to say something. As for us, though, we can always say this: we were national champions.

I went on to play two more seasons at Chapel Hill. We made it to one more Final Four, in my senior year in 1995, but lost to Arkansas. I had some injuries and never had another moment quite as good as those in New Orleans, although we did have some very good wins in those last two years.

I didn't make it in the NBA, but I played for more than a dozen years overseas. I played everywhere—France, Poland, Sweden, Spain, Korea, and the Philippines, plus the CBA and a little time with the Harlem Globetrotters, too.

When you're on a winning team overseas, the season goes really well. When you're losing, the American players take all the heat, because there aren't very many of them on any one team. Then it is stressful.

Now I've stopped playing and have just begun to coach. Right now I'm in Raleigh and back at the high school level. I've run basketball camps for kids for years and have always enjoyed that. I've coached some girls' teams. I want to be like Coach Smith or Coach Williams, teaching the game the right way.

Donald Williams was named the Most Outstanding Player of the 1993 Final Four. He broke three Final Four records that weekend. His 10 three-pointers over the two games was one more than Steve Alford had for Indiana in 1987 and UNLV's Anderson Hunt in 1990. His three-point shooting percentage for the championship and his total for the Final Four—71.4 percent—were also records at the time.

In 2009 the UNC administration changed the rules for the jerseys they hang in the rafters at the Smith Center. The Final Four MOP was added to the list of criteria for allowing a player's jersey to hang in the rafters, which earned both Wayne Ellington and Williams admission into the "Jerseys in the Rafters" club.

Williams' shooting barrage ensured Coach Dean Smith's second and final NCAA title in 1993—both of them coming in New Orleans. "He was in a zone," Smith said of Williams shortly after the title game. "I thought he was going to make it every time he went up."

Williams scored 12 of his 25 points in the national final in the game's last 7:37. "He hurt us," Michigan coach Steve Fisher said. "He hurt us a great deal."

Michigan star Chris Webber's 23 points and 11 rebounds matched exactly the totals of another great player who lost to the Tar Heels in a national final—Patrick Ewing for Georgetown in the 1982 championship game. But Webber may be most remembered for his infamous timeout—and an incident nine years later.

In 2002 a former Michigan booster named Ed Martin said he had provided illegal payments to Webber, at least some of them in college, giving Webber and his family $280,000 in cash, loans, and gifts. Martin also said he gave substantial amounts to three other ex-Michigan players—$616,000 in total.

Michigan found enough evidence to believe Martin that it imposed sanctions upon itself in the hopes that the NCAA would treat it more gently after an investigation. In November 2002 Michigan announced that it would forfeit 112 regular-season and tournament victories from five separate seasons.

It was a "day of great shame," the school's president said. Michigan also took down basically every reference to the "Fab Five" on campus. Included in all those forfeits: every Michigan win from the 1992–1993 season. In the NCAA's official bracket from the 1993 tournament, Michigan is now listed as having "vacated" its participation.

In other words, let's say Webber was a little more poised and didn't call the timeout. So there never were any technical foul shots for Williams to shoot. Instead, let's pretend that Webber threw a pass to a teammate, who made a three-pointer at the buzzer to beat UNC 74–73.

Nine years later, everything still would have been reversed. Michigan would have had to give back everything from the 1993 tournament, including its title.

The Tar Heels, who would have finished in second place in this hypothetical scenario, would have finished first after all—nine years after the fact, and with an asterisk. It's quite likely the 1993 Carolina team would have been reunited for a somewhat hollow victory celebration, and a championship banner would have been raised at the Smith Center.

That would be an odd way to win a championship, though, wouldn't it? Better to just beat your opponent fair and square, even if the opponent turned out to be cheating. And that's what the Tar Heels did in 1993, behind a streaky sophomore named Donald Williams who hit a hot streak at just the right time.

DANTE CALABRIA

GUARD

1992–1996

I THINK THE No. 1 THING ABOUT WHY TAR HEELS basketball is so special is that they win. They almost always win. They've had that history for a long, long time. When you win, lots of people want to follow you, so they have a big following throughout America. And when you win games, do it in the correct way, and follow the rules, you become one of the teams that even people who have no affiliation with it at all follow.

UNC is one of those teams in college basketball. The place is always sold out. You walk down Franklin Street, and they have an array of shops that you can buy paraphernalia from. Once you're a Tar Heel—player, fan, student, whatever—you're always a Tar Heel.

I have spent a large part of my adult life in Europe playing basketball, and I'll talk about how different the European and American cultures are. I didn't grow up in Europe, though. Even though the name "Calabria" is Italian, I grew up in Beaver Falls, Pennsylvania. That's Joe Namath country—the old quarterback. He's the most famous athlete to have come out of Beaver Falls.

My mom worked in the travel industry and my dad was a regional manager of appliance sales. My parents and my grandparents both played big roles in my upbringing. We lived in a nice area—just a great area for sports. My father played basketball at the University of Iowa. All my uncles played sports. I had two sisters who played sports. I played baseball and football in-season but whenever the opportunity was there, I played basketball. That was my year-round sport and my favorite.

The first time anyone from Carolina saw me play was before my sophomore year. I was on an AAU team, and we were playing in a tournament in San Antonio. Coach Ford happened to be at the tournament, and I had one of the better weeks I had had in my life. Our team played pretty well and won some games. After that I got a letter, and they inquired at my school, and it just progressed from there.

I played with a group of guys in high school—we were basically together since the fifth grade. We won a state championship in my senior year, and in my junior year we got to the semifinals—we were something like 62–2 in those years. I played a little bit of everything—everything except center. We had a good group of guys who were pretty interchangeable—all between 6′3″ and 6′7″.

When I was being recruited, it came down to Iowa, Villanova, Florida State, UNC, and Pittsburgh. I chose North Carolina, but not because of the reasons a lot of people do. I really didn't know much about the history. I was more of a Big East guy—St. John's, Syracuse, Georgetown. I knew UNC was always good but never knew the history. When I came, I had really never been in the South. I did know about Coach Smith, of course, and obviously I consider him one of the top two or three coaches of all time.

174

But the South was appealing to me, first of all, for the weather. You could get a beautiful day in North Carolina in October or November. In Pittsburgh that's a day you only get in the summer. I just wanted a change. I wanted something different. I wanted to get away from home.

I was a freshman on the 1992–1993 national championship team. There were a lot of guys on that team who knew and played their role. It was difficult for me, though. I had been averaging 28 or 30 a game in high school and was used to always being on the court. Suddenly, I was fighting to get on the court eight or 10 minutes per game. But it was a big learning experience for me, to be on a team that good, and it helped me a great deal. One of the biggest moments that year was when we played at Butler—it was the "home" game for Eric Montross, since he was from Indiana—and I played well. I didn't score a lot of points, but I felt like I belonged. And I'll always remember the comeback we made that year at home against Florida State.

That season was really a good season with a great group of guys. A lot of times our practices were better and more competitive than the games.

Dante Calabria was known for his outside shooting touch, but he could also slice through the middle and get to the basket, as he did here against Duke.

My sophomore season was a little more difficult. We had a lot of guys graduate and a lot of new ones coming in. Sometimes things worked wonderfully, sometimes they didn't. Rasheed Wallace, Jerry Stackhouse, and Jeff McInnis were all freshmen. That was quite a squad, really—you could have taken "UNC 1" and "UNC 2," and both teams would have done well in the NCAA tournament. But there are only 40 minutes in a game, and when you have 12 guys on a team who all feel like they should have been playing a lot, that's tough on the coaching staff and the players. We had some good and bad moments, and ended on a real bad one with Boston College, losing in the second round of the NCAA tournament.

In my junior year, in 1995, we went to the Final Four again. We had some talent on the team. Coach Smith changed his style of coaching some that year—we weren't really that deep, so we didn't do all the pressing and trapping that Carolina is noted for. That showed his brilliance—he could take different types of teams and be successful with all of them. We ended up in the Final Four and got beaten by Arkansas when Stackhouse got a thigh injury in the first minute of the game. He still played, but he wasn't the same. And I had a bad shooting night.

Then in my senior year, after Jerry and Rasheed had left, we brought in Vince Carter, Antawn Jamison, and Ademola Okulaja. Antawn was phenomenal right away. But we were young and thin. We got off to a great start in the ACC but couldn't keep it up. We lost in the second round of the NCAA tournament to Texas Tech, but we did win 21 games that year, and a lot of people were not expecting us to do that.

I didn't get drafted. I went to an NBA camp, played in the CBA a little, but ended up settling in Europe. I knew that I had relatives from Italy—my great-grandparents. I was able to locate all the documents. They came from the southern part of Italy.

Because of that, I was able to get my Italian citizenship—I have dual citizenship now—and make a career for myself. I was able to count as a player from Europe, not one of those from America, which helped a lot. You can only have a certain number of Americans on your team—usually two to four—so they have to be the stars. The scorers.

I played more than a dozen years in Europe—in Greece, France, Spain, and Italy. Most of it came in Italy—nine years of it. I was able to learn to speak some Italian. I have spent more of my adult life in Italy than in the United States, although I always spent the off-season in Wilmington, North Carolina.

Italy really fits me well. I love the culture. The people are so friendly, especially when you can speak to them in their language. I had nothing but a great time there. I still weigh about the same—6′5″, 193 pounds—as I did in college. The key is that the portions there are a lot less. It's not a buffet. You get small portions for your meals—a small circle of pasta or whatever. In the United States, it's all large. Everything is big. The houses are like that, the cars are like that. It's a totally different culture.

In Italy, it's mostly all small. You have smart cars both here and there, but in Italy, you really need them because there is nowhere to park. Things seem more family-oriented there to me. Everyone takes off just about the whole month of August. Families go on vacation. I think people work more in America.

One of the downsides of playing overseas, though, is you don't always get paid. I still have teams owing me money from 1998.

As my career winds down, I plan to keep a home in Wilmington and would love to get into coaching or broadcasting. I still want to be involved in basketball, and hopefully my Carolina connections can help me with that.

Dante Calabria was known as one of the Tar Heels' best pure shooters of the 1990s. He counts as one of his greatest achievements at Carolina being able to go 7–1 against Duke in his career. Calabria was a freshman on the Tar Heels' 1993 national title team. Besides his three-point shot, he was known for his low-cut sneakers and floppy hair during his college career.

Following graduation, Calabria played for more than a dozen years overseas—mostly in Italy. As a holder of dual American and Italian citizenship, he even played for the Italian national team for a while. He lives in the Wilmington, North Carolina, area and would like to get into sports broadcasting or coaching.

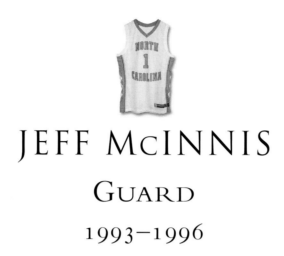

JEFF McINNIS

GUARD

1993–1996

MY RELATIONSHIP WITH CAROLINA and Carolina basketball—I think it's great. A lot of people misjudged me when I was at Carolina and thought I was a bad guy. People who don't know me sometimes think that. But when they get to know me, they're like, "Man, I was so wrong about you."

I've got a lot of friends in Chapel Hill who still live there, and I still appreciate the Carolina family very much. I have stayed in touch with Coach Smith, off and on, throughout the years. When I was in the NBA, he'd call me sometimes. I'd think I had just had the greatest game, and he'd say, "Oh, I don't know about your defense." He doesn't like NBA games much. He says nobody plays good defense. You've got to love him for that.

Coach Smith has been a friend and a father figure to me and to so many others. You can call him anytime. When I was in the CBA, trying to get into the NBA, I'd call him. "Coach, what's up?" I'd ask. "You don't have any friends in the NBA or something? Why am I still here?"

He'd say, "You're on your way. I've had conversations with people about you." He always kept it real with you, though—he didn't just tell you what you wanted to hear. I have always liked that about him.

I grew up in Charlotte, on the west side of town. The tough side. I'm a big football guy, I never really took basketball seriously until I was in sixth grade. I was kind of introduced to basketball by Ed Sockwell, my old AAU coach, who passed away a couple of years ago. First of all, I played football. I was a tall quarterback and was always fast. Some of the older guys in the neighborhood were already playing AAU, though, and they came and asked me if I wanted to do it. From that day on, I started liking basketball.

We had a pretty good AAU team. Jerry Stackhouse was on it, and Jeff Capel, who went to Duke, and several other guys who could really play. One year we thought we were going to win it all but we lost to a team from Virginia that had Allen Iverson and Joe Smith on it.

My mother, Cynthia, and grandfather, Frank, mostly raised me. I have a big family. I've got three sisters and seven or eight uncles were around a lot.

The place I used to live is now Time Warner Cable Arena in Charlotte. That's why I was so amazed when I first saw the building and later got to play for the Bobcats for a while, because I know what it used to be. I'm so fortunate I got that chance to play at home for a while. When I was growing up, I always dreamed of playing for the old Charlotte Hornets when they were out on Tyvola Road.

I've had to knock down a lot of bad rumors about me for a long time, like the one about me being a hothead. That one comes from my youth. I just like to win. I can't play the game quietly. I'm not the average guy who can do that. That's just me. When you grow up on Beatties Ford Road playing the game, you can't be quiet. If somebody tries to do something wrong to you, you've got to defend yourself. I've learned to channel that streak more as I've gotten older. I didn't always go about it the right way when I was younger.

179

I played for high schools in Charlotte for two years and won a state championship in 10th grade with West Charlotte. That was in 1991. Then I did what an older friend of mine in the neighborhood did—I went to Oak Hill Academy in Virginia for my last two seasons of high school. Charlotte had turned rough for me, man. A lot of my friends were getting into crazy stuff. And having won a state title, there wasn't much to do. Junior Burrough had grown up in the neighborhood, gone to Oak Hill, and was successful enough he signed at Virginia. I thought I needed to go there to play in the ACC.

Myself, Stackhouse, and Rasheed Wallace all ended up signing with North Carolina and coming in together in the fall of 1993. We stuck together. That made it easier. Of course, they left me after a couple of years.

The game I remember the most was at Duke in 1995. Double overtime. Capel's shot. All that. It was an absolutely incredible game. I think we were a little overconfident going in because they were having such a bad year [this was the season that Duke coach Mike Krzyzewski took the rest of the year off midway through due to his back injury, and Duke entered the game 0–7 in the ACC]. But we got over that in a hurry when we saw how they were playing.

The Duke and UNC players got haircuts a lot of time at the very same place. It was this barbershop about halfway between the two campuses called Forty Below. Robert Massey, who used to be a cornerback in the NFL, owned it. We had a lot of friendly fun in that place. Everyone would talk, but it never got serious. We UNC guys had our barber—he sat in the back. Then another guy, named Teddy, was the Duke barber. They were separated by one guy in the middle. I remember being at Forty Below a couple of days before the game with a lot of the Duke players and our guys. We were just saying how we were going to blow them out and put an end to their terrible season.

I loved playing in Cameron. I always remember getting off the bus there. They'd have what seemed like 3,000 fans meet us at the bus. They'd all be singing, "Go to hell, Carolina," or else they'd be reading newspapers when we got off, ignoring us. I've got a lot of memories getting dressed in that visitors' locker room, too. It seemed like their fans were right on top of us. So when they'd bang on it, it would seem like they were about to come through the roof on top of you. You'd be trying to get dressed two hours before the game and it'd sound like, "Boom, boom, boom!"

That year we came out for the pregame shootaround wondering what they were going to do. That was also the year we pretty much knew Rasheed and Stack were going pro. Some sort of story had come out about Rasheed not going to class much and all that stuff. So as soon as we walked out there, two hours before the game, they started throwing books at him and chanting, "Rasheed can't read." It was crazy. To me, though, that kind of stuff just made me play better.

We were always excited to play Duke. Coach K wasn't there for this one because of his back problems, but that didn't matter. The Cameron Crazies do so much and act so crazy before the game that it really hypes you up to play.

We got off to a big start. We were up 26–9 after Stackhouse dunked on Cherokee Parks and did a funny little walk. Rasheed was dunking. I think we got overconfident. We started thinking, *This is going to be easy.* Duke started coming back. Cherokee Parks had a good game for them, but what I remember most is the way Chris Collins would act when he made a three, like the world was coming to an end or something. He'd jump all over the place.

Point guard Jeff McInnis counts as one of his fondest memories at Carolina the 102–100 win over Duke in double overtime in 1995.

Anyway, credit to them—they fought their way back. Next thing you know, we don't have a 17-point lead. It's more like six. And then in the second half, they started winning big [Duke was ahead by 12 points with 9:56 to go in regulation]. We had to make a comeback of our own, and it was nip and tuck after that.

We got into the first overtime and were really playing well. We should have closed the door on them then [UNC was ahead by eight points with 16 seconds remaining in the first OT]. But Duke made another great comeback. Serge Zwikker was at the line for two free throws with five seconds to go and us up by three points. Dean Smith actually took Stackhouse and me out at that point—he went big all the way across the free-throw lane trying to get the free-throw rebound, because we all knew Serge wasn't a great free-throw shooter. I've still got a picture of Stack and me in my home of that moment—we're holding onto each other on the bench.

Remember, Stack, Capel, and I all played AAU ball together. And Capel was always practicing these long-distance shots in AAU—and he was always making them, too. I saw him make a whole lot of them in practice. That's what got me doing it. I actually practiced them, too, throughout my career.

So Serge missed both free throws. Capel got the ball. I grabbed Stackhouse, and he grabbed me. And from the angle where we were, it felt like Capel shot it right in front of us. We watched the ball, and man, he made it. Then we just looked at each other. You couldn't talk. It was too loud. It was an amazing shot, and it put the game into double overtime.

I'm sure the Duke fans thought that the momentum from that shot would carry over and Duke would win, but that's when I knew Dean Smith was a great coach. After all that, he said in our huddle, "This is where we want to be. Isn't this fun?" He regrouped us. Then we came back out again, and we won it.

In the second overtime, I had noticed they had been pushing the ball in really quickly on the out-of-bounds plays after we'd score. They were throwing it in pretty recklessly. So we had just gone up 100–98 with about a minute when Donald Williams made a jumper, and I faked like I was running back on defense and then sprinted toward the Duke inbound pass instead. The Duke guy [Greg Newton] threw it right to me, and I just laid it right back up.

It happened so fast, they didn't even register it on the scoreboard. Nobody saw it. The scoreboard guy, the TV, nobody. Well, Coach Smith saw it. He was going crazy, trying to get the points put on the board. I was running back on defense, this time for real, holding up two fingers, telling them to put two more up there. That turned out to be important, because they had two shots at the end to tie it. Steve Wojciechowski took the first one, and I nearly fouled him on that. Then Newton missed a follow shot, and we won 102–100.

I kind of passed out after that. Honestly. I was so tired. I had told Wojo at one point in the second OT, "Look, either y'all win it, or we'll win it, but somebody needs to. I'm ready to go." Stackhouse basically carried me to the locker room, I was so exhausted. And so happy.

We got to the Final Four that year, 1995, and played Arkansas in Seattle. Stackhouse got hurt on the opening tip with a deep thigh bruise, and he wasn't himself. Rasheed had what was just about his worst game of the year. So it was just a bad night. That's the tournament for you—one bad game, you're out of there.

I played one more season for Carolina after that, and then I left a year early for the pros. Rasheed and Stack were already gone by then. That caused some hurt feelings, but I wouldn't change that decision now for anything in the world. My granddad was real sick. He had had a bad stroke. I wasn't fortunate to have a lot of money growing up. I wanted to provide for my family. I wanted to get him the best medical care I could. And the only way I thought I could do that was by going to the NBA. I don't regret doing it. If I hadn't have done it, he probably wouldn't have lived as long as he did.

I got drafted No. 37 overall by Denver, got waived in the middle of the season, played in Greece, and then later became the CBA's Player of the Year. That got me back into the NBA. I like the way I came through to the NBA. I had to take the tough road. I always tell these NBA guys they're prima donnas, that they should see what a CBA road trip looks like sometime. That's why I appreciate the game so much.

I've matured a lot, I think. I've got a son—Jeff McInnis Jr.—who is starting to play a lot of ball now and will be in high school before too long. Once, last year, I was eating with Rasheed at his house. His wife is pretty tough on him. He said something like, "Well, I'm going to get ejected in tomorrow's game." She said, "How do you think your son is going to feel when he sees you get ejected? Then you come home and try to discipline him? He's not going to listen." Rasheed was like, "You're right, baby." And I learn from stuff like that. You can't be on the court acting a fool and then go home and tell your own kid not to do the same thing.

183

The game Jeff McInnis described in detail—UNC's 102–100 win over Duke in double overtime in 1995—is considered one of the best games in series history. As part of ESPN's season-long celebration of its 25th season of college basketball coverage, the network revealed that that Duke-UNC game was selected as the No. 1 moment in ESPN college hoops history by a panel of current and former ESPN college basketball staff.

McInnis played three seasons for the Tar Heels. He didn't stick in the NBA his first time around, but then played in Greece and the CBA and got called up by the L.A. Clippers in 1999. He stayed in the league for most of the next nine seasons, bouncing among various NBA teams. His best season came with the Clippers in 2001–2002, when he averaged 14.6 points and 6.2 assists per game. Slightly oversized for a point guard at 6'4", he grew adept in the pros at shooting over smaller guards and playing under control.

McInnis now lives in Charlotte, where he does some basketball coaching at the youth level.

VINCE CARTER
GUARD/FORWARD
1995–1998

Each time I go into another NBA city, I check up on the Carolina guys. It's great. I don't have everybody's phone number anymore—not for some of the younger guys in the league—but I always find them in the layup line. The respect we have for each other is amazing. We pay homage to each other. Each guy comes to the other guy and speaks—we just check up on each other. Not just players. Coaches or announcers who went to Carolina, guys who are doing our games for TV like Scott Williams or something—whoever.

Everybody on our teams, they'll get kind of angry at something like that. They'll say, "You Carolina guys always have to stick together. You do this together, you do that together. Can't you leave each other alone?" But we can't. Our tight-knit relationship with each other is understood throughout the league.

My NBA career has been longer and more spectacular, I guess, than the one I had at Carolina. But I understood that. Coach Smith's style was inside-out. We were always taught to look for the inside man first and to play as a unit. And that was fine. What I learned at Carolina really jump-started me in the NBA. I hit the ground running.

I grew up mostly in Daytona Beach, Florida. My mother was a teacher and did a whole lot for me. I had a great high school basketball career, but I did other things as well. I played on the volleyball team and was the head drum major for the school as a senior. I love music. I started off playing alto sax,

Vince Carter's otherworldly ability to dunk the basketball was part of the reason Dean Smith has called him the best leaper he has ever coached.

and I learned to play all the saxophones. I can also play the trumpet, tuba, drums, clarinet, and trombone a little. Bethune-Cookman even offered me a music scholarship.

I was going to play basketball in college, though. My final four choices came down to Florida, Florida State, Duke, and North Carolina. I just had a gut feeling that Carolina was the right place for me, and I still think it was one of the best choices I ever made.

My freshman class included Antawn Jamison—who is still one of my best friends—and Ademola Okulaja. The three of us were joined at the hip for three years after that. We have always had each others' backs.

But when I came in, it was Antawn who was making the big impact as a freshman, not me. It was frustrating at first. After all I had done in high school, I had to learn to do what was asked of me. It was one thing to hear it while being recruited, but another thing to actually go through it. By my junior year it all made sense to me, but not at the beginning. Every young guy who gets into college wants to produce.

One of the games that I still remember in college came in my sophomore year, 1996–1997. We had started 0–3 in the ACC—our worst start ever in the conference. In one of those games, Wake Forest had really handled us easily at their place. Tim Duncan had really killed us. So later in the season, we had that game targeted. We were going to play them again about six weeks later, and we wanted to use that as a measuring stick.

That was a very big game for us. We knew we were good and could compete against anyone. This was Ed Cota's freshman year, remember, and it took us all a while to adjust. Jeff McInnis had been our veteran point guard the year before and we were comfortable with that. Ed was good, too, but it took us some time. Coach Smith puts a lot of trust in his point guards, and once Ed got comfortable running what Coach Smith wanted, we were fine.

So early in the season there was a buzz, an "Oh, no, what's wrong with Carolina?" sort of thing. I remember that well.

Wake was very good that year. Tim Duncan was such a challenge for Antawn. Duncan had such great skills already at that point—he was already getting close to being the player he is today. It's more defined now. More fine-tuned. But he already was a great rebounder, and he had a turnaround jump hook and shot off the glass. He was Mr. Fundamentals already.

For some reason in this game I got it going like I hadn't had it going since high school. I was slashing, hitting threes, dunking—it was an incredible night. In the first half, when we got so far up [38–18 at halftime, with Carter scoring 21 points], it was like a dream. Everything was going in.

I may have had the best moment of my college career in that game, too. I was dribbling off the right wing with my left hand. Duncan was defending the middle. I decided to challenge him and took it right to him. Boom! I dunked with two hands on him.

And it was an "and one," too. I got fouled, so I got to shoot the free throw and made it. I won that battle with him, although, believe me, he's won many of them with me over the years.

But that night was mine. When you have one of your best nights against one of the better teams in the country, that's the sort of high where you can walk around campus with your chest out the next day. And that's what I did. I ended up with my career high—26 points—in that one.

We were really ahead the whole game. Wake made one run at us in the second half, but we finished it off after that. We knew after this game that we were good—very good. In fact, this team was the best one I played on in my three years at Carolina. We really should have won the whole thing, but we ran out of gas a little bit against Arizona in the Final Four. At the end of the Arizona game, I remember thinking, *Wow. What just happened?*

That turned out to be Coach Smith's last team. It was special to get to play on both his last team and on Coach Guthridge's first team, too. We made the Final Four in my junior year, too, but then we lost to Utah.

Antawn and I both turned pro a year early, in 1998. He was drafted fourth overall, I was picked fifth, and then we were traded for each other. It was strange. We've never played on the same team again, but we still communicate a lot. And we meet up and have a good time whenever we play each other.

I spent my first six seasons in Toronto—that's where the "Vin-sanity" and "Air Canada" nicknames came from. I later got traded to the New Jersey Nets and now am in Orlando. I'm going to play for as long as my body—especially my knees—will let me. I really want to get an NBA championship. But I'll be able to accept when I need to step down and move on. I'd love to be able to win a championship before that's done. But the biggest thing for me is I want to go down as a consistent player—someone who came out and played well for many years.

And I'll be carrying Carolina with me all the way. When you have Carolina in your back pocket, that always helps.

Vince Carter has been almost a perennial All-Star since entering the NBA in 1998. As a Tar Heel, he helped lead UNC to ACC championships and Final Four appearances in both 1997 and '98. He is still known as one of the most spectacular dunkers in UNC history. Dean Smith has said Carter remains the best leaper he ever coached.

Carter won a gold medal with the U.S. Olympic team in Australia in 2000 and also completed one of the most famous dunks ever in that competition. Against France, Carter got the ball on a fast break but had 7'2" French center Frederic Weis (a former first-round NBA pick) between him and the goal.

What did Carter do? He actually went over Weis. Scissoring his legs in the air, Carter leaped over Weis's head, slammed the ball home, and came down pumping his fist. The French media would eventually dub the play *"le dunk de la mort"*—the dunk of death.

Now with the Orlando Magic, Carter is back in his homestate. In a dozen NBA seasons, he has averaged close to 23 points per game, almost double his career average of 12.3 points per game as a Tar Heel.

Carter returned to school to get his degree in African Studies in May 2001—he calls the degree his most significant accomplishment. He also has started his own nonprofit foundation, called Embassy of Hope. Details can be found on Carter's official website, www.vincecarter15.com.

ANTAWN JAMISON

FORWARD

1995–1998

I LOVE CAROLINA. THERE'S SOMETHING ABOUT IT that is so special. When I see Michael Jordan somewhere, it's just, "What's up, Carolina?" That's something a lot of schools wish they could duplicate, but they can't even come close.

When I got married, pretty much everybody on the team was either in the wedding or at the wedding. I attribute that—the feeling, the Carolina vibe, whatever you want to call it—to Coach Smith and Coach Guthridge. They always made it feel like a family.

I grew up first in Shreveport, Louisiana, and then we moved to Charlotte when I was 13. When we got to Charlotte, my dad, Albert, put up a basketball goal. It helped me not be quite so homesick for Shreveport. But he didn't measure it, and he put it up a little high—11 feet maybe, or 12. I could dunk on a 10-foot goal by the time I was in ninth grade, but the backyard goal was a challenge. The high, looping shot I have today comes from shooting over that rim.

I wanted to be like Mike when I was younger. The baggy shorts, bald head, the way Michael Jordan played—all of that. I was one of those guys who idolized him. So when Coach Smith came to the house to recruit me, it wasn't that hard to sign me up. I remember him talking mostly at the time about the importance of education. He has kept in touch with my parents for years after I left, making sure they're all right.

I was in the same recruiting class as Vince Carter, although he was a lot more highly recruited at the time than I was. He was Mr. Basketball in Florida, while I came in under the radar. We became friends right away and have stayed friends all this time—great friends. His daughter and my daughter are best friends. He's always had my back when times were tough when I was in the NBA. We were the same way in college. Even though we're not from the same family, we have a very brotherly relationship. We've had our ups and downs, but nothing has ever broken that bond. Coach Smith would sometimes have to get on us because we were acting like a couple of fools, acting like we were nine years old.

Now Coach Smith—I know I wouldn't be where I am right now if it weren't for him. The way he cares about his players, the way he keeps in contact with the families even after they're gone and have left the university—he's done so much for so many people. He's taught me a lot, and I mean about being a human being. He's meant so much. He always found a way to put the attention back on the players. I love Coach Smith dearly. He's like a second father to me.

When we had the big alumni game for the current pros to celebrate the 100-year anniversary of UNC basketball [in September 2009] and they introduced Coach Smith and everyone cheered for so long—that was unbelievable. I choked up then and several other times during the night. You just realize how much he's done—not only for you but for all the guys in attendance. He truly cared for everybody he has encountered.

191

As a player, I had the unique opportunity of playing both on Coach Smith's last team and Coach Guthridge's first team at Carolina. The Duke games are the ones I remember the most. Every year in my three-year tenure at UNC, it seemed like the Duke games just got more and more spectacular. And nothing was more fun or exciting than a Duke game at home.

The game I remember the most was the one we played against Duke in 1998 at home when Duke was No. 1 and we were No. 2. There was always a lot of hoopla for our games with Duke, but this one was special. A few days before the game, some Duke students had sneaked into the Smith Center, crawled out on the rafters, and cut down Michael Jordan's No. 23 jersey that hangs out there. It was finally found, but it took several weeks, and they never figured out who from Duke did it. And you had to be crazy to go up there. There's no way you can just get a ladder and get it—that thing was practically on top of the Dean Dome. That was definitely dangerous, but just goes to show how far people will go in this rivalry.

As a guy who went to high school at Providence in Charlotte, as someone who not too many people knew how good he could be, the games against Duke in college really gave me some confidence and helped make me the person I am right now. For some reason, I always played well against Duke.

Elton Brand was hurt in that game, and there's no doubt that helped us. He was a load. But Duke still had [Shane] Battier, Wojo [Steve Wojciechowski], Trajan Langdon, Chris Carrawell, and a whole lot of other guys.

Our game plan was to get it inside on offense. We didn't think they could really stop us in there. By that time, I had really developed my inside game. In high school, I was so much taller than everyone else that just about everything I shot was pretty much a dunk. I took my time with those.

But when I got to Carolina and started dealing with seven-footers, I started to use my quickness a lot more. It's really something I never worked on until I got there, but Coach Guthridge and Coach Smith helped me take it to another level. I never kept the ball in my hands long. I just shot.

[Dave Odom, then the Wake Forest head coach, said of Jamison while he was still playing at UNC, "I don't think I've ever seen a player who has the sense of presence on the court that Antawn has. His feel, his sixth sense—all of that is unprecedented. You could almost spin him like a top, blindfold him, and throw him the ball. He could shoot without looking, and it would go in."]

ESPN put a clock on me during that big UNC-Duke game to see how often the ball was actually in my hands, though I didn't know it at the time. But they came back with this stat I still remember—I scored 35 points and only had the ball in my hands for a total of 53 seconds.

I don't remember many shots in particular in that game, just the overall performance of our team. I didn't miss too many and got off to a really good start [Jamison had 23 points at halftime, and UNC was already ahead by 16]. Everyone in the world seemed to be watching that one. Maybe a game like that helps a guy like Marvin Williams to go to UNC down the road or something—he sees what is going on and wants to be a part of it.

I actually remember a shot Vince Carter missed in that game more than any that I made. It was a *missed* dunk—and it still made ESPN. It's one thing to get on ESPN with a dunk that you made, but how many people get on there with a dunk that they miss? On the play, Ed Cota threw it off the glass on an alley-oop and Vince took off about a step inside the free-throw line for the dunk.

Antawn Jamison often caught opponents like Duke's Greg Newton off-guard with the "shoot first, ask questions later" style that made Jamison the consensus National Player of the Year in 1998.

Someone got an awesome picture of that one—Vince is so high he's looking down at the rim. It's a great picture to look at. I remember the whole gym just got silent as the play developed. And then Vince missed it!

We still laugh about that one—we call it the best missed dunk in basketball history. Of course, the play still worked out well—the ball bounced out to Shammond [Williams], and he knocked down a three. That's just the way things went for us that night—even when they went badly, they went well. It was one of those games I will always feel grateful to be a part of. [UNC won 97–73, and Jamison scored 35 points and had 11 rebounds while shooting 14-for-20.]

We actually thought we should have won the national title that year, and I still think we should have. But we picked the wrong time of the season to play our worst game. We got back to the Final Four. But Utah got off to a quick start [an early 16-point lead for the balanced team coached by Rick Majerus and featuring future NBA first-round picks Michael Doleac and Andre Miller]. We never could recover from that.

If I could go back and redo anything in my college career, I'd redo those two Final Fours. I would have slowed down. I would have calmed down. Of course, when you're more mature now, you say that. But we were young. We did our best, and it just wasn't quite enough.

I turned pro after that season. I was only at Chapel Hill for three years. Sometimes I think of all the history before and after me—100 years of Carolina basketball. To be part of those 100 years is special.

I had a great career at UNC. I had fun. For me, to be part of it is something I'll treasure for the rest of my life. When I go into the Dean Dome now, I point out jersey No. 33 to my son. We named him Antwan, but it's spelled differently than my name. Did you know my parents misspelled my name on my birth certificate? It's true—that's why my name is pronounced "Antwan" but spelled "Antawn." My wife, Ione, and I weren't going to do that to him, too. My son is a little boy now. But my jersey is always going to be there—No. 33—so I can point it out to him again and again until he gets it.

Those are the sorts of things you cherish. And there's so much to cherish about Carolina. I'm blessed and grateful to be a part of it.

Antawn Jamison was the unanimous National College Player of the Year in 1998 at North Carolina, and his No. 33 jersey is retired at the school. Jamison led UNC to ACC tournament titles and to the Final Four in both 1997 and 1998.

As an NBA player, Jamison was the fourth overall pick of the 1998 draft. He has played for more than a decade, mostly with the Golden State Warriors and the Washington Wizards. Jamison was traded in 2010 to the Cleveland Cavaliers, where he got to briefly team with LeBron James and have a chance to be on a consistent winner for the first time in his NBA career.

Although Jamison hardly ever shot three-pointers as a college player, he developed a three-point shot in the NBA and has made more than 800 of them in his career. That's one reason why his career scoring average hovered around 20 points. Long involved in charitable endeavors, Jamison has twice been named by the *Sporting News* as one of the "Good Guys" in sports. He and his family maintain an off-season home in Charlotte.

The
NEW
MILLENNIUM

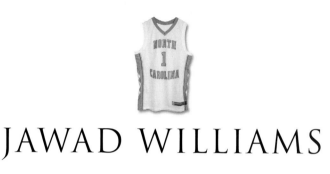

JAWAD WILLIAMS

FORWARD

2001–2005

I GREW UP IN INNER-CITY CLEVELAND. We lived on the east side of Cleveland, in a neighborhood called St. Clair. It was the roughest neighborhood in Cleveland. But I was fortunate enough that my mother and father made the right decision and sent me to a suburban school, which was St. Edward High School. I had a pretty rough upbringing. My environment was rough. But my parents kept me on track, and I found basketball to be a way of keeping myself out of trouble.

I got serious about basketball probably around the age of 11. I have five sisters and two brothers. One of my older sisters is Na'sheema Hillmon—she played in college at Vanderbilt and then professionally, so I kind of followed in her footsteps. I wanted to be the next one in line for that.

Both my parents were in the home, so that was good. My mom was a probation officer. My dad ran a local recreation center, so I spent a lot of time in the gym. My father was once a professional boxer, and so was my brother. So I was going to be spending a lot of time in a gym one way or the other, either boxing or playing basketball.

The gym my father ran was called Glenville Recreation Center. I actually tried the boxing thing, but I found out boxing was not for me when I tried to fight my brother one time. I quickly had enough of boxing, and I stuck to basketball after that.

My parents wanted me to get out of that neighborhood, and so they sent me to St. Edward. I had to get some financial aid—there was no way we could afford it. But it worked out.

We won the state championship when I was a ninth-grader. I didn't play a lot on that team, every now and then I'd get a few minutes. But as I got taller, I got better. My growth spurt came between eighth grade and ninth grade. I was 5′10″ in the eighth grade and shot to 6′6″ in three or four months. I had a lot of painful days—literal growing pains. But my body developed, and everything started to catch up with itself. I'm 6′9″ today. My father is 6′1″, and my mother is 6′2″, so I guess my height came from her. I have a grand-mother who also is 6′2″.

I was Ohio's Player of the Year as a senior. I was recruited by every major school except for Kansas. That was the crazy part. Coach Williams was at Kansas and didn't recruit me, but then I ended up playing for him. He told me later he figured he didn't have a chance at me or something.

My finalists were North Carolina, Duke, Florida, Southern Cal, and Cincinnati. I kind of gave a verbal commitment to Maryland to start. But then I went on my official visit to Carolina and had a change of heart imme-diately. I remember going to the football game, hanging out with Jackie Manuel, and after that I was convinced Carolina was the place for me.

I played two years under Coach Matt Doherty first. Yes, I was part of the 8–20 season of 2001–2002. That was my freshman year. And that was the one time I really didn't want to play basketball. I thought about transferring, about running from my problems. I just didn't want to be there anymore. Myself, Jackie Manuel, Melvin Scott—we were the freshmen on that team. And we stuck together. We did everything together. But we all stayed. We decided since we came in on a low note, we wanted to stick together for all four years and leave on a high note.

Why did I think about transferring early in my career? It was the losing. I definitely wasn't used to losing. Throughout high school and AAU ball, I don't think I had lost 20 games in my career. To lose 20 in one season—that was tough for me. I didn't know how to take that. And then I was only allowed to do so much as a freshman—that bothered me a lot, too. It was tough.

Then, in my sophomore year, we got some help. Raymond Felton, Sean May, Rashad McCants—they all came in. We got a lot better even though we didn't make the NCAA. We went to the NIT, and things got better.

200

Jawad Williams was part of the Tar Heels' infamous 8–20 season but then started on the 2005 national championship team.

Before my junior year, I actually thought about leaving school early at that point and going into the NBA. We were in between coaches at the time—after Coach Doherty and before Coach Williams. I got a personal trainer and started training extremely hard. I was actually thinking about coming out. So I met with Coach Williams, and we had our first individual workout. I thought maybe I should just give it one more year and see what happens.

What changed with our team once Coach Williams got there? We stopped being so selfish as individuals. A lot of guys put aside their accolades and just started working as a team. We were a pretty good team my junior year. We were a dangerous team. But at the end of the season we started to tank out and lost in the second round of the NCAA tournament to Texas.

I thought about leaving again after my junior season, but I had a lot of concussions that season. I broke my nose that year and had two or three concussions, too. It kind of slowed me down and took me a long time to get my mental state back. I wore a mask for several games that season. So I stayed one more year. And I'm so glad I did.

My last team, 2004–2005, was close to the same team, except Marvin Williams came in as a freshman. We were something. We still believe we were the best team in college basketball—ever.

That team really knew how to sacrifice as a team. Coach Williams always said if we play well as a team, we'd all get our rewards. And it worked out that way. One of his quotes of the day was: "Be led by your dreams, not pushed by your problems." I kind of use that as my motto. Sometimes things go wrong, but there are bigger things ahead.

We had a great group of guys. We worked hard each and every day. We had so much talent that our practices were sometimes more competitive than our games. We had a half-dozen guys who would play in the NBA and some others who ended up having great careers overseas. And we ended up getting the championship.

There really weren't that many low points that season. We lost at Duke and at Wake Forest. We lost the first game of the year when Raymond was out. But every time we lost, we felt like we beat ourselves. We didn't ever feel that anybody could really beat us. I started as our power forward, and Marvin was the top sub off the bench. A lot of my offense came from the perimeter, and they ran a lot of lob plays for me.

When we got to that final game in St. Louis, and we beat Illinois in the championship, I was just so thankful. I knew where I had been—at 8–20. That's when everybody had pretty much turned their backs on us. I remember myself, Jackie Manuel, and Melvin Scott—we said a prayer at halfcourt right after the national championship game. We had come a long way. Only

God could do that for us, and it was a special moment for us. We were praying while the confetti was coming down.

From there, I had a long road to the NBA. I wasn't drafted. I went to training camp with the San Antonio Spurs that first year, but that didn't work out. Then I ended up going to Spain and playing. After I came back, I had a few other workouts. I went to training camp with the L.A. Clippers but didn't make the team. I went to the NBA's developmental league, but that didn't work out. I went to Japan and had a great time. I absolutely loved it. So I was actually thinking about just staying in Japan and living over there. I also went to Israel for two months. I had a chance to stay overseas and make a lot of money.

But then I got a call from Cleveland and had a chance to come and work out for them. I thought I'd give it one more shot, since I was a hometown kid, and see what happens. I went in there and was fortunate enough to finally win the job. Still, it wasn't that easy. I signed a couple of 10-day contracts, got released and picked back up, went to the D-League for 19 games, and then came back. Finally, I got picked up by the Cavaliers for a long stretch.

Because of that, I've been around LeBron James a lot. LeBron mania is crazy, but it's a lot of fun. When you have a guy who's such a high-profile player who cares about all his teammates and their families, that's a great thing. He really took care of me from day one.

Our relationship goes back to high school. We've known each other for 11 years. I'm a couple of years older, and we only had one scrimmage against each other and never a real game, but we used to always watch each other play.

In the off-season I live in Morrisville, in the Raleigh-Durham area. I have a house four exits from the airport. Everybody whom I played with, we all have houses there. Rashad McCants, Marvin Williams, Sean May, Melvin Scott, David Noel—we still see each other a lot. We get together and work out all day.

When we had that alumni game in 2009 in the Smith Center, we really wanted to play our 2005 team against the 2009 team to see which one was better. That's what we wanted. But I don't think they really wanted it. A fight might have broken out, because we would have definitely beaten them by at least 20.

Our versatility would have been the difference. We had so many guys who could do so many different things. We always have arguments about that in the summertime. We think Rashad would be a mismatch for Wayne

Ellington because Rashad could post him up. Marvin and me—we think we could do whatever we wanted to do on the court.

My long-term goal is to open a recreation center in Cleveland. But more than just a rec center, a place where kids can have Bible study or get tutoring if they need it. Something to keep kids off the street. I want to do a 24-hour type thing. I want a safe environment where kids can come and go as they please in the St. Clair area where I grew up. I think it's going to work out.

When I think of what it means to be a Tar Heel, the first thing that comes to mind is pride. We take a lot of pride in all that we do. We're a family, all of us. From the guys who played way before me—Mike O'Koren, Mitch Kupchak, Lennie Rosenbluth—we all know the struggle. A lot of guys come from rough backgrounds. But when we come together and meet up with each other, it's all about family.

Jawad Williams played four years at North Carolina—two under Matt Doherty and two under Roy Williams. As a senior starter, he averaged 13 points and four rebounds per game for the 2005 UNC team that won the national championship. After several years playing overseas, Williams—a Cleveland native—made the Cleveland Cavaliers in 2008 and has been a backup with the Cavaliers since then. He hopes to one day open a recreation center in his Cleveland hometown.

RAYMOND FELTON

GUARD

2002–2005

COLLEGE BASKETBALL IS SO GREAT. I miss it. I miss the intensity of it. I miss the way it feels on game day on campus.

Don't get me wrong. I love the NBA, where I am now. It's the ultimate dream for every player. But even today—thinking about games like the one we played against Duke in Chapel Hill in 2005—that makes me miss college.

I grew up in Latta, South Carolina, kind of close to the South Carolina coast. We're about an hour away from Myrtle Beach.

My father, Raymond Sr., was a star in an industrial league down there. He was an incredible player and could flat-out shoot. Latta is a really small town, maybe 1,500 people. We played in a 1A conference. The Latta High School enrollment was about 400 when I went to high school there, but we'd draw a lot more than that for most of our games. I played center on defense a lot in high school, because we had a small team, and then point guard on offense.

My mom and dad both worked hard at jobs that didn't pay much. Sometimes, my dad worked third shift. But they always raised me well—to know right from wrong—and encouraged me when I needed it.

When I was little, I'd go outside sometimes to dribble in the dark. I knew how to dribble pretty well by the time I was two.

Our basketball goal was stuck in the grass behind our house. There was no asphalt out there. It was mostly dirt. When you dribbled, you had to try and figure out where the ball was going to bounce next. It really made you work

Raymond Felton could dribble a basketball by the time he was two and ultimately became the point guard for the Tar Heels' 2005 championship team.

on your dribbling, and I think that helped me develop my point-guard skills that I still use today. I got really good dribbling with both hands. I have always been able to switch-hit in baseball, too.

I played on an AAU team, and that's where Coach Matt Doherty first saw me play, in a game in California. I think he was recruiting somebody else at the time. I wasn't that into the Duke-North Carolina rivalry when I was in high school, being from South Carolina, but once I got to Chapel Hill, I got into it in a hurry.

My first year was tough. We made it to the NIT, but not the NCAA tournament. Coach Doherty was forced to resign. Then Coach Williams came in, and we started to get better.

Still, though, we had trouble against Duke. By my junior year, 2005, I read that the Blue Devils had beaten us 14 of the last 16 times the two teams had played. Then they made it 15 of 17 at their place when we couldn't get off a shot in the final seconds and they beat us by a point.

In that game we had the ball at the end with a chance to win. But I picked up my dribble and then tried to make a tough pass to David Noel. We ended up never getting a shot off.

There was no question that that was a very tough moment for me. I wish I had the chance to go about it differently. I should have either given the ball to David in a better situation or probably just kept the ball and penetrated. So I put that on myself, that we lost that game. Coach Williams had told me not to do that—that we won and lost as a team—but I did anyway.

And, following that, I started playing better, and we started playing better. By the time we got to the second Duke game that year, we were flying high. And I really think winning that second game against Duke was what set us on a path toward the national championship we'd win a month later. I know Sean May talks about the national championship game elsewhere in this book—that was such a great game for him—so I want to tell you some about that Duke game that was so huge for us instead.

First of all, the Carolina-Duke games I played in were just crazy. It's tough to explain it in words. It's best to experience it, to be a player in one. But I'll try to explain it to you. It starts off early in the morning, with this weird feeling in your stomach. You get it for Carolina-Duke and for nothing else. You've got butterflies all day. The hype that goes along with that game—it's tremendous. So that particular game, it was special. There was all the hype around campus. All the hype on TV.

Finally, the game started. I wasn't shooting that well, but I was determined to make something happen. I wasn't going to let myself get tentative like I had on the last play the first time against Duke.

It wasn't looking good, though. Duke was really playing well. We were holding J.J. Redick down in the second half—Jackie Manuel was just relentless on him. But Lee Melchionni had five three-pointers in the second half and was really hurting us from the outside. Finally, with a little under three minutes left, we were down nine points. Sean May was playing great—he always ate Shelden Williams for dinner. No offense to Shelden, but Sean always had such big games versus Duke.

But we just weren't scoring, and we weren't getting stops when we needed them. And then all of a sudden, it happened.

To be honest with you, I can't remember everything that happened. I just remember it in a blur—stealing and scoring, and we kept doing things right and then, all of a sudden, we were just down by two [73–71]. I had the ball, and I was going straight to the basket this time—I had learned my lesson! I got fouled by DeMarcus Nelson and had two free throws. The chance to tie. I made the first one, but as soon as I shoot the second one, I knew it was off. So I went after the rebound, just like everyone else, and I managed to get a finger on it and helped tip it out.

Marvin Williams grabbed it with about 17 seconds left and shot fast, and the ball banked in. And he got fouled! That's when the wood seemed to start peeling back from the floor, or at least that's what it felt like. I'm serious— the whole floor was vibrating. At the end, when we were taking the lead, I actually thought the wood was about to come up off the floor. I've heard Coach Williams say that moment was the loudest the Smith Center has ever been, and I believe it.

Marvin made the free throw to finish off the three-point play, and we were up 75–73. Duke set up a great play at the end—they were so well-coached by Mike Krzyzewski—but J.J. Redick missed a three, and we won. And that game taught us something. It really brought us together as a team and showed us we could come back and win games, even in situations like that, as long as we stayed together.

That was my last game against Duke, and I still think about it a lot today. It was a good one to end on, too. I went pro after that season and stayed in the state, playing for the Charlotte Bobcats for five seasons. I'm a true blue Carolina man. I try to be very loyal to my school and to make sure everyone knows about that loyalty. It's a very special place, and I miss it.

Coach Roy Williams calls Raymond Felton the "most indispensable player" in the Tar Heels' run to the 2005 national championship. Felton's ball-on-a-string dribble was essential in controlling games for that talented UNC squad, which broke up almost immediately following the title.

Felton was one of the Tar Heels' four lottery picks in the 2005 NBA Draft, joining May, Marvin Williams, and Rashad McCants. He was taken No. 5 overall by the Charlotte Bobcats, where he played his first five NBA seasons—150 miles west of Chapel Hill. Roy Williams bought two season tickets to watch Felton and May (who are no longer with the Bobcats) and came to several Bobcats games each season. Felton signed with the New York Knicks as a free agent during the summer of 2010.

Felton regularly started for the Bobcats almost from day one and has improved each season—especially once former Tar Heel Larry Brown was named the Bobcats' coach in 2008. He is known for his work ethic, his ability to play through injuries, and the way he accepts blame anytime something goes wrong for the team. In the summer of 2010 Felton took on a new challenge—he signed a two-year deal to be the new point guard for the New York Knicks.

SEAN MAY

CENTER/FORWARD

2002–2005

I LOVE THE UNIVERSITY OF NORTH CAROLINA and I love Chapel Hill. The place means so much to me. I am always going to go back there in the summers, because there is always somebody playing, somebody to hang out with, somebody to talk to. It's a special place. Anyone who ever went there knows that.

The most special time of my career at Chapel Hill was our run through the NCAA tournament in 2005, and then especially the championship game itself. I still think back on those days. People still remind me of them wherever I go, especially if I'm in North Carolina. They'll want to talk about our title game against Illinois, or that regular-season game against Duke—my last real game in the Smith Center—when I had 26 points and 24 rebounds and we won right at the end.

It took a long time to get there and to win that championship. It started for me in Indiana. That's where I was raised. My father, Scott May, was a basketball star for Indiana University. His 1976 Indiana team went 32–0—still the last team to win the title and finish undefeated.

My older brother was Scott Jr., and he played at Indiana. I didn't want to go there, though. I was pretty highly recruited—I was Indiana's Mr. Basketball as a senior—and I wanted to be my own man. I knew I would always be compared to my father if I went to Indiana, and I also didn't know Mike Davis as well as I had known Coach Knight. Mike Davis was the coach by then at Indiana when I was graduating high school. Coach Knight had been fired.

So I decided to come to North Carolina in the same recruiting class as Raymond Felton and Rashad McCants. I did honor my father by wearing No. 42, the same number he wore at Indiana. We all were recruited by Coach Matt Doherty and got there right after the 8–20 season. When Raymond and I signed, I remember we called each other and said, "Hey, one of the greatest programs in the history of basketball is at its lowest point right now. We can help take it back to the top."

But for the first couple of years we were there, no one thought it was going to happen. We had one year under Coach Doherty—I broke a bone in my foot, we made the NIT, and then he was forced to resign. Then we had a year under Coach Williams in which we made the NCAA tournament but lost in the second round.

Then came our junior year. We had a great team, one we knew had a chance to go all the way. Now, I'm not a nervous person. That's in contrast to my dad—I don't know why he does it, but every game I've ever played, he's never been in his seat. He can't stand to sit still and watch. He'll go out to the concourse and walk around and watch instead. He won't sit there for my NBA games, either.

I'm not like that. I'm usually calm—an even-keel guy. I was the one who—if everyone got riled up—I would calm them down. I never got nervous for any game in my career until I walked back out into the arena with two minutes on the clock, right before the starting lineups were announced for the NCAA final—North Carolina versus Illinois in St. Louis. There were so many people. There were cameras going off everywhere. It was amazing. The whole night was amazing.

Now to just get there, we had to get a little lucky. Every good team has a scare somewhere down the line, and Villanova was our scare in the NCAA tournament. We shouldn't have won that game in the Sweet 16 the way they played. So getting past them [67–66] kind of gave us a second chance. We really stayed in the moment after that.

In the Final Four, our first game was against Michigan State, and the Spartans were ahead of us 38–33 at halftime. Coach Williams told us at halftime that teams could run with us for 20 or 25 minutes, but no one could run with us for 40. So we just kept trying to run. At the end of the game, they kind of folded.

So that got us to the title game. It was played on my 21st birthday. It was a really long day, just waiting for the game to start. To pass the time, I watched this DVD of my father's championship game—Indiana versus Michigan in 1976. I had gotten it for Christmas, but for whatever reason, I hadn't watched it yet. I watched it the night before our game and then again the day of the game, when it got me through a good hour. It got me thinking about something else other than who I was guarding or what was going to happen— about the short shorts they wore and stuff like that. Jackie Manuel watched a little bit of it with me.

Then, before our game, they were showing clips from different games on the Jumbotron scoreboard in the arena, and there his game was again, big as anything. It was like karma.

As enormous as the championship game was, we approached it like we had a task at hand. We started running and going inside right away, and at first Illinois just couldn't handle us. We kept scoring, and I was able to get James Augustine in foul trouble early. We were running, and at first Illinois didn't seem to be able to run with us. And I was getting a lot of good looks once Augustine had to sit out with foul trouble [Augustine would play only nine minutes before fouling out and was held to zero points]. Roger Powell was good but undersized for a big man, and Nick Smith, one of their main substitutes underneath, just wasn't very good.

211

We were ahead 40–27 at halftime—Rashad had scored all 14 of his points by then—but we knew they would make a run at us. They were too good not to, and they did. Luther Head was really hurting us for a while from outside— he made a lot of tough shots. Deron Williams, who we knew would be a really good NBA player, ran the show. But in college, that was really Dee Brown's team more than anyone else.

They just kept taking threes, and they were hitting some. Of their 70 shots, 40 of them were threes. That's just unheard of. Head was shooting them constantly, and he hit some of them. But my teammates just kept giving me the ball. I had hit this stride the past month of the season where I was getting a double-double just about every game, and it felt so great that my teammates had such confidence in me. I'll never forget against Wisconsin [in the Elite Eight] in a timeout huddle, Coach was drawing up a play. In the middle of the timeout, Melvin Scott just grabbed Coach Williams and said, "Just give Sean the ball. He's eating right now—feed him!" Coach said, "Fine," and he called a play for me.

Sean May celebrated after the 2005 national title game, in which he scored 26 points and grabbed 10 rebounds in the Tar Heels' victory over Illinois.

That carried over into the Final Four. I just felt like it was my moment. I was going to step to the plate. I had it going. I just felt like I wasn't going to miss.

But it was still nerve-racking, because they kept shooting so many threes. In one possession, they got four attempts, and they took a three every time. We'd get one stop after another, but we couldn't get the rebound [Illinois outrebounded UNC 39–34 for the game]. But they kept missing the threes, and I was just like, *Thank you, thank you.*

In the final minutes, they tied us up at 70–70. And then I'll never forget this play. Rashad McCants had come off the bench and was upset at the time because he'd been out for a while. He had had a really good first half and really hadn't done much in the second half. So he came off the bench, drove baseline, one against four, right into the teeth of the Illinois defense, and threw up a reverse. I was like, "Whoa, whoa—what are we doing here, guys? We may never have a chance to do this again." It was an outrageous shot.

But Marvin Williams and I both went up for the rebound, and Marvin got up just a little higher than I did and tipped it in. And that, to me, was the biggest play of the game. Because after that, I knew we would be okay. That was the most outrageous shot I had ever seen, and we still came away with a bucket.

The only other time I was nervous, beside right before the game, was when Raymond went to the line when we were up 72–70 [with 26 seconds left] and then missed the first one. We were celebrating too much too early. But he made the second one. And then Luther Head missed a three-pointer that could tie, I got the final rebound, and it was all over after that. I went over and gave Coach Williams a bear hug. It hurt me when we were going through all those press conferences before the game and there were all these questions about whether he needed a national championship to validate himself as a Hall of Fame coach. The confetti was falling all over us. I was so happy. It was great.

I found my mother and my older brother after the game. Not my father. He doesn't sit in his seat, remember, so I didn't see him right then. My brother told me he had seen my father right after the game for a second and that he was a little emotional, but of course he won't tell me that.

Then we went back to the hotel, and it was like we were the Beatles or something. People were just everywhere, all over us. Wes Miller's parents gave me a bottle of Dom Perignon—my first legal alcoholic beverage, since I had turned 21 that night. So that was fun. We drank that in the room. We had a good time.

I finally caught up with my dad in the hotel, too. The first thing he said was, "Congratulations." And the next thing he said was, "You missed a couple of boxouts."

"I was like, 'Dude, are you serious? I just played the best game of my life.'"

I originally planned to go to this party that we were invited to thrown by Nelly, the rapper. A couple of the guys did go. But they left me, Wes Miller, and Marvin Williams at the hotel. We were supposed to be downstairs in 20 minutes. We took our time, got down there in 25 to 30 minutes, figuring they wouldn't leave us. And they were gone. So we ended up staying at the hotel, just having fun.

That was a great end to my college career, although I didn't know it was the end of it at the time. I had always said I would be a four-year player at UNC, so I figured I'd try for a repeat in 2005–2006. I thought I was the kind of player who needed to stay four years, to prove myself and give myself the best opportunity. I wanted to stay.

On the plane ride back home, a couple of us talked about it. Marvin Williams and I sat next to each other and talked about it. I asked him what he was going to do, and he said, "It really depends on what everybody else does." He was like, "Maybe if we can get Ray or Rashad, I'll definitely stay." I knew Ray wasn't staying, and Rashad had said before the season he was leaving. We all knew he was gone, although it hadn't been announced. But I still wanted to stay and get a couple of guys to stay with me.

I went to talk to Coach Williams. I asked him to pull a little information and just see. He came back to me and said he had talked to three agents he knew and three scouts, and they all said I'd be picked between No. 8 and No. 15. They told him if I stayed, I'd still probably go between eight and 15. I sat down with my family and with Coach. Meanwhile, Marvin had information that he'd probably be a top-five pick, so his decision was pretty much made.

So I started thinking about it. I've got five freshmen coming in, and I don't know if they can play a lick [one of those freshmen was Tyler Hansbrough]. And I've got three guys who I know are great players who are leaving. I ended up declaring, too. And I'm glad I did. With what's happened with my knee in the NBA, if I had stayed, I would have been pretty much out of luck. Everyone knows my heart and my passion is with Carolina. But it's hard to turn down that opportunity when it's right in front of you.

I've had a lot of injury problems in the pros, and that has hurt me. I was in the best shape I've ever been in when I first got hurt. There was nothing

I could do. It's the luck of the draw. It happened. I don't know what your particular passion is, but it's like somebody taking it away from you. You're going to work your hardest to try and get it back. That's all I can do. That motivates me every day. If I go out to a restaurant or whatever, somebody always says, "I love what you did at Carolina." And I love that. That's nice for people to say. But I want them to say something about my NBA career because I've proven myself in the NBA. That's part of my motivation now.

Sean May had 26 points and 10 rebounds in North Carolina's 75–70 win over Illinois in the 2005 national championship. He was named the Most Outstanding Player of that Final Four. He also averaged a double-double in his career as a Tar Heel—15.8 points and 10 rebounds.

After declaring a year early for the NBA Draft, May was drafted No. 13 overall by the Charlotte Bobcats in 2005. Former UNC teammate Raymond Felton was selected No. 5, also by the Bobcats. But May's early NBA career was dogged by injuries. In his first three NBA seasons, May played in only 82 of a possible 246 games because of his troublesome right knee, which underwent three surgeries in that time period.

The Bobcats and May parted ways in 2009, and he signed with the Sacramento Kings. He played sparingly for Sacramento in the 2009–2010 season and as of this writing was still trying to find his niche in the NBA.

MARVIN WILLIAMS

FORWARD

2004–2005

WHEN I TALK ABOUT CAROLINA, it's hard to know where to begin. There's a tradition there—a brotherhood. It's a family. And not just among the basketball players—I'm talking about the entire Carolina family. Anyone who ever went to school there. Anyone who cheers for the sports teams—those people are part of it, too.

When I'm at the gas station or in the grocery store and I see someone with a Tar Heels T-shirt or bumper sticker or something, I'm always like, "Go Heels!" Moments like that just make you feel good.

When I was getting recruited, I cut my list down to two: the University of Washington, which was a lot nearer to where I lived in Bremerton, Washington, and North Carolina. My father is from North Carolina, and so he really wanted to see me in Carolina blue. My mom wanted me to stay around. So you can see I had a tough decision.

I watched Carolina growing up, so that helped. I was a big fan of both Antawn Jamison and Shammond Williams—those were my two favorite Carolina players at the time. The tradition helped me decide to go there, but also Coach Roy Williams was so important. Every chance he got, within the rules, he would come and see me play or practice or something. And I know how hard that trip is. Chapel Hill and Bremerton are about 3,000 miles apart. Yet he seemed like he was there all the time.

Marvin Williams made the most of his one year as a Tar Heel, winning a national championship as the team's sixth man and then turning pro.

The thing I liked about Coach Williams' recruiting, too, was the fact that he never promised me anything. He said I'd have to earn whatever playing time I got. I liked that. I didn't want any promises. Well, he did make me one promise: he said if I got hurt in college and couldn't play anymore, he would still guarantee I'd stay on scholarship and be able to get my education.

When I went to Chapel Hill on my recruiting visit, Sean May was my host. Now that was a good move—Sean can sell anybody on just about anything. We're still very close today.

At the time of that visit, though, I was just about worn out. I had visited Arizona one weekend and then Washington on the next weekend, and going to Carolina was going to be my third straight weekend visit in a row. It's a long trip across the country, and I didn't really want to go. But I ended up going because I said I would, and before long I realized it was the place for me.

I only played one year at Carolina—a lot less than most of the other players who are telling their stories in this book. But I crammed a lot into that one year. It was such a great overall experience.

My best memory, of course, is winning the national championship. That was fantastic. I was able to make a basket toward the end that helped us in that game against Illinois, tipping in a shot that Rashad McCants missed. The game was tied at the time at 70–70 with a little under two minutes to go, so that shot turned out to be the one that put us ahead for good. It was just a case of "right place, right time." And then we got to celebrate afterward— that was something I'll never forget.

But close behind would be our home game with Duke that season. We were nine points down with 2:40 to go, and I remember Coach Williams telling us during one of the timeouts toward the end, "Stop hanging your heads! This isn't over. There's so much time still to go."

Toward the end, Raymond Felton was at the line and we were down two. He made the first, missed the second, and was able to tip it out to me. I grabbed it, shot a bank shot, and got fouled. I've never heard the Smith Center louder when that shot went in. I was fortunate to make the free throw, too, for a three-point play. We won by two points, 75–73.

I was a sixth man for us that year, and that didn't bother me at all. I didn't start games, but I usually finished them. Sean May, Jawad Williams, and I all played a lot underneath. Coach Williams told me that I might not start at the beginning of the season, and it stayed that way, and that was fine. I've always

218

been a team-first kind of guy. The thing is that we were all good friends on that team. That team was about more than just basketball, and that's why we had such good chemistry.

After that season, I went to the NBA. And you know what? I didn't really want to. That was probably the toughest decision I've ever made in my life. I prayed and prayed about it. My family situation really made the difference— I needed to help them financially. My dad was always working. My mother worked two jobs most of the time when I was growing up. I had two younger brothers in school who were going to need to go to college.

So my father and I met with Coach Williams, and he went out to gather information about where I might get drafted. He came back to us a few weeks later and said, "It sounds like you'll probably get picked in the first three picks." That made it just so hard to turn down, all that money. Coach said, "I wouldn't blame you at all if you took it. I wouldn't be upset, because that's a lot of money to pass up."

So finally I decided to go pro, and I ended up getting drafted No. 2 over-all by Atlanta. In the NBA, I always try to talk to the Tar Heels guys on the other teams. And in our own locker room, we compare stories about our college experiences. A lot of players wish they had the kind of experience that we all get at Carolina.

219

Although I only spent one year at Carolina out of the 100 years that the basketball program has been in existence, I feel like a part of it. Sean May and I get a place every summer and stay in Chapel Hill for three or four months. I take a summer-school class and work out there during that time. We get some great pickup games. Jackie Manuel and David Noel—I've stayed close to those guys, too.

I also came back to play in the big Carolina/NBA Alumni game in September 2009, and that was something else. To have more than 20,000 people watching a game like that was great. I was so proud that Coach Williams asked me to play in that. To be part of that 100-year Carolina basketball tradition— it's really special.

In the pros, I feel like I can have a long career. I'm trying to get better every day. I know I made the right decision to leave Chapel Hill when I did—you can't turn down being the No. 2 pick in the draft in my situation— but sometimes I do wish it had turned out differently. If I didn't feel like I had to go, I would have absolutely stayed a lot longer, because Chapel Hill is such a special place.

Marvin Gaye Williams (born in 1986 and named for the late Motown singer) is currently a standout NBA player with the Atlanta Hawks. The 6'9" forward played one year for the Tar Heels as the sixth man on the 2005 national championship team before getting drafted No. 2 overall by the Atlanta Hawks. In 2009 Williams signed a new five-year, $37.5-million contract with the Hawks.

BOBBY FRASOR

GUARD

2005–2009

THE THING ABOUT CAROLINA is that no matter how good your team was or how good you were as an individual player, you were always part of something bigger. You were part of something that was more than just you. I always have liked that.

I grew up in Illinois, in a place called Blue Island. It's about 30 minutes outside of downtown Chicago. My dad was a high school basketball coach, so I grew up around basketball at an early age. The thing I enjoyed most as a kid was going to college basketball games. My dad, Bob Frasor, played basketball at Wisconsin. So we'd go to Badgers games occasionally, and I was a big Wisconsin fan. We'd go to the United Center in Chicago some, too, whenever there was a good college game there. It was a longtime dream of mine to play Division I college basketball.

Not many people know that I grew up as a Duke fan, too. I went to Duke's basketball camp when I was in eighth grade. Duke never did recruit me, though—they already had Greg Paulus—and I kind of got away from my love for them before I ever went to college, and then particularly after I got to Chapel Hill.

I didn't play for my dad in high school. He taught at a public school, and I ended up going to a private school instead. I have three older sisters, and we've got a pretty athletic family—two of my sisters played volleyball in college. When I started getting recruited, I liked Bo Ryan a lot at Wisconsin. I

Bobby Frasor was one of only three point guards in school history to start every game as a freshman—Phil Ford and Raymond Felton were the other two.

was being recruited by a lot of mid-majors at first, and then I had this tournament where I blew up and a lot of people saw me. Then more people started recruiting me, and at the end it came down to either Michigan State, Marquette, Stanford, Wisconsin, or Carolina. But when Carolina came knocking, I knew that's where I wanted to go.

I lived with Tyler Hansbrough pretty much the whole time at college, from the time we got to campus in the summer of 2005 until the end.

Marcus Ginyard, Mike Copeland, and Danny Green lived with us a lot of that time, too.

I really embraced college. When I say that, you might be thinking of the pictures of me and Tyler Hansbrough jumping off a second-floor balcony into a swimming pool. That was in 2008. It was the last day of class, which is always a celebration.

We went to this frat house and were on the balcony, and people were urging us to do it. I felt like I couldn't back down. So I got up there and riled up the crowd, and then I jumped. Because I did that—delaying a little bit to get everyone fired up—I think people all had their cameras ready when Tyler jumped after me. Then it just blew up from there. That picture of Tyler jumping was everywhere. College was easily the best four years of my young life—so far.

Some of my fondest college memories actually come from my freshman year. That was right after the 2005 national championship, when all those guys left, and everyone was kind of down on Carolina basketball. We thrived in that scenario. We were still pretty good—we had Tyler and David Noel and Reyshawn Terry. And I became the answer to a trivia question. Do you know which three UNC point guards started every game of their freshman year? Phil Ford, Raymond Felton, and myself. That's pretty cool.

I got thrown right into the fire as a freshman and played point guard the whole season. One of the big highlights was our win at Duke that season, which spoiled J.J. Redick's senior night. We had kind of a bittersweet ending that season, though—we lost to George Mason, which we probably should have beaten.

Before my sophomore year, I felt probably the best I ever had skill-wise. I was starting, and I was scoring well. But then I had a stress fracture in my foot. I ended up sitting out 10 games in my sophomore year. I never quite got back into the same shape. I even thought about redshirting that year, but I knew we had a chance to play in the Final Four. That was the year we lost to Georgetown in the Elite Eight—we should have won that game.

In my junior year, I had my foot feeling great again. But then I blew out my knee two days after Christmas, against Nevada. That was the end of that season for me. We petitioned the NCAA to let me have a fifth year after that—to be a medical redshirt. But I had played in something like 34 percent of our games, and it needs to be 30 percent or less—that's what they told me anyway—so the petition was denied. It was a bittersweet year for me for sure. We went to the Final Four, and I got to see everything first-hand, but I wasn't wearing a jersey.

Then came my senior year. My goal was to stay healthy after those two big injuries. I wasn't quite the same player, honestly—I didn't have quite the same killer instinct offensively. But I got on the court a good bit because I could still play defense. I was the defensive player of the game for a lot of our games, including both of them in the Final Four, and got the award at our banquet for Defensive Player of the Year. There were some personal highlights for me that season. I hit a couple of big shots against Gonzaga and had some good moments against Villanova in the Final Four. It was just so great to go out as a champion with such a great group of guys.

After that, I wound up in Bulgaria, playing professionally. It's funny how I got there. Vasco Evtimov, who is from Bulgaria and played for Carolina in the late 1990s, was over in Bulgaria practicing. A point guard got hurt, and Vasco knew about me and said they should take a look at me. So I got the job in Bulgaria in part because of my Carolina connections.

Bulgaria is an interesting country. We play games once a week on Saturdays and have two practices a day—but the practices are not taxing. One practice at Carolina is harder than two of these. You can only have three Americans on the court at the same time during the games—that's one of the league rules. It's a country of contrasts—some people are still on horseback and some are driving around in the latest $100,000 Mercedes. There's a lot of American fast food around. I tried not to go into those, but I would go into Burger King occasionally if I missed home.

I played a lot that first year and started to get some of my offensive confidence back. I made it into the all-star game in Bulgaria. I even dunked in a game once, after a steal and then a breakaway. I tell people I took off from the free-throw line to do it, but it wasn't quite like that. I really did dunk, though—something I think I did only once at Carolina in a real game.

Over Christmas in 2009 I had some time off and flew back to the States. I had dinner with Tyler. We were talking about pro basketball and how different it was to get paid to do something you loved—of course, he's getting paid a lot more than I am. We were talking about the 2009–2010 Carolina team and all its struggles, and then I think we really realized what we had done. It was like, "Did that really happen? Did we really win the national championship together?"

I'm going to play basketball professionally for as long as I'm having fun. I like being able to travel some while I'm still young. But eventually, I really want to coach. I think I could be a great coach. And I definitely want to do it at the college level. I saw how hard it was for my dad in high school. He'd have to teach driver's education or P.E. or English from 8:00 AM to 3:00 PM and then he'd have to get ready for practice. I'd rather be able to devote all my time to basketball.

I really wish I could have gotten back to Chapel Hill for the 100-year anniversary in 2010, but I was playing in Bulgaria. I do keep up with a lot of the guys, though—through email and Twitter and Skype and Slingbox, which allows me to watch American TV from anywhere. Technology is a wonderful thing.

And sometimes the Carolina family just reaches out to me unexpectedly. I recently got an email from Steve Previs, who played guard at Carolina about 40 years ago. He lives in London now and just said maybe we could get together sometime if I ever get over there and to keep him in mind if I ever needed anything.

That's Carolina for you. When I was a sophomore we celebrated the 25th anniversary of the 1982 national title team and the 50th anniversary of the 1957 national title team. That was really, really cool. It's just so great to know you're going to be part of something like this for the rest of your life. Maybe in 2034 we'll be having our own 25th anniversary of our national championship team, although that's really hard to imagine now.

Bobby Frasor played both guard positions for the Tar Heels from 2005 to 2009 and was an instrumental part of the 2009 national championship team. Although a reserve on that team, he was selected as that team's best defensive player. He started every game as a freshman point guard for the Tar Heels and then was a part-time starter for the rest of his career.

Frasor graduated in 2009 with a degree in communications and a minor in business. He played his first professional season in Bulgaria, where he averaged 12 points and five assists per game. Frasor said he would like to continue playing basketball professionally for several years and eventually wants to pursue a coaching career.

DANNY GREEN

FORWARD

2005–2009

I DIDN'T KNOW WHAT IT WAS LIKE until I got to become a Tar Heel. The rivalries, the pride, everything like that. The hard work. The desire. Doing things the right way. Chemistry. Family. Tradition.

That's the way Carolina has always been and always will be. Carolina basketball—we've always done it the right way and to the best of our ability. It's hard to find the words, really, to explain it.

I think the key is the hard work. Behind closed doors, when everybody is sleeping and not working, when the TV cameras are off, we're doing a lot of hard work. Off the court, on the court, in the weight room.

I played in more victories than any other player in UNC history—123 of them. That means a lot to me. I hope that shows the kind of person and player I am. I don't care about my individual stats, my individual stuff. I want to win. Guys will tell you, even in the summertime and in pickup games, I would be there every day, play as many games as possible, and try to win as many as I could. Ty Lawson and I, we battled it out the last couple of years. But my first couple of years, I was the summer league pickup ball champ. I held the record for highest percentage of winning—it was 80-something percent at some point. Yes, we really keep stats on that. You don't have to be there—it's not mandatory—but the coaches keep up with what you're doing and who's working hard.

Danny Green was a versatile player for the Tar Heels' 2009 championship team, whose pregame dance moves to the song "Jump Around" became a cult favorite among UNC fans.

So it's not just about the season, it's about the off-season. And you have to keep working and not make a big mistake off the court. Everybody's always watching. Eyes are always on you.

My senior year couldn't have ended any better. Each of the first three years before that, we took a bad loss in the tournament to end our season. Not that senior year, though—we went out on top. We all came back and did what we were supposed to do. We started off a little shaky, but each game we got better and better. The chemistry was there as a team.

In the NCAA tournament, we really built some momentum. Our tougher games were actually early on. I think the LSU game early in the NCAA tournament in the second round was actually our toughest, even though we won it 84–70. From then on, we built some momentum and knew what we had to do. Basically it came down to defense, picking it up defensively, because that's what we were lacking earlier in the year. We knew we could score. But we started talking more on defense—that's what defense is about, communicating.

I was a reserve my first three years and then started as a senior. My junior year I was a sixth man—the two years before that I didn't play quite as much. My junior year was when I started playing a lot more, and that's when the "Jump Around" thing started.

If you didn't come to any of our games that year, let me explain what that means. There's this song called "Jump Around" that they would always play over the speakers at the Smith Center just before tip-off. I kind of got known for dancing to it right before the game started. I feel like I started a little tradition there. A lot of guys like to get loose on the sideline right before tip-off. Once the ball goes up, it's business. But before that, guys like to have a lot of fun.

And Coach allowed it. We used to do it as a group all the time, like in my sophomore year, and then it ended up more or less being a solo thing when I was a junior. We have guys doing it now that I'm not there.

When I was a sophomore, we had more guys doing it, and it wasn't as big of a deal. And then all those guys either left or were starting, so then it was just me. We just had fun with it, doing it every game. Coach is a little superstitious—just a little bit—and the one game we didn't play that music and I didn't do "Jump Around," we lost. So ever since then, Coach Williams made it a point—we've got to play that music.

I've gotten to be teammates with Jawad Williams during my first year in the NBA, with the Cleveland Cavaliers. I heard he said elsewhere in this book that his 2005 national title team would beat the 2009 title team by 20 points. Let's see now—the 2005 team did well, but let's look at the NCAA tournament. We won all of our games by double digits. They had some very close games. They really weren't as good there as we were. They may have won their tournament, too, but they didn't do it the way we did it. We ran the table pretty well in that tournament, and we could run the table on them, too, if we needed to!

I grew up in Long Island. My father put us in New York City pretty quickly, though, at a very young age. If you were from Long Island, you didn't get much respect in the city, you kind of had to earn it. For whatever reason, Long Island players have always been known for being soft. So we had to earn that. I am the oldest of three brothers. My brother right beneath me, Rashad, we're really close. He became a college player, too—he's now at the University of San Francisco. We did everything pretty much together. We traveled borough to borough, making a name for ourselves. I didn't get much respect until high school, I guess. I wasn't really highly recruited until my junior year, when I went to an ABCD camp. I always wanted to go to Carolina, though—I was a fan from the beginning.

One of my most memorable moments at Carolina came when I dunked in a Duke game on Greg Paulus. That game in general was a great game for me. It was a high-intensity game, and I was just running the floor. It was off a long rebound, on a three-on-one fast break, and I was thinking about catching it and going up. I was in the middle on the break. I dribbled most of the way down, passed off, then got it back and went right over Paulus. He was trying to draw a charge, but there was no call. I just caught it, went up, and hung on the rim a little bit. People still remember that one.

I've got two boa constrictors now. One's a baby, one a little more grown. They're low-maintenance pets, and I always liked them growing up because my uncle had boa constrictors. So being around him, snakes became interesting to me.

Now I'm just getting started in the NBA. I got on a really good team with Cleveland, so it's very interesting to see how someone like LeBron James handles himself—how he plays, how he deals with all the attention, all of that. I think it will make me a better player down the road. I'm not sure where I'm going to spend off-seasons yet, except I know that Chapel Hill is going to be involved a lot. That's my second home now. Always will be.

The interview with Danny Green was conducted in the Cleveland Cavaliers locker room, and LeBron James (who had yet to leave for the Miami Heat) listened to a lot of it in a stall just five feet from Green's. When Green started talking about his dunk over Duke's Greg Paulus in 2008, LeBron perked up.

"What, you dunked on somebody?" LeBron asked.

Green nodded, smiling. "And you should have seen me today," Green said, referring to a Cavs' practice and gesturing at LeBron. "I looked like a young you out there."

That's what the Cavaliers would love to see, of course. Green was a second-round pick in 2009 but played very little as a rookie due to the Cavs' stacked roster.

Still, Green certainly knows how to win. He was known as a stat-stuffer at North Carolina. At 6'6", he had great leaping ability and was a surprisingly good shot-blocker as well as a fine three-point shooter and rebounder. Green finished his career as the only player in ACC history to tally at least 1,000 points, 500 rebounds, 250 assists, 150 three-pointers, 150 blocks, and 150 steals. He was also an all-conference defensive player as a senior.

TYLER HANSBROUGH
CENTER
2005–2009

WHAT DOES IT MEAN TO BE A TAR HEEL? It means a lot. There is a Carolina connection. And not just for the basketball players. You have a connection with everybody there who ever went to school there or cheers for the Tar Heels. There's something about the place that just binds people together.

I should know because I spent four years there. Some people thought I should have left early for the NBA, but I have no regrets about any of it, no matter whether it helped or hurt my draft stock.

I'm a national champion. I had a great time in college at North Carolina. I got my degree. And I got to be around people I really enjoyed for four years.

Now I'm with the Indiana Pacers in the NBA, and things are a lot different. The athleticism is the big difference from college. The majority of the guys are bigger. There are seven-foot guys who can move and things like that. And there are little adjustments to the rules and things like that.

Some things are the same, though. We like to run a lot at Indiana, and that part is the same as at Carolina. I'm used to that. And this is the same: it still feels good to have a good game, but I'm always just trying to help us win, just like at Carolina. I'm still not concerned about individual stuff. My role is different now, but that's fine. Whatever I can do to help us win is what matters.

And I guess you could say hustle plays and things like that carry over. When does hard work not carry over? But there's more to my game than just hard work.

My mom lives in Chapel Hill now, so I get back there to see my family and my basketball family, although not as much as I'd like. I'm trying to get settled in Indiana, too. I'm going to come back every summer and play in those great pickup games at the Smith Center for as long as I'm healthy.

My No. 1 memory from UNC is the championship, definitely. But not too far behind that is my memory of graduating and getting my degree in communications in 2009. That was very important for me, too.

Will I ever be a great NBA player? I'm sure going to try. People are going to say what they want about me. Reporters will ask me, "Why do people doubt you?" I don't know, but I'm not doubting myself. I'm confident. I'm a guy who has a lot of energy, a high motor. But I'm also a guy who can step out and shoot the mid-range jump shot, who is more skilled than a lot of people give him credit for, and who is a very good rebounder offensively.

[Hansbrough has already impressed one Hall of Fame NBA coach. Said the Charlotte Bobcats' Larry Brown of Hansbrough during Hansbrough's rookie season, "He's going to be great. Anybody who plays as hard as he does every possession is going to be successful in our league. He does what he does best. He pursues the ball. He runs on the break. He does all the little effort things that you can't teach."]

To tell my story, you have to start in Poplar Bluff, Missouri. I grew up there. It's a town of about 17,000, in between St. Louis and Memphis. It's just a great town. I still have a lot of friends there, and when I go back they always treat me exactly like they did when I was young.

I have two brothers. My dad, Gene, is a surgeon. My mom is named Tami. I'm close to both of them, although they aren't together anymore. My younger brother, Ben, played college basketball, too. We won two state championships together in high school. He's just a great brother. He'll tell me anything. I yell at him, he yells at me, and off the court he's one of my best friends.

My older brother, Greg, might be the family's best athlete. But when he was eight, he got a brain tumor and had this big surgery. There was a chance he wasn't going to make it. And even when he did, people said he wasn't going to be able to do normal stuff. To walk. To ride bikes. To play sports. Greg came back and did all of that. He's even run marathons. He's been my role model through everything. And he's a big goofball. He doesn't take anything seriously, and when I have a serious issue, he helps lighten it.

233

Tyler Hansbrough, the No. 1 scorer and rebounder in UNC history, was well-known for finding just enough space to make difficult shots like this one.

When I came to Chapel Hill—and at first I was shocked a school like Carolina was even recruiting me—it was right after the 2005 team won the national championship. Then, just about everybody left. So nobody knew much about us. But we had a lot of success, and in my junior year we made the Final Four. The game we played in Charlotte to beat Louisville that year in the Elite Eight is still one of my favorite college games.

We had had heard a lot about losing in the Elite Eight in 2007—a whole year's worth of hearing about it, really. And here we were again, in the exact same place, getting ready to play Louisville.

I had my usual pregame routine that night. I always do the same thing. I get stretched out by our strength coach. Then I go out on the court, get some shots, get loosened up. Then we go out as a team. I always have to make two free throws in a row before I go in.

The part of this that makes it one of my very favorite games came very late. I hit two big jumpers in the last three minutes—the sort of shots that people don't expect me to take. But I had been working on those kinds of shots every day, before practice and at practice, all season. I try to make 150 to 200 shots before each practice, which takes about 45 minutes. That's free throws, three-pointers, post moves—everything. I really work on my shot.

And in this game, it paid off. The first jumper came from the top of the key when the shot clock was running down. I just let it fly and fortunately it went in. Then on the second one, I was going to shoot but it might have gotten blocked. So I pump-faked one guy. Then I saw [Louisville center David] Padgett coming at me, and if you look at the replay, it barely gets over Padgett's hand. But it goes in, and after that we're far enough ahead that they run out of time. The Final Four was one of our goals. I remember pointing to my mom in the crowd after it was over and cutting down the nets. It was just a very exciting moment for everybody on our team. And for me.

That year, though, ended suddenly after we made the Final Four. In the semifinal, we ran into a Kansas team that was really hot and would end up winning the national championship. To be honest with you, it was just Kansas's night—we got way behind [it was 40–12 at one point] and never could quite catch up. They just outplayed us.

So I came back for my senior year in 2008–2009. The first reason was that I hoped to win a national championship. But getting a degree was also very important to me. A good education is a big part of why I came to UNC. I learned a lot of things I never knew anything about before—I even took

Swahili while I was at Chapel Hill. I loved being in college, really. If I didn't love it, I would have probably been gone before my senior season. But I had great roommates, great teammates, a great house to live in, and great classes. There's a lot more to the University of North Carolina than basketball, though, and I tried to take advantage of all of it.

We had some bumps in the road. I had a stress reaction in my shin early in the season. But we got back to the Final Four a second time. And this time, I think we were a little more prepared. We were more used to a big stage. And it all went right for us. There were so many questions in Detroit and all through that season beforehand—things about whether I would be a great college player if we didn't win a national championship. I didn't like that. But when we won, we put all that to rest. Against Villanova in the semifinal and then Michigan State in the final, we were ahead pretty much the entire game. It was a storybook ending, to be honest with you. It couldn't have been any better. We even got to go see the president in the White House. Nowadays, I still have a hard time believing all the things we were able to accomplish. No matter how bad a day I'm having, that sort of thing brings a smile to my face.

Then came the draft. I had been dreaming of that day for a long time, too. I always wanted to go to New York, to be there for it, so I could get a picture with the commissioner after my name got called. It was special for me to get picked by Larry Bird and the Pacers since Bird was such a favorite player of mine growing up.

Now I'm just trying to get adjusted to the NBA. I've had some setbacks. But I'll always remember my years in Chapel Hill. And when those Carolina guys come to Indiana, I'm always calling. When you see another guy from Carolina in the NBA, you're always catching up, making sure you make and keep that connection, because it is very special. We all know that.

Tyler Hansbrough, nicknamed "Psycho T" as a freshman at UNC, left Chapel Hill in 2009 as the No. 1 scorer and No. 1 rebounder in school history. His No. 50 jersey has already been retired at the school.

Hansbrough counts his biggest accomplishments as obtaining the 2009 national title and his UNC degree in communications, but there were dozens more. He was first-team All-America for each of his four seasons, the only player in ACC history to accomplish that feat.

Hansbrough's 2,872 career points ranks him first in ACC history. He also holds an NCAA career record for made free throws (982). He went 4–0 in games played at Duke. In 2008 he was the consensus National Collegiate Player of the Year. The Indiana Pacers drafted Hansbrough No. 13 overall in the 2009 NBA Draft. Hansbrough's rookie year was short-circuited by injuries—including a serious inner-ear infection—but the Pacers have high hopes for his future.

At UNC, Hansbrough was renowned for his toughness—he earned the "Psycho T" nickname in the weight room—and for his desire.

Hansbrough's coach, Roy Williams, once said of him, "When that young man takes the Carolina blue uniform off and doesn't put it on again, I'm going to sit on top of the Smith Center. I'm going to sit there for an hour and realize how lucky I am to have coached that youngster."

Hansbrough's 2009–2010 rookie season with the Indiana Pacers, however, was an injury-riddled disappointment. He played in only 29 of a possible 82 games because of a strange dual injury—a concussion combined with an inner-ear infection that caused him a serious case of vertigo. It is hoped that Hansbrough can fully recover from the injury and that it won't affect his future NBA career.

MARCUS GINYARD

FORWARD/GUARD

2005–2010

BEING A TAR HEEL MEANS BEING A PART of a special family. I don't mean only an athletic family with the basketball team, but just a special family of people in the Tar Heels community—people who attended the school, who cheer for the UNC teams, or who work here and make up the institution. There's a real sense of togetherness among all of us.

In terms of basketball, it gets even more intense. There's that fraternity of people, that family feel. It also brings out a sense of responsibility, to keep up that reputation of excellence. You don't want to embarrass the university. And of course you want to win.

When you're at the university, you become a part of something so much bigger than yourself. You understand the rich history of the school, and you know that you'll be able to put a mark on this. I don't think there's a lot of people who feel that way when they go to college. I think they just feel like they're going to school, just taking classes. They don't feel quite as bonded. I think most people who go to the University of North Carolina feel that special tie with their university, like it's a second home.

I was one of the easiest recruits Carolina ever had. I grew up in northern Virginia and was exposed to a great deal of basketball early. Luckily, I got a good chance to follow Joseph Forte pretty closely—he was a big inspiration for me. He came from the same area and went down to Carolina. He and my older brother played in the same league, and we all went up to the same gym on weekends to work out. I really focused on Joe, and that was really cool for me. He ended up being a big star at Carolina, and that helped make me want to go there.

My mother and my brother, Ronald Jr., were huge influences on me to play basketball at all. My brother ended up playing for a small Division II university up in Manhattan. Then he went into coaching. He coached at my high school for a while and now is an assistant coach at the Naval Academy.

My mother, Annise, and father, Ronald Sr., both spent time in the Marines. My dad spent 23 years in the Marines, and my mom spent five years there. We were a very disciplined family, and that helped me to get my academics straight. I always have tried to maintain a good balance of athletics and academics. I was a National Merit Scholar and in the National Honor Society in high school.

My mom was always in very good shape—she's a personal trainer and even did some coaching at my high school in terms of strength and conditioning. So when I was growing up, she was a big help to me in terms of telling me how to work out and what to do and pushing me some. There aren't a lot of moms like that.

When I was 12 or 13, I first realized that I could probably play at a program like Carolina. I had always wanted to play at a big school. When I was 13, my team won the AAU national championship. I figured we were the best team in the country at that age group, and that was probably a good sign for me.

When it came time for the recruiting process, it was very stress-free for me compared to most. I had seen my brother go through it—just boxes and boxes of mail—and he hated it. So we decided to see if I could get ahead of the curve a little bit. I made a decision very early, the summer after my sophomore year. I had gone to Carolina's basketball camp and wanted to play there.

When Coach Williams took the head-coaching job there in 2003, I went down on an unofficial visit and met with him once. I think he had had the Carolina job no more than two weeks.

My mom and I went to his office, and I said, "Coach, this is where I want to play." He said, "Well, I've never seen you play, but I've heard some good things, so I'll come watch you play this summer, and then we can make a decision." So he came to watch me, and a few of the other assistant coaches did, too. They offered me a scholarship at the end of that summer. I verbally committed right then and never wavered.

Marcus Ginyard was the Tar Heels' Defensive Player of the Year as both a sophomore and a junior but could also get to the basket off the dribble.

I joined a great recruiting class—Tyler Hansbrough, Bobby Frasor, Mike Copeland, and Danny Green. There's no question that you really grow and blossom with whatever group of guys you're with. We were all together four years, and that doesn't really happen that often anymore. We became great friends, too. Bobby, Dannny, Tyler, and I lived together all four years. Then in my fifth year—I had to redshirt my "first" senior season due to a foot injury—I moved in with Deon Thompson and Marc Campbell.

I became known as a player first for my defense—both in high school and in college. I like defense. It comes down to pride, really, being able to stop that man in front of you. It's obviously a huge part of the game. I got a chance to start on my high school team—Bishop O'Connell in Alexandria, Virginia—as a freshman because I was the best defender out there. I love the challenge of having to guard a great player. I was a part-time starter at Carolina in my freshman year, too, for defensive reasons. That's my pride.

As for highlights of my career, beating Duke at Duke in my freshman year probably sticks out to me the most. In fact, beating them my first four seasons in a row at their place—that was pretty cool.

And being a part of a national championship team—that was unbelievable. There's no doubt that for me it was a little difficult at times. I had a foot injury that season and ended up as a medical redshirt. I only got to play in three games at the beginning of the season. But toward the end of the season, I was probably 80 to 90 percent, and I was going hard in every practice.

I felt I was helping my team get better at practice late that season. I could push my teammates some. And then when it came time for games, I decided to try and be the best cheerleader on the team. I just had to forget about myself. We all did. That's why we were so successful at the end of the season. We put our personal agendas aside, and that's why we won.

So the rest of my freshman class left me behind after that season, and I became a fifth-year senior on a very young team. Deon Thompson and I were the only two seniors in the regular rotation on my last team—the 2009–2010 team. It was another great challenge. It was certainly tough at times, and we didn't do as well as we wanted, there's no doubt about that. But it was still a fun season.

As for the future, I definitely want to be a pro basketball player on some level. I want to do everything I can do with that. After my career ends, I've always been interested in business, and I've always been interested in cars. I'd love to own my own business dealing in cars—a car dealership or something like that. My dad in the past 10 years or so has also been getting into real estate, and that's also something that interests me. And I've thought about trying to come back and be part of the athletics department at Carolina. So I've got a lot of things to sort out. But I already have my degree—I got it in 2009, in communications, and spent my fifth year at Carolina working on a second undergraduate degree in sociology. Plus, I just took some other classes at Carolina—just in things that I thought I would be interested in. There are so many things to do at Carolina—it was great spending a fifth year there.

Marcus Ginyard spent five seasons on the Tar Heels basketball team. He was known as a defensive stopper and often guarded the other team's primary scoring threat at either shooting guard or small forward. At 6'5" and 210 pounds, he played every position except center for the Tar Heels during his career.

Ginyard was the Tar Heels' Defensive Player of the Year as both a sophomore and a junior and was a team captain of the 2008 Final Four team. He was also a member of the ACC all-tournament team in 2008.

Ginyard took a medical redshirt due to an injured foot for the 2009 national championship team, but still won the team's Most Inspirational Player award in a vote of his teammates and coaches. Ginyard played in more than 100 wins as a Tar Heel, was named Defensive Player of the Game more than 20 times, and served as president of UNC's Student-Athlete Advisory Council.

WAYNE ELLINGTON

GUARD

2006–2009

BEING A TAR HEEL MEANS A LOT OF THINGS. Excellence. Tradition. Family. Hard work. Greatness.

No question that the Tar Heel tradition was a big reason I came to school there. Once Coach Roy Williams and Coach Joe Holladay started recruiting me, that was something I really wanted to be a part of. They really expressed to me how it was a family and the tradition of excellence. And when I went down to my visit, looked up, and saw all those banners, saw all the guys who had already graduated coming back around, I knew I wanted to be part of that.

I grew up in Pennsylvania, where I was a high school teammate with Gerald Henderson, who ended up going to Duke. He's one of my best friends and has been for a long time, which made it kind of weird when he broke Tyler Hansbrough's nose. But let me back up to tell my story.

I started playing basketball when I was about five or six years old. My dad put me into a YMCA league, and I fell in love with the sport. I was always getting in trouble for dribbling a ball inside our house. I'd be throwing it in the air, practicing my shot, shooting inside—got in trouble for that, too. But for years, I was always doing something with a basketball. When I got older, I started getting a little into football, too. But in high school, I decided to stick with basketball. My dad was very helpful—he never coached me, but he was always the guy trying to help me find good teams to play on, get me into tournaments, and let me be seen.

I went to Daniel Boone High as a freshman in Pennsylvania, and then I transferred to Episcopal Academy in the Philadelphia area. It wasn't just for basketball reasons—it's a good academic school, too, and my family wanted to move into that area. At the time, Episcopal wasn't a basketball powerhouse or anything like that. My best friend, Gerald Henderson, had been going there since he was in about second grade. He was continuing to get better and become more well-known. So we joined up with each other starting in my sophomore year.

Carolina started recruiting me during that sophomore year. My final decision came down to Villanova or Carolina. My home school was Villanova, and there was a lot of pressure from people at home for me to stay home. It was a very tough decision to make. But finally I took Carolina, because it seemed like it was more than just basketball, it was something that lasts forever. I wanted that family-type atmosphere. I wanted a situation where we would all be like brothers.

[Villanova coach Jay Wright said during the 2009 Final Four that Ellington's decision "broke my heart, man. Broke my heart. But I'm very, very happy for him. He's had a great career, and I know he loves it down there."]

When I came out of high school, I was mostly a shooter. The jump shot was my specialty, and that was something that had just developed for me with the help of some of my coaches. I kept working on it until it became natural.

As a freshman, I had a chance to make a jump shot against Georgetown in an Elite Eight game in the NCAA tournament that would have put us into the Final Four. I missed it, the game went into overtime, and we lost. That was a very tough experience for the team and for me. It made me spend all that summer working hard—it was a motivator. I knew I had to work on getting better defensively, on getting stronger, on being able to penetrate. I didn't want to be so one-dimensional as a shooter. I wanted to be a lot of things.

My freshman year was also the year when Tyler Hansbrough got fouled by Gerald and had his nose broken. That situation got really hyped up [Henderson was suspended for a game, and Hansbrough wore a protective mask for several games]. I tried to mediate as best I could. I got in contact with Gerald, who wanted to talk to Tyler and apologize. Then I talked to Tyler to make sure Gerald had the right number. We didn't need any bad blood the next time we played Duke.

It was kind of different to have Gerald as a close friend on our biggest rival. But we just kind of got used to it. When we stepped on the floor, we

Wayne Ellington came into UNC known primarily as a shooter, but once he started driving to the basket regularly, he became even more dangerous offensively.

were enemies, but otherwise wee were friends. And he can't ever say anything to me about the rivalry. I was 5–1 against Duke.

In my sophomore year, it felt great just to get to the 2008 Final Four. That
was such a focus for us. But I think it was too much of a focus. When we got
there, we didn't focus on the bigger picture, on winning the whole thing. We
got there kind of wide-eyed and we weren't really that hungry, I felt like. We
were satisfied. We came out in that first game, and Kansas opened on us
pretty good, and we never could catch up.

Then I had a decision to make. I could have gone to the NBA at that point,
and I considered it. I put my name in without hiring an agent, so I could
return if I wanted to. Finally, I decided to come back for my junior year, just
like Ty Lawson, Danny Green, and Tyler Hansbrough all did. That was definitely the best decision I ever made in my life, because we came back and
accomplished all the things I wanted to accomplish. As a team, we got so
much better. The national championship was such an amazing feeling—it's
hard to understand it until you experience it.

The weird thing was playing Villanova in the Final Four. I had come to
Carolina to compete for a national championship and yet here I was playing
Villanova, which had made it to the Final Four, too.

I really was hungry throughout the Final Four—the Villanova game, the
championship against Michigan State—through the whole NCAA tournament, really. I just didn't want the same thing to happen to us that had happened my previous two years. I wanted to be one of the leaders on our team,
lead by example, attack, and be aggressive. I didn't want to lose again. Getting voted as Most Outstanding Player of the Final Four was just a bonus.
The part I liked the most about that Final Four in Detroit was that we were
a very close team and we were able to share that with each other.

I didn't come back for my senior season at Carolina because I knew that
the main core of our team was going to be gone. I felt, after winning a
national championship, it would be a great time to take it to the next level. I
got drafted by Minnesota late in the first round, and that's actually a good situation for me. I've been able to be on the floor and get some game-time
experience that a lot of rookies don't get, so that's been good. It's been an
adjustment—the guys are a lot bigger, stronger, faster, taller, all of that. And
smarter, too—the players here use their advantages so well. Everybody's just
very good when you're playing in the best league in the world.

245

The hardest part of the NBA? I lost more games halfway through my rookie year than I think I had lost in my entire life up until that point. That's tough, but it's a learning experience, too. You always have a game the next day. You always have a chance to redeem yourself.

I keep up with all the Carolina guys in the league—it sometimes seems like there is one in every city. The older guys in the league that I didn't play with—I always try to talk to them when I see them, too. It's fun. No matter where you go, if you went to Carolina, you've always got family somewhere close by.

Wayne Ellington was voted the Most Outstanding Player of the 2009 Final Four, which earned his jersey a spot in the rafters of the Smith Center. He shot Michigan State out of the game in the first half of the title contest, scoring 17 points in the first 20 minutes as Carolina took a 55–34 lead. Ellington also had 20 points and nine rebounds versus Villanova in the national semifinal. He averaged 19.2 points and 5.7 rebounds throughout the NCAA tournament, shooting 55 percent from the floor.

Ellington finished his three-year career with 229 three-pointers, second in UNC history. Besides the 2009 NCAA tournament, he may be most noted for a 36-point effort in a 2008 win at Clemson. That game ended when Ellington hit a three-pointer to win the game at the buzzer for the Tar Heels. The Minnesota Timberwolves drafted Ellington with the 28th overall selection of the 2009 NBA Draft.

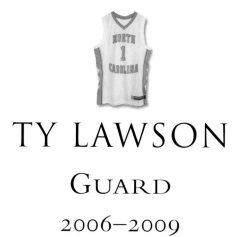

TY LAWSON

GUARD

2006–2009

Want me to tell you what sold me on North Carolina? In 2005 I was going to Oak Hill Academy in Virginia. I was being recruited by a lot of schools. Carolina had just won the national championship, and yet Coach Williams was there practically the next day to recruit me.

He came up to Oak Hill—which is two or three hours from everything else—with this big presentation. He was showing me his national championship ring, too. Stuff like that. That was a sign to me that he was real dedicated, that he really wanted me to sign with his program, and so that's what won me over.

The tradition was important, too, of course. Year after year, a lot of great players go to Carolina, come out, and become stars in the NBA. So it's a great tradition, and it's like a family.

My NBA career has started with another Carolina guy coaching me. George Karl of the Denver Nuggets was my first head coach in the NBA. He played point guard for the Tar Heels, too. That makes it easier because I have someone who can relate to it—who has been in the same place and knows where I'm coming from. But it also makes it harder because he expects that much more from me.

When I was growing up, I modeled myself on AI—Allen Iverson—or more recently Chris Paul. I liked really small point guards who were really quick. That's who I mostly looked at.

That's why it meant a lot to me when I was a rookie in the NBA and Iverson told some reporters that he thought I was the fastest guy in the league. That made me feel really good, because he's one of my idols and I've been watching him play since he entered the league.

The year I'll always remember at Chapel Hill was my junior year—the 2008–2009 season. We won the championship, of course, and so many good things happened. That was the year I got more aggressive. I started taking charge more and being a leader on the team. I knew I could always be really good and take over the team, but that year was the year I finally went out and did it. Plus I ended up shooting the three-ball well.

Most of us on that team were together for three years. We all came in together except for Tyler. So we were really close. I still stay in touch with Danny Green, Wayne Ellington, Deon Thompson, Ed Davis, and Larry Drew. Those are the ones I talk to the most. I plan to come to Chapel Hill in the summers.

It wasn't too tough a decision to go pro after my junior year. I accomplished everything I wanted to there. I won a national championship. I won the Bob Cousy Award as the nation's best point guard. I won an ACC title and was the conference's player of the year. There was nothing else for me to prove at that level. But as far as just being a kid and staying a kid one more year, yeah, I do miss that. It was tough to leave that. Now I'm grown up and I've got bills and stuff.

My best memories are really about the Final Four in 2009. In the first game, against Villanova, I remember playing my old teammate. When I played elementary and pee wee basketball, I played with Dante Cunningham. So I remember talking trash with him, saying we were going to beat them and there was no point in them showing up, stuff like that. And also just making a strong point because a year before we had gone out there and lost by a lot in the Final Four against Kansas. So there was no way we were going to be coming out slack in that game. And we didn't.

Then, in the final against Michigan State, we knew we had to stop Kalin Lucas. I was supposed to guard him. That was just my focus, that was all I was trying to do. I wanted to make sure he didn't get to the basket.

And while I was doing it, I got eight steals. That was a career high for me and a high for anyone in a national championship game, so I broke a couple of records. I was surprised. I thought it was four or five steals while I was doing it. Eight really is a lot.

248

Known as the "one-man fast break," Ty Lawson may have been the fastest point guard in school history and directed North Carolina to the 2009 national championship.

We won it, really, without it being too close [UNC led by 21 points at halftime and won by 17]. They always play the song "One Shining Moment" during highlight reels, and at the end of the game, I was just wanting to hear that song so badly. And to see the highlights—that was probably the main thing I was looking forward to, and then just getting to go home and celebrate with my teammates.

As for the NBA transition so far, I find it very easy. Coach Williams prepared me a lot for it. It's not too much of a difference. There are bigger guys who are a lot stronger, but otherwise it's the same as college. You've got to figure out your place in the league. I still feel for the most part like I'm the fastest guy in the league. Now T.J. Ford, he's pretty fast. Tony Parker, he's fast—but he hides it a lot. But I feel like I'm still the fastest.

Ty Lawson's jersey hangs in the rafters at the Smith Center, a tribute to his being honored as the ACC's Player of the Year in 2009. Lawson was the first true point guard to win that award since Phil Ford did so in 1978. Lawson also won the Bob Cousy Award, given to the best point guard in the country.

Renowned for his speed—he was known as the "one-man fast break" at UNC when he got the ball in transition—Lawson ran the Tar Heels team throughout the 2009 championship season. His career assist-turnover ratio was 2.78 in college, second-best in ACC history. In the championship game against Michigan State, Lawson led everyone in points (21) and steals (an NCAA-record eight) while also adding six assists against just one turnover. Lawson was chosen 18th overall in the 2009 NBA Draft by Minnesota, then was immediately traded to the Denver Nuggets, where he began his NBA career coached by former Tar Heel George Karl.

"He's quick and very strong," Karl said of Lawson midway through his rookie season. "I think the biggest thing that has surprised me is how fundamentally good he is defensively."

NIE ROSENBLUTH · TOMMY KEARNS · YORK LARESE · LARRY BRO
ADWICK · BILL CHAMBERLAIN · GEORGE KARL · BOB MCADOC
RTHY · JIMMY BRADDOCK · MATT DOHERTY · BUZZ PETERSC
LIAMS · GEORGE LYNCH · ERIC MONTROSS · BRIAN REESE · DC
TAWN JAMISON · JAWAD WILLIAMS · RAYMOND FELTON · SEA
NSBROUGH · MARCUS GINYARD · WAYNE ELLINGTON · TY LAV
OWN · CHARLIE SHAFFER · BILLY CUNNINGHAM · CHARLIE SC
ADOO · BOBBY JONES · WALTER DAVIS · JOHN KUESTER · PHIL
ERSON · BRAD DAUGHERTY · STEVE HALE · JOE WOLF · JEFF LEB
ONALD WILLIAMS · DANTE CALABRIA · JEFF MCINNIS · VINCE CA
Y · MARVIN WILLIAMS · BOBBY FRASOR · DANNY GREEN · TYLER
NNIE ROSENBLUTH · TOMMY KEARNS · YORK LARESE · LARRY
VID CHADWICK · BILL CHAMBERLAIN · GEORGE KARL · BOB M
ES WORTHY · JIMMY BRADDOCK · MATT DOHERTY · BUZZ PETE
LIAMS · GEORGE LYNCH · ERIC MONTROSS · BRIAN REESE · DC
TAWN JAMISON · JAWAD WILLIAMS · RAYMOND FELTON · SEA
NSBROUGH · MARCUS GINYARD · WAYNE ELLINGTON · TY LAV
OWN · CHARLIE SHAFFER · BILLY CUNNINGHAM · CHARLIE SC
ADOO · BOBBY JONES · WALTER DAVIS · JOHN KUESTER · PHIL